ADVANCE PRAISE FOR *OF FLOATING ISLES*

"Kawika Guillermo's experiences with games and gamers may be shocking to some, but they reflect the everyday lives of people I've known who sought games in their most challenging times, and who now have this book to call their own."
—Minh Le (a.k.a. Gooseman), designer and co-creator of *Counter-Strike*

"*Of Floating Isles* is an invigorating work of gaming memoir and history that reveals how our virtual experiences are inextricably linked with our off-screen lives. Through their own story, Kawika Guillermo convincingly demonstrates that the time spent in games is as real as anything else—that games construct monuments within our memory, engraved with hidden facets of ourselves. *Of Floating Isles* is a testament not just to the power of video games as art, but to the kaleidoscopic meanings that can result from recognizing games as an active element within our lives."
—Marina Kittaka and Melos Han-Tani, game designers of *Sephonie* and *Anodyne 2: Return to Dust*

Of Floating Isles

KAWIKA GUILLERMO

On Growing Pains and Video Games

ARSENAL PULP PRESS
VANCOUVER

OF FLOATING ISLES
Copyright © 2025 by Kawika Guillermo

All rights reserved. No part of this book may be reproduced in any part by any means—graphic, electronic, or mechanical—without the prior written permission of the publisher, except by a reviewer, who may use brief excerpts in a review, or in the case of photocopying in Canada, a licence from Access Copyright.

ARSENAL PULP PRESS
Suite 202 – 211 East Georgia St.
Vancouver, BC V6A 1Z6
Canada
arsenalpulp.com

The publisher gratefully acknowledges the support of the Canada Council for the Arts and the British Columbia Arts Council for its publishing program and the Government of Canada and the Government of British Columbia (through the Book Publishing Tax Credit Program) for its publishing activities.

Arsenal Pulp Press acknowledges the xʷməθkʷəy̓əm (Musqueam), Sḵwx̱wú7mesh (Squamish), and səlilwətaɬ (Tsleil-Waututh) Nations, custodians of the traditional, ancestral, and unceded territories where our office is located. We pay respect to their histories, traditions, and continuous living cultures and commit to accountability, respectful relations, and friendship.

Arsenal Pulp Press is committed to reducing the consumption of non-renewable resources in the making of our books wherever possible. We make every effort to use materials that support a sustainable future. This book is printed on paper made with 100 percent sustainable recycled fibre content.

Lyrics from *Hades* are reprinted with permission of Supergiant Games.

Cover and text design by Jazmin Welch
Cover artwork by Chris Kealoha Miller
Edited by Catharine Chen
Proofread by Alison Strobel

Printed and bound in Canada

Library and Archives Canada Cataloguing in Publication:
Title: Of floating isles : on growing pains and video games / Kawika Guillermo.
Names: Guillermo, Kawika, author.
Description: Includes bibliographical references.
Identifiers: Canadiana (print) 20250153173 | Canadiana (ebook) 20250153386 | ISBN 9781834050065 (softcover) | ISBN 9781834050072 (EPUB)
Subjects: LCSH: Guillermo, Kawika. | LCSH: Patterson, Christopher B. | LCSH: Video games—Social aspects. | LCSH: Video games—Psychological aspects. | LCSH: Video gamers—United States—Biography. | LCGFT: Autobiographies.
Classification: LCC GV1469.34.S52 G85 2025 | DDC 794.801/3—dc23

To Cameron, my brother

It's dangerous to go alone!

Take this.

—Old Man, *The Legend of Zelda*

CONTENTS

9	**INTRODUCTION** Straying from the Path
29	**CHAPTER 1** Of Floating Isles
47	**CHAPTER 2** Playing Roles
67	**CHAPTER 3** War and the Terror of Teenagers
87	**CHAPTER 4** Final Fantasies
107	**CHAPTER 5** Would You Like to Continue?
129	**CHAPTER 6** Pleasures of the Open World
151	**CHAPTER 7** Game-Sensing the System
173	**CHAPTER 8** Hair, Hips, and Other Blueprints
193	**CHAPTER 9** Of Dark Dungeons
215	**CONCLUSION** A Poetics of Interaction
229	Acknowledgments
231	Notes
237	Bibliography

INTRODUCTION

Straying from the Path

I play as a virtual girl named Robin, a nine-year-old in a hooded raincoat, lantern red. I stand in the sun on a brightly lit path leading to Grandmother's house. The path is bordered on both sides by a dark yet inviting forest. I am alone, with only the instructions my mother has given me: "Go to Grandmother's house. And stay on the path."

I stray from the path.

Among the forest trees, I collect early-blooming flowers. I find a rusted shopping cart, climb inside, and pretend to drive. I play hide-and-seek with a whimsical girl in a white dress. I happen upon a graveyard and, with my bare hands, dig in an open grave. "People die," I tell myself. "It's hard to imagine for a kid like me. They die and we put them in the ground. Like flowers."

Gasps and cries echo through the forest.

I see a dark, fuzzy, fanged creature pacing around the cemetery, half human, half wolf. I love wolves, so I leap onto its backside. The wolf tries to buck me off, but I hold tight and ride until the screen fades to black.

When I come to, I am in the dark, in heavy slanted rain, my body contorted, soaked, and injured upon the wooden slats of a narrow bridge. Slowly, I rise and limp to Grandmother's house.

Inside, intense blue-and-red walls move me through psychedelic passageways of torn wood, hovering white balloons, and an open grave. I reach a mattress covered in red tape where my bedridden grandmother should be. As the screen again dissolves into darkness, images of the wolf's teeth and my injured body flash before me, images I cannot pause and cannot unsee.

~

These experiences happen in *The Path*, a video game that depicts the horrors of growing up, making choices, and living with the consequences. It is also about the playfulness and disobedience of many gamers, who, unwittingly perhaps, take risks when we venture into the digital unknown. Curious and enchanted by darkness, we are not here to walk the path's Edenic safety, but to leave it, to give ourselves to play.

The Path was first conceived as an art project by two digital artists turned game makers: Auriea Harvey, a Black digital artist and modeller from the United States, and her husband, Michaël Samyn, a Belgian artist and programmer. Though both Auriea and Michaël stopped making games in 2015, *The Path* is today a cult classic, a grim and Gothic version of the "Little Red Riding Hood" fairy tale that, like most fairy tales, speaks through symbolism and metaphor. The game's horror elements come not through jump scares or physical violence but through atmosphere, story implication, suggestive imagery, and fade-outs that leave violent incidents to the players' imaginations. The path itself is the first metaphor: it doesn't turn or wind or change colour or terrain. It's just a straight road, sunny and bright and accompanied by a melodic track. Once you leave the path, it disappears entirely. Then, as you move through the forest, the camera pulls back and darkens, simulating the blind panic of being lost in the woods and losing daylight.

Players of *The Path* take on the role of six sisters—"Reds"—aged nine to nineteen who are one by one tasked to travel to Grandmother's house. Each Red's story begins by straying from the path; their forest adventures end when they meet the Big Bad Wolf. Each of the girls has her own wolf, specific to her age and personality, and, like gamers themselves, each of the girls will always choose to play with her wolf.

In Robin's story, innocence turns to blind naïveté. As she plays with the wolf, I think of my own son, eight years old, also young enough to play with a creature capable of nightmarish violence. Surrounded by graves, Robin's encounter with the wolf implies injury and death, and she must live in the shadow of those implications forever.

Many would refuse to call *The Path* a video game, seeing it as too linear, too mature, too artsy, and too unfun. *The Path* can hit deep—too deep, perhaps, for many gamers. Even so, I begin this introduction with *The Path* because it conveys many of this book's aims to intimate the experiences, feelings, and transformations of growing up with video games. Like riding a wolf, video games can be intensely pleasurable, exciting, and rewarding but can also result in injury and mayhem. *The Path* depicts youth the way only a game can, by moving through its experiences and playing them out to see what feelings, what memories, what traumas and fears such play lets loose. And like many games that never meet mainstream popularity, *The Path* feels dangerous. You don't just play it; *it* plays *you*, marks you, hurts you, and transforms you. But only if you let it.

The main feeling I get from *The Path* isn't fear or anger but a lingering unease. Since I first played it in 2009, *The Path* has never left my mind. This is because, unlike most depictions of youth, *The Path* portrays the pains, the violences, and the erotic desires of growing up. While other media encourage us to envy youth, to valorize our teenage years, *The Path* gives us our youth as many gamers remember it: feeling trapped, helpless, constantly alert to danger, and expecting abuse. Each of the sisters, the Reds, gives us a different form of this darker side of youth. Each girl plays different, thinks different, and desires different. Yet, like we who decide to stay within the game, each Red chooses to stray from the path set before her. And there is always, always a wolf.

~

I am on the path, this time as Rose, an eleven-year-old girl known by fans as "Innocent Red." I stray from the path. I cannot help it. The forest's beauty awakens me.

I find the grave I played in earlier, back when I was Robin. This time, I take a skull that has somehow unearthed itself and place it back in its grave. "The dead go in the dirt," I say, "while their souls fly to the sky." Later, I play patty cake with a darker-skinned girl in a white dress who appears and then flits away.

Gasps and cries echo through the forest trees.

I collect little white flowers until I happen upon a misty lake. In the centre, an ethereal being made of clouds hovers over the water. I am not afraid, but fascinated. "Welcome, clouds!" The being is elegant, angelic, and invites me to dance. We levitate and spin. Then, darkness.

I wake up—weary, defeated, soaked—on the bridge facing Grandmother's house. Inside, furniture flings about in a violent whirlwind. Grandmother's bed hurtles toward me, and I collapse.

~

Like me, Rose was raised to imagine clear distinctions: good and evil, right and wrong. Nothing is due to blind luck. And yet, the universe's inconceivably vast and complex nature withholds a certain madness, a dark but wondrous cosmos that lures us in and invites us to dance.

I am a scholar and writer specializing in video games who has taught video game analysis to university students for over a decade. I have published an academic book about games, as well as an edited collection featuring game scholars and game makers. I have led a team to design and make my own game. I have presented my research on games across the world, from Osaka to New York to Hong Kong. And yet, when I try to grasp this concept, *video games*, I cannot help but think of Rose's clouded wolf. I feel him whenever a student in my class asks me, "What is a video game, anyway?" and I sink into that misty lake of uncertainty. My attempts to answer this question as a lifelong gamer, games researcher, and game designer have led to patches of messy argumentation. Games are playful, except when they get really serious. Games are a type of interactive technology you use with others. But then again, so is a book, once you read it out loud. Studies show that games cause violence! Except that, according to other studies, games relieve anger and have been shown to decrease violent acts.

There is a vastness to games that makes them inconceivable. My own clouded uncertainty as a player, teacher, scholar, and maker hits a stark personal chord. Questions about games feel intimate, as though they're about my very being. The question "What is it like being a gamer?" feels similar to questions such as "What is it like being Asian in North America?," "What is it like being a twin?," and "What is it like being neurodivergent, or queer, or gender nonconforming?" I don't know, because I've never *not* been these things. What is it like to grow up *without* a twin, or *not* being Asian, or being perceived as "normal"? What is it like *not* to play games nearly every day of your life? What is it like to have your earliest memories *not* revolve around a rotating joystick?

Perhaps the question of what video games are is often a way for non-gamers to ask how they can deal with friends and loved ones who *do* play games, because those friends and loved ones are having a riot of a time without them. This is how I feel whenever someone discovers that I play video games and starts on a familiar path of questioning: "Are games violent?" "Are games healthy?" "Do games make you an addict, or stupid, or subsumed into an ideology?"

I feel uncertainty spin around me. This wolf is an agent of chaos. He is the always-present possibility of losing ourselves in the clouds.

~

> Make short and intense games:
> think haiku, not epic.
> Think poetry, not prose.
> —Auriea Harvey and Michaël Samyn,
> "Realtime Art Manifesto"

The French philosopher Jacques Rancière once took on the challenge of defining the hazy and misunderstood category of *poetry* by comparing it to something equally hazy and undefinable: rhetoric.[1] Ancient Greek philosophers had also compared poetry to rhetoric, but for Rancière, these philosophers had it backward. For them, rhetoric was real, public, and engaged in the arts of argument and persuasion. Poetry, by contrast, was seen as a perversion of the "real," a realm of private imaginings of pleasure and pain. For Rancière, however, rhetoric and poetry were the opposite. Rhetoric, in imposing itself as truth and in persuading readers to action, was the actual perversion of reality. Poetry, in having no claim to truth and in choosing to speak not through argument but through emotion, body, and art, was far closer to truth.

Over the years, my feeble attempts to understand games compel me to imitate—or perhaps *simulate*—Rancière and to reapply his points about poetry to video games. I've come to rely upon a similarly upside-down way of describing what video games are and how we play them. It begins with a category definition: Video games are a genre of interactive media, similar to how poetry and rhetoric are two genres of writing or how television and film are two genres of moving pictures. And in the wider world of interactive media—where input on a digital device expects a reaction—video games are the naughty, annoying sibling to another genre of interactive media: the internet.

Like rhetoric and poetry, the internet and video games are two sides of the same interface, from the spoken word to the screen. Like rhetoric, the internet gives us a visible identity and a stage to perform ethical conduct, to be a "truth teller," to embrace a moral performance. And like rhetoric, the internet's promise of giving us these truths—time and again, as we've come to learn, with the circulation of "fake news" and fake identities—is, in many ways, a perversion. Games, in contrast, are the poetry of the digital age. They offer emotion, stimulation, and art, and they confront us with the realities of our world. By allowing us to unmask the mimicry pressed upon us by social media, chat groups, and YouTube videos, games refuse the realities that these media curate for us. Like poetry, games claim to have no essence of truth. Thus, they allow deeper unspeakable truths to be told—or, in this case, to be *played*.

~

Back on the path, I am Ginger, an adventurous tomboy. Of course I stray from the path. I'm not into going straight!

I plunge into the forest, present for it all: the sound of footsteps on dry leaves, the smell of pine trees, the dim sunlight through filtering clouds. I light a campfire, mull around a shack, open and close doors.

A girl in white walks me back to the path. I stray again. Gasps and cries echo through the forest.

A sun-drenched field of flowers lies within a grassy meadow canopied by power lines and a murder of crows. "If I get rid of the flowers," I say, "nobody can hide here anymore." In the field, I approach a woman in a red dress. We hug, turn away, then hug again, a full embrace as she lifts me off the ground. We collapse under a tree, and I go still. The light fades.

I awake in the dark, in heavy rain, soaked and injured upon wooden slats. I limp slowly to Grandmother's house. Inside, the floor is wrapped in barbed wire. The walls tighten. I crawl under a bed and hear someone come in. I see only their feet. I am trapped. I am terrified.

~

The Path sees youth as a continual process of becoming—not becoming something else or something new, but just the act of becoming itself. We experience the pain that accompanies growth, as well as the possibilities of experimentation, of creating blueprints for what we aspire to become.

Ginger's desire to experiment, to take control, reflects the most common gamer personality of seeking to act upon the world and to play with it. Looking inside a shed, Ginger comments, "There is always a door, and a door can be either open or shut. The difference is me!" Climbing a barbed-wire fence, she exclaims, "You cannot stop me! I am never still." In the end, the Big Bad Wolf that threatens Ginger's rambunctious attitude is not male ego but femininity itself: the social demand that Ginger adhere to the boundaries of good womanhood. Ginger can only be a tomboy for so long before it becomes a "problem." She is growing up, and soon the barbed wire around her will tighten.

Like Ginger, video games aspire to retain the playfulness of youth, because adulthood means being watched from all sides and feeling labelled, tightened, identified, stuck in our roles. In games, we can refuse the seriousness, the fear, and the overbearing surveillance of our everyday relationships. In games, we become anonymous, untethered to the roles that once enclosed us in little boxes.

Ginger's story draws attention to how, in many cases, transformation does not come from doing safe things, and growth comes from learning not just what we are, but what we are *not* (straitlaced, straitjacketed, or just straight). But *The Path* offers no resolution to Ginger's story. We don't know if she will embrace her queer self or find more comfort in the promises of traditional womanhood. *The Path* does not presume that childhood growth is always good. Like most games, *The Path* is not a lesson but an experience, a gateway to a different sensibility, one that has the power to shift our sense of the world and how we grow within it.

~

I am Ruby, a fifteen-year-old girl with long black hair and bangs that float over my wondering, averted eyes. Also known as "Goth Red," I watch the world decay. I wear a brace on my left leg, but I'm still mobile enough to stray from the path.

I try to climb a playground tower and give up. "I must be getting old," I think. "It's about time!" I find a cigarette and consider trying to smoke.

"They say it shortens your life." I chase away a girl in white. Despite my leg brace, I'm faster than my sisters. I find a knife in a tree stump and wonder what it would be like to use it on myself: "Cut my veins and make me bleed. A valley or ocean. Desire or need?"

My wolf looks like a wolf—not a real wolf but a man-wolf, a hunter. He wears all black, sits with legs widened on an old park bench, and smokes a cigarette. He offers me one, and I join him, fulfilling my wish. The screen goes black.

~

Ruby or "Goth Red" was by far the most popular girl in *The Path*. The first of the Reds conceived by Auriea Harvey and the cover girl for the game's publicity art, Ruby epitomizes traits of nihilism, defeat, and self-destruction, characteristics that the world has repeatedly cast upon video games and the people who play them.

In the early 2000s, when *The Path* was developed and released, the internet resembled the possibilities of techno-utopia, collaboration, connection, and achievement through AI, while video games appeared as a perversion of technology, played only for pleasure, self-gratification, isolation, and the glorification of violence. Ruby resembled all of these qualities of video games and was proud of it.

Like Ruby, video games often appear as an injured and destructive force, refusing the optimism of the digital age. Games are the dark world of a new and unpredictable technology, one that emerged not from the friendly faces of Steve Jobs or Bill Gates, but from obscure US military training exercises, the labs at MIT, and the Japanese, a foreign people who were once remembered through tales of war, violence, restricted immigration, forced incarceration, and the atomic bomb. The first video games ever made (*Spacewar!* and *Galaxy Game*) were direct products of US military funds. The very first video game developer, William Higinbotham, who developed the game *Tennis for Two* in 1958, also led a team of engineers in the Manhattan Project to create the ignition mechanism for the first atomic bomb.[2]

Today, the shadow realm of video games is ever expanding. Video games outpace every other entertainment medium in revenue, with over 180 billion USD estimated in 2024, dwarfing movies, television, publishing, and music.[3] They are played by around 60 to 70 percent of the population in North America (about the same amount of people who watch sports), and by over 3.5 billion people the world over.[4] And yet, despite having been part of our daily lives for over a quarter century, games still feel otherworldly. They seem to offer a dark view of the world, one that the real world would prefer to dismiss as irrelevant. Whereas internet platforms like Facebook and Twitter are hyperpoliticized social arenas that garner constant news coverage, games lack political interest, even though one single video game (like PUBG: *Battlegrounds*) can carry twice as many users as Twitter and may contain just as much political wrangling within its live chats. A single game of half a million people resembles far more than an escape—it's an unwatched, unobserved realm where anything can and often does get said and done.

Ruby's story is about living in this shadow realm, about the desire for self-destruction and the thrills of flirting with danger. Games, of course, often lean into these thrills, and the consequences of doing so, as with Ruby's wolf, have at times been catastrophic. In 2014, the fanciful disobedience of game cultures combined with the male-dominated industries of information technology created a perfect storm that led to the massive harassment campaign against women journalists and game makers known today as Gamergate. The campaign's main targets were the popular YouTube feminist media critic Anita Sarkeesian and game developers Zoë Quinn and Brianna Wu, yet Gamergate affected all women gamers, creating what Sarkeesian and game critic Katherine Cross called "a never-ending, violent, and steady eruption of toxic misogynist hate."[5] According to many studies of Gamergate, this "steady eruption" of sexism helped produce much of the misogynist rhetoric that was later used in Donald Trump's 2016 presidential campaign to eliminate his rival Hillary Clinton, and has had effects to this day that reach far outside gaming communities.

The lowbrow territory of games makes perfect stomping grounds for our disobedient, pessimistic, perverse, and Ruby-like selves. But games also help us understand that such disobedience can feel cathartic precisely because it upsets the policing of our daily lives. Ruby's pessimism does not come from nowhere—she is living deep within the barbed wire of womanhood that Ginger knows will be her future. Ruby feels its piercing metal on the daily. After encountering her wolf, Ruby must enter Grandmother's nightmarish house, where she is locked inside a birdcage above a school gymnasium and must swing herself out, injuring herself all over again, before crawling to Grandmother's empty bed.

Like Ruby's nightmares, the dark realms of video games are reflections of how the world has done us harm. Even within their pessimism, video games have always been in critical conversation with the military, the media, and the internet. In games, you can play as a border control guard (*Papers, Please*), as a COVID-19 quarantine officer (*Novel Containment*), as a prison manager (*Prison Architect*), as a drone bomber (*September 12th*), or as a heavily armed soldier (too many games to mention). As a medium that sees not identities but roles, not abstracted communities but bodies that feel and play, the shadow worlds of games are not mere signs of our maladjustments—they are expressions of our refusal to adjust to our barbed-wire world.

~

I am Carmen, "Sexy Red," a flirtatious seventeen-year-old with purple highlights. I grab attention with ease, and I know it.

I step breezily off the path and into the trees. I wander over graves, seeking nothing from them. I compare dresses with a free-spirited girl in white. I take a jog, then crawl into a rusted bathtub and imagine soap suds. At an abandoned theatre, I sit on a cherry-red bench and flirt with the air: "Oh, come on, have a seat. Have a kiss."

Gasps and cries echo through the forest.

I happen upon a campsite where a middle-aged woodsman hacks at a tree with an axe. I take his hat, wear it, and laugh. He doesn't seem to mind and hands me a beer. We drink, and the screen goes black.

I awaken in the rain, my hands on my face. I return to Grandmother's house, bracing my injured neck with my arms. The house is filled with moans, perhaps my own. I reach Grandmother's bed, skewered by a humongous tree. Images of the man in the woods flash before me.

~

Like the fairy tale "Little Red Riding Hood," *The Path* depicts the gruesome experiences of youth. If the "Little Red Riding Hood" story seeks to discipline young women, *The Path* explores the wayward curiosity inherent to the medium of video games—it assumes that you, the player, will always choose the undisciplined route, the dangerous and wayward forest where no paths exist and where awful, regretful things can take place. This is terror, haunting trauma, and it is part of many of our youths. Youth wakes us to the excitement of powerlessness, of submission, of being fragile, human, helpless.

Like fairy tales, video games are often the last place we expect to find depictions of humanity's darkest traits: exploitative violence, sexual assault, trafficking, cruelty, and death. But, as I will show throughout every chapter of this book, games do not shy away from these subjects—quite the opposite. Like fairy tales, video games are inundated with traumatic events and stories, though these are often expressed through symbolism and metaphor. The idiosyncratic activity of playing a video game is not merely about pleasure or experimentation or reclaiming our youth. Though we might see games as isolated experiences, as "virtual worlds" divided from our "real world," this only denies their actual truth-telling power. Games are about acting upon the world, about understanding power: the kind that we hold over others, the kind that controls us, and the kind that we can and must let go.

~

In his book *Mondo Nano*, games scholar Colin Milburn uses islands as a metaphor for video games, claiming that games provide islandic laboratories, "place[s] for melodrama as much as alien experimentation."[6] In literature, islands are often metaphoric thought experiments that can create mouldable exemplars of all humankind. They are, as Milburn writes, "incubator[s] for the future" that offer a "discrete space for prototyping the world of tomorrow: a crucible for futurity."[7] Think of the idealistic islands of Thomas More's *Utopia* and Francis Bacon's *New Atlantis*, or the tropical deserted islands of *Robinson Crusoe* and *Lord of the Flies*. Such islands work well for experimental thinking, but also for reductive thinking. These islands are abstract, totalizing places that imagine mankind as a singular, individual being only by cutting them off from the real histories and power dynamics that have defined humanity: those of colonialism, capitalism, empire, and racism.

Playing as any of the sisters in *The Path* does not feel like an islandic experience, an experiment free of humanity's darker inclinations. Games might appear as isolated islands from afar, but they are less like the islands of utopian literature and more like literature's "isles": imaginary, mist-covered lands that invoke myth, legend, and imagination, as well as fear, violence, and power. Though *isles* can refer to geographical formations (the Black Isle, the Isle of Wight), they are only named as such by those on the mainland, outside of the salt and the sea, who can only speculate on what happens on the isles or how the people on them might also be seeing and naming *them*, the people on a distant shore.

In literature, *isles* name lands of uncertainty. They are not spaces of isolated experiments but unknowable and threatening mysteries. They are the mythical realms of exotic danger in *The Odyssey*, the satirical remote nations of *Gulliver's Travels*, the magical exilic islet of *The Tempest*. These isles do not sanctify "Man," but condemn him by putting him face to face with those he has colonized, enslaved, exploited, abused, and hurt. The isles of video games are troublesome. Like Carmen's story, they can pierce us deeply and open up new wounds. But in doing so, they also allow us to face the darkness and, from out of its splintered materials, grasp the future on the horizon.

~

I am Scarlet, the eldest of the Reds. I am tall, elegant, and mature, with my hair tied in a bun and a red shawl keeping stray hairs firmly in place. Still, I stray from the path. The music of the forest calls.

I clean up a used syringe. I beat dust from a hanging rug. When I clutch my arms in fear of the forest, a darker-skinned girl in white, a full head shorter than me and visually much younger, gives me a long hug.

Gasps and cries echo through the forest. I am drawn in still.

My wolf is an older gender-ambiguous person who hangs around an abandoned theatre, leaning on a lamppost. I approach the ruined stage and sit at an old piano. I think to myself, "Art is where the nobility of humanity is expressed. I could not live in a world without it." As I play the keys, my wolf approaches. They mentor me from over my shoulder, encouraging me to play. The theatre curtains slowly fall.

~

Scarlet's story is the closest glimpse we get into the everyday lives of the Reds. Through her, we discover that their mother is mostly absent, perhaps working overtime to provide for her six daughters. The father, if there is one, is entirely absent, never warranting a mention. Scarlet has had to be the caretaker, the diligent, responsible sister nicknamed "Stern Red," who has had to suppress experimentation, youth, art, and dreams. She mourns the childhood she never had. Having hidden her love for art and music, she has remained deeply unfulfilled.

Scarlet may not seem to reflect the youthful, pleasure-seeking gamer, but that's because most gamers aren't really youthful or pleasure seeking. The typical gamer, according to a 2024 report from the Entertainment Software Association, is not a playful and experimental youth, but a thirty-six-year-old working adult (about half men, half women).[8] Many gamers are not dreamers but instead, like Scarlet, are facing the loss of their dreams, the defeat of realizing they'll never have time to pursue their childhood aspirations. Though gamers might prefer to see themselves as a playful Robin, a rambunctious Ginger, or a pessimistic Ruby, we are, truthfully, Scarlets, treasuring the few liberated moments of the day when we can stray from our paths and immerse ourselves in imaginary worlds, where we can dream again.

The first person to speculate on the page about the imaginary worlds of video games was also not a typical young male gamer, but a thirty-two-year-old woman named Mary Ann Buckles. Though her 1985 dissertation on interactive games is better known today, at the time, Buckles's ideas had little impact, and their rejection by even her own mentors (professors of literature) led her to leave academia entirely. And yet, Buckles had perhaps the greatest insight into games of any scholar at the time. For Buckles, games were not important because they represented something immersive or even fun, but because they created worlds for the player to imagine differently, which they could use to create their own stories. Buckles called this the "supra-story": a story created by the reader in their imagination before they write it down or share it with others.

Supra-stories thrive when they are given space to play—worlds that feel insular and logical (in their own way), but most importantly, that are both complete and incomplete: complete in the sense that everything in them seems to work independently of the player; incomplete in the sense that the player's own stories have yet to be told. The player joins the game world but also creates it anew, imagining strange, untold stories within it. This is why Buckles found games less similar to tightly woven fiction novels and more similar to the open imagination of lyrical poetry. Games do not dictate stories to us but, like poems, speak in metaphors, images, similes, allusions, and allegory. As Buckles writes, the player's attachment to game worlds can "unlock strong feelings and memories of associated events from their own lives which they then build into the imaginary world they are creating."[9]

Buckles's ideas are the longings of Scarlet, our "Stern Red": the desire to escape to an imaginary land free of our daily responsibilities and defeated dreams. Yet Scarlet's wolf, the artist promising fulfillment and nourishment, also reveals the flaw in how we come to understand the supra-story, which is one of insularity. In Buckles's own diagram, supra-stories work in a feedback loop, coming from the game world to the imaginary universe shared with the game and the player to the player's own supra-story, which then manifests in text that feeds back into the game world through actions in the game. But Scarlet's story reminds us that even in this desire for release and escape, the Big Bad Wolf can still feed on us, can exploit this desire, as he can all desires.

1. The author's account
   ↓
2. The imaginary universe ← 5. The reader's text
   evoked by the author
   ↓   ↑
3. The imaginary universe → 4. The reader's
                                supra-story

Mary Ann Buckles's diagram for the supra-story, a gamic version of Tzvetan Todorov's diagram showing the chain of connection among the reader, the author, and the text. Both diagrams show a closed loop (from "Interactive Fiction: The Computer Story Game *Adventure*," by Mary Anne Buckles).

In my own experiences growing up with games, the effects of supra-stories went far beyond looping back to the game world. They manifested throughout my life in various ways: from my own sense of self, to my decision to leave my religion, to my sexual awakenings, to my anorexia, self-harm, and suicidal ideation, to my decisions to travel, to living abroad, to receiving a PhD, to becoming a games scholar and an author of imaginary worlds myself. Games may be feedback loops between ourselves and a machine, but they create worlds that compel and shape our decisions outside the machine. Scarlet's wolf is a reminder that our pleasures can never be compartmentalized, and neither can our pains. Our supra-stories bleed into our lives, often in ways that elude us. This is the power not of games, but of the stories we build from games: the power to reflect, to reimagine, to merge.

~

Inspired by Mary Ann Buckles, this book sees supra-stories as a description not for the isles that video games *are*, but for the floating isles that video games *create*. The isles of video games are not hidden away by a daunting dark sea. In video games, isles float. They float above but always within eyesight, within earshot, of those on land. Isles are the magical realms that many of us can't wait to float toward, while those who have never been can only speculate, can only ask, "What is so interesting about those bits of rock in the sky?"

Floating isles are no strange concept in games. They are the homeland of Sonic the Hedgehog, the levels of tantalizing coins that Mario can bounce and run toward. Floating isles bring balance to the world (*Final Fantasy vi*), protect idealistic utopias (*BioShock Infinite*), and are sometimes just a cool place to shoot demons (*Doom*). While growing up, I often filled in the blanks of game worlds with my own floating isles. I played *Sonic the Hedgehog* and imagined a thousand new adventures, each featuring a cast of talking animals. I played *Final Fantasy vii* and imagined myself as one of its characters, venturing on far-out sexual escapades upon floating airships. I played *Counter-Strike* and entered an isle of war and terrorism, one that spoke to my own involvement in a nation whose enemies looked like me, like my family members, like my friends.

This book is about the floating isles of video games and how those who inhabit them are not just seeking forms of escape or having their heads in the clouds. I want to show how these floating isles are also forms of introspection and self-observation, where we gather the experiences we've had, the emotions we feel, the ethical and philosophical questions we've dwelt upon, the challenges we are facing, and manifest them into another world, a place where we can take risks, fail, learn, and start over. Even as they take place in their own worlds, the floating isles of video games are never themselves complete. They arise from our personal and often intense attachments toward a game's characters, worlds, objects, and the feelings we get from play. Floating isles are formed after we have dwelt within a game's world for many weeks, months, years. Even if we're not technically good at the game, we feel we've understood its world. We get its sensibility, we feel attuned to its ways of moving with us as we play it and inside us after we've put down the controller.

The nine chapters of this book walk through formative moments in my life and the lives of those I've known to account for how video games allowed me to process the joys, confusions, and pains of growing up. I tell these stories from the view of my floating isles, which have always been there, hovering just above my real-world self. In moments when the world's sprawling clamour felt overwhelming, the isles offered consolation, as well as a digital hearth where fellow outcasts could gather. Tethered to the ground but far above it, these isles have been in constant interaction with every change, every love, every tragedy. And they will remain there, lingering, until my end.

~

I am the girl dressed in white. I am darker skinned than the other girls, and I remember myself in their worlds: I was the free spirit in the forest; I was innocence itself. Unable to speak, I communicated through performing cartwheels, sharing flowers, and kissing foreheads. When one of the girls fell into a panic attack or a crying spell, I was the one who led them back to the path.

Gasps and cries echo through the forest. I hear them, and I do not stray from the path. I am never injured, and I have no wolf. I go straight to Grandmother's house.

The house is maturation, a shedding of childhood. Inside, I have no trauma to overcome. Instead, I witness all the other girls' nightmares.

Robin couldn't see danger, only play. Rose put her faith in a pure, orderly world. Ginger dared to be fluid, unrestricted. Ruby romanticized the darkness. Carmen yearned for touch. Scarlet couldn't live through the day without imagining the dream.

I relive each of their nightmares, but I do not experience the events leading up to their traumas, their joys and desires. I see only their regret and pain. Finally, I approach Grandmother—an elderly woman lying in bed, looking up at the ceiling. I crouch at her bedside and stare intently at her. I am young, only beginning my life; Grandmother nears the end of hers.

Perhaps, I think, if Grandmother weren't here, none of the sisters' pain would have happened. There would be no path, no forest, no nightmares. Perhaps Grandmother is the real wolf.

The screen fades to black.

I, the girl in white, stand alone in the centre of a red room, hands folded. My eyes jerk upward. A gash of blood is smeared across my white dress, crimson red. The sisters, the Reds, enter the room one by one. They don't see me—I am the innocence they have lost, the youth they can never reclaim. I can never grow up. I am beautifully, airily free. I sneak away, looking for the next flower to pick, the next game to play.

The Reds position themselves around the room, silent. I, the player, have spent many hours with them, living their lives, seeing their flaws, listening to their desires, and shaking from their terrors. One by one, they strayed, they fell, they sank, they lost something dear to them. But now they are here, and they are together. If they can help each other, if they can share their pain, maybe they will be okay.

CHAPTER 1

Of Floating Isles

I am the child that television hosts, pundits, schoolteachers, and scholars once feared: the child raised by video games.

The deepest and most enduring memories of my childhood are times when I held a game controller in my hands. When I remember my happiest times, I think of me and my twin brother hip-checking each other into the stratosphere in *Super Smash Bros*. When I think of friendship, I remember group sleepovers where friends and I stayed up all night planting proximity mines in *GoldenEye 007* and then raced through our explosive obstacle course. When I think of sadness, I remember sobbing into my shirt at the end of *Sonic the Hedgehog 2* after I, hurtling down from outer space, was caught in mid-air by my childish accomplice, a fox named Tails. When I think of longing, I remember me and Tails flying away together toward a floating isle in a bright azure sky.

I say I *am* that child, not I *was* that child, because most of the world still places me within the categories of the juvenile, the callow, the undeveloped. This is for several reasons. First, I am variously browned. My mother is Ilocana, her family from the Philippines. Through her, I carry the legacies of American colonization, of people whom Rudyard Kipling once called "half devil and half child" and whose leaders were once referred to as "brown boys" by the future American president William Howard Taft. As a half-Filipino, half-white person (or "hapa haole," as my family in Hawaiʻi puts it), I am invariably seen by others as Latinx, Southeast Asian, or "Islander." To be browned in North America is to be assigned to low-level service and custodial work, but it is also to be stamped as infantile, unready, and—unless met with a firm hand—a touch too wild.

I am also cast as childlike by my sexual interests, my gender deviance, and my neurodivergence. To be queer—whether sexually queer, genderqueer, or neuroqueer—is to be characterized as immature, as involuntarily seeking pleasure and love in all the wrong places, as being unable to make adult connections that result in a stable family life. Fixating on one's sexuality, gender, and mind state is something society likes to quarantine to the phase of adolescence. Acts of queer sex are dismissed as something adults are too mature to care about, something even queer political movements need to grow out of, or at least keep out of streets, classrooms, and parades. Self-exploration, self-remaking, self-transformation: these are the political equivalents of navel-gazing, of sex for pleasure's sake. These are things we do in our youth, when we're free to experiment and haven't much else going on. Adults, it seems, are done experimenting, done playing around.

Multiply browned, multiply queered, there are many ways I have remained a child trapped in a grown-up's body. But of all these, the most incriminating reason I am seen not only as a child but as someone who *revels* in my own childishness is that I have never left the playgrounds of video games. I am forty years old. I have a child of my own. I am a professor and a writer. Yet I still play video games for at least an hour a day, as I have since I was old enough to press a button. Through the five countries and many cities I have lived in, through fluctuations of love, career, grief, and joy, games have been there, dwelling with me, pulling me back.

What is life to a person who, according to some, has never really lived in the "real world"? How does one remember their childhood when every memory is entangled with the urge to dodge a fireball or to hear the *ping* of a virtual coin? Is a life in video games any life at all?

~

I don't remember it, but I often imagine the first time I touched a game controller and felt that strange smooth rectangular surface, cool to the touch. Then how it became a heat vessel fused to my hands as I anxiously mashed its buttons. Then how I had to wipe sweat from its grey plastic, which would soon fade to white. Was it like finding a lost limb? Did I know then that this angular hardware would build calluses on my palms? Did any part of me sense that over the course of my life, this machine would reflect back the warmth of my own body heat?

~

> Video games crash any cocktail-party rationale you attempt to formulate as to why, exactly, you love them.
> —Tom Bissell, *Extra Lives*

I grew up in Portland, Oregon, the whitest big city in the United States, as a mixed Asian boy in the 1990s. This meant that everyone assumed I played video games and that I was good at it. Indeed, video games were the one thing I had going for myself. I wasn't good at sports, I couldn't be attractive to girls, and unlike other Asian Americans, I was too brown to be considered a star student. Games were all I had, and my life with games was written in the stars: I was born in 1985, the same year as the Nintendo Entertainment System. My birth was concurrent with the arrival of the console that defined gaming so broadly that for decades parents referred to all video games as "the Nintendo."

I was not alone; I had Cameron, my twin brother. From kindergarten through to sixth grade, we were the only non-white kids in our entire class. Meaning, we were relentlessly bullied, harassed, and made to feel dumb, fat, and ugly. Our bodies stood out in our white working-class religious school. We were feminine, had long hair, and wore shorts with

T-shirts that went down to our knees, long as dresses. People on the street would often ask if we were boys or girls, and we were usually too afraid to give an answer. We had no self-esteem, so we would never defend ourselves, but we did get into our fair share of fights—always one of us defending the other. We did have friends, sometimes two or three. They were white kids we met near the school dumpsters, where we could avoid the terrors of slouching down the hallways and getting our cheeks slapped, our nipples twisted, of seeing the girls hold their noses from our presumed stench. For us malodorous outcasts, video games were our refuge. But they belonged truly to my brother and me. Games were the one cool thing our fat, effeminate Asian selves could claim as our own.

In my memories of playing games as a child, Cameron is always there beside me. Our parents both worked full-time, so we were independent, raised by Nanny Nintendo. We didn't play to win but to entertain each other. Controllers in hand, sitting in comfy lotus positions on our bedroom carpet, we played with the sole goal of making each other laugh. I would play *Sonic 2* as the flying fox Miles "Tails" Prower, and pick up my brother, only to ram him into spikes or off a cliff. We hunted each other in *GoldenEye 007*, shamelessly looking at each other's split-screens, until eventually we only played with our sights pointed down at the ground, steering our bodies through the level maps we had memorized, sensing our locations through the tiled textures of pavement, sand, and brick. When we finally encountered each other, we would jump at an angle and try to shoot each other's rectangular feet until we collapsed in convulsive laughter.

The delight my brother and I took from games, often by dying in ridiculous ways, lifted us to a different world, a place akin to the Japanese sense of ukiyo or "floating world": a fleeting and transient realm far above the earthly plane. At that height, bringing each other joy was our only concern.

~

Like many twins, Cameron and I spoke in a language only we could understand, a broken English of curved consonants and inexplicable vowel shifts. "Hello, Christopher!" turned to "Huwwo Qwittafa!" "Play a game?" turned to "Pwrey o gayme?"

The adults thought our shared language was an accent we'd inherited from our mother, who could easily code-switch between Hawaiian pidgin and an overeager Pacific Northwest English. As time went on, their amusement turned to concern. We had to repeat ourselves half a dozen times before grown-ups understood us, though most of the time they'd just hazard a guess. In kindergarten, we and our garbled English were often sequestered in the shoe-shelf corner. In sixth grade, we were sent to speech classes and told to mimic the voices of advertisements and newscasters on AM radio. None of these attempts changed how we spoke. For us, our speech, indecipherable to the world, was only a minor inconvenience. We could understand what others said, and we didn't care if they understood us. We had something more going on.

~

Before J.R.R. Tolkien could envision Middle-earth, he had to create the Elvish tongue. For me and my twin brother, our broken tongue was the magic that spoke new worlds into being.

We conjured these worlds after bedtime, in the total darkness of our bunk beds. One of us would begin with an opening line—"Wheeee, I'm Tails and I'm zooming across the island!"—and the other would respond—"*Blam!* You run into *me*, Amy!" We would take on the voice of a different character—usually someone from a video game and especially from the *Sonic the Hedgehog* universe—pal up, then set out on an adventure to rescue a friend or find an emerald or defeat a supervillain who was minutes away from destroying the world. But regardless of whatever urgent deed needed doing, we never kept to our quest for very long. Every night, we'd delay our crusade to wander off and find some side mission, some random encounter.

Needless to say, our habit of inventing stories late into the night annoyed our parents to no end. Their bedroom was directly above ours, and after hours of giggling, imagining our game characters charging through fortresses or fainting from seeing someone's private parts, we would hear our mother or father stomp down the stairs and scream, "IT'S THREE IN THE MORNING! WE HAVE TO WORK TOMORROW!" After a minute of silence, we would continue our stories in whispers.

Eventually, we called this nightly practice TALK, an acronym that didn't stand for anything. TALK was our way of telling improvised, imaginative stories where we role-played video game characters and set them wandering on mischievous escapades. In one of our most memorable outings, we paused our quest to help a woman plug a leaky faucet. Our characters, better at squashing robots than fixing sinks, burst the lady's pipes and then tried to soak up the flood water by pouring tons of salt into her kitchen (in our imagination logic, this worked just fine). While the evil villain came one day closer to turning every being on the planet into a member of his soulless robotic army, Cameron and I celebrated our small victory, frolicking in a sandbox of salt.

~

The earliest photo I have of my brother and me is during our first trip to the Hawaiian island of Oahu, where my mother's family has lived for over a century. In the photo we are only a few months old, held by our mother on the airplane. Somehow she brought us, two screaming, ear-plugged infants, all by herself from Portland to Hawai'i, along with our luggage.

My other pictures from this trip are of my brother and me with our grandmother Prisca Guillermo. In these pictures our grandmother sits in a wheelchair, enervated from chemotherapy. She would pass away shortly after this trip, along with the traditions that we, as a family, had entrusted to her. My brother and I never inherited these traditions: the Filipino foods of pancit and adobo she cooked, the Ilocano language she spoke during religious ceremonies, the stories of our ancestors and brethren living in the Philippines she told. Her husband, my grandfather, was a Christian preacher and had little interest in carrying on these traditions. Without ancestors, my brother and I could only speculate on our origins, our cultures, our backgrounds, our selves.

My twin brother and I: fat brown Asian kids in a white city, in a conservative religious school, knowing nothing of our background or the colonial histories that made us different. Untethered to our legacies, and our very selves, we began to drift from the world around us—it was the only way to see our lives as something other than raw slabs of flesh churning through a ruthless and unstoppable meat grinder. In the night's whispers, upon our bunk beds, we shape-shifted into magical beings snapped up in a dragon's jaws. Together, we found new ways to conjure ourselves out.

Like our favourite games—*Sonic the Hedgehog, Super Mario Bros., Super Smash Bros.*—our stories took place upon floating isles. With our broken tongues, we shaped these isles into fabled spheres of myth and imagination. From our isles, the people below us—the ground dwellers—were still visible. But they were small, unimportant, distant. Their voices could only reach us in ancient echoes.

~

When most people think of video games, they think of platformers—the scrolling worlds of *Mario* and *Sonic*, playable paintings that unspool landscapes of touchable, jumpable objects. In platformers, what lies beyond the edge of the screen is a mystery. No mountain peak vantage point can reveal the landscape. The skyline, the atmosphere, the horizon, whatever might occupy that space is left to the player's imagination. As games journalist Tom Bissell writes, platforming games like *Super Mario Bros.* were "among the first video games to suggest that it might contain a world."[10] Mario was not merely a character but represented a surreal fantasy, a hallucinogenic realm of magical mushrooms, fire flowers, coins spinning out of bricks, and genderless anthropomorphic fungi people inexplicably called "Toad."

In *Sonic the Hedgehog*, the unspooling scroll of the platform unravels like toilet paper in a typhoon. Sonic pinballs through cities, casinos, and oil factories, turning his body into a whirling razor blade that slices through red-eyed killer robots. Whereas Mario's psilocybinic world is a trip to a land of deliriant dissociation, Sonic's world is a euphoric rush of blurred lights, spring pads, speed boosters, and television monitors that, when bashed open, sonic-boom you right off the screen, often to an enigmatic death.

Mario and *Sonic* vibed different, but both evoked worlds that invited players to help invent, to make their own. Stand still, and you cannot see very far. But start moving, and the world manifests around you.

~

The TALK stories Cameron and I shared every night were a small comfort in a world that felt days away from total collapse. Always, our parents argued. Often, they slammed doors. Sometimes, they hit walls and threw things. Our father often drank himself into a stupor, sometimes in laughable ways (like when he came home and puked in my bed), sometimes in sad ways (like when he fell asleep in his own vomit) and sometimes in scary ways (like the morning after). We were often robbed, sometimes by the boys our older sister brought home. When one of them stole our Super Nintendo, Cameron and I brought its characters back to life in our TALK stories.

Our older sister was nine years older than us and, due to having a different father, was also darker: part Filipino, part Black, and part Indigenous Kānaka Maoli. Her colour, against Portland's white pallor, was easier to target than our own. When she went to jail and then got cast out of our home, our stories became full of hungry thieves looking for someone to help them, or someone to rob. When she got pregnant at fifteen years old and became a single mother at sixteen, our stories became about castaways on pirate ships longing for home.

Our TALK stories were not merely a form of escape, and neither were video games. These activities gave us space to discuss the hardships of our lives, even as we floated above those hardships. We did not need direct speech to converse about hardship; we did not need the AM radio voice to express our worries. Even the roots of the word *conversation* suggest other means of communication: *con* meaning "together" or "with"; *versare* meaning "to turn" or "to raise or hold suspended." Conversation need not be direct or instant or even between two people. For us, it came from suspending time, from lifting ourselves just off the ground.

As our lives became more tumultuous, Cameron and I would TALK during the daytime, at all hours, whenever we were alone. We TALKed in the back of our parents' car on the way to church, pretending our characters were running behind us, trying to keep up. In the malaise of uncertainty that was our lives, our imaginations gave us a place of ease, creativity, and safety where we could always drift away.

~

When I became a father myself, I remembered my own upbringing as a linguistically challenged social outcast. I did not have an easy childhood, and I did not want the same hardships for my son. But during the first years of his life, I saw him performing the same eccentric tics that had always made me feel out of place: spinning around in circles, repeating scenes from a movie verbatim, being fixated on numbers, spreading his arms and hands and fingers like he could sense radio waves. My family too recognized his behaviour. "He's just like you were!" I heard, again and again.

When my son was only two, his pediatrician also recognized his behaviour. ASD, she called it: autism spectrum disorder. After months of testing and consultancy, other doctors confirmed her diagnosis: high-functioning ASD. The doctors told us this with some hesitation, because neither of those phrases, ASD or *high-functioning*, is well defined. They are always being redefined, recreated, renarrated.

It took months to settle funds for caregivers, consultants, and interventionists. Once we did, I began to wonder: was my son's behaviour *really* on the autism spectrum, or was he just like me at his age? Couldn't his behaviour just be a result of my paternal pathways? Like father, like son, right?

Our child psychologist, Dr. Dhami, stated the obvious: Couldn't it be both?

"But," I told her, "I was never diagnosed with autism."

"Okay, would you like me to test you?"

Dr. Dhami knew the results before she even tested me. She had been trained to see the signs: wavering eye contact, conversations full of non sequiturs, all the stimulations ("stims") that autistic communities recognize.

Yes. Most definitely yes, on the spectrum.

According to Dr. Dhami, I was moderately autistic in "speech," and severely autistic in "obsession" and "repetition." Further testing noted my more excessive proclivities. I had "rigid habits," "obsessive tendencies," and, perhaps most alarming for me as a writer, teacher, and academic, I had a nearly complete "lack of empathy" for other people.

I couldn't stomach it. What kind of professor was I, if I had no empathy? How could anyone trust a writer who was unable to pick up basic social cues?

Over the next several months, I began to read my past through what author M. Remi Yergeau calls the *autism narrative*, "a lens through which others could story my life."[11] Under the autism narrative, the spaciness of my youth, where I often imagined other worlds with my head in the clouds, was a form of disassociation. My continual longing for the floating isles of video games was an early sign of lacking "joint attention." My constant playing with my hands in kindergarten was not a form of role play, but a sign of stereotypy, of "self-stimulatory gesticulation." My ability to recite every line from a video game like *Donkey Kong Country* or a movie like *The Lion King* was not a sign of a sharp memory but of "echolalia." And my ability to invent new languages with my twin brother was not a bridge for conversation but merely a form of "babble," of "aberrant vocalization," of "lack of volubility."

I bargained with the psychologists. "Do you know that I am an author who has written *four books*? Do you know that I am a professor and a known scholar of video games?"

Oh, yes, they knew I was a writer. Perhaps I wrote too much. Maybe I wrote *obsessively*. And yes, they knew I played video games, that I wrote about video games. Maybe I played games too much. Perhaps *compulsively*. And maybe none of these achievements was really, totally my own.

For the medically trained evaluators, my lifetime of playing and writing about video games was not a proof *against* autism but a sign *of* autism. My love for games was not an imaginative sprawl into exciting virtual worlds but an act of succumbing to the temptations of compulsive social avoidance.

The research was clear: kids with autism have a risk of becoming addicted to games, of playing them for far longer than their peers, and for preferring their isolating virtual worlds to the bright and loving environments of reality. There was no denying it. Autism seemed to be at the core of it all.

~

> Suddenly, with the neuropsychologist's signature on my diagnostic papers, I was no longer my body's author.
> —M. Remi Yergeau, *Authoring Autism*

After my diagnosis at thirty-six years old, every childhood memory began to be reshaped by the autism narrative. My views on video games began to shift, my love for them becoming overshadowed by "asocial tendencies." My love for writing, my imagination, my need for TALK stories, my constant longing to float away—all of the things that had made me feel weightless and free, it turned out, were caught within an invisible web held together by my neurodivergence. I began to reach out on online forums for other adults who were diagnosed with autism later in life. Many, it turned out, also played a lot of video games. They too were also haunted by the abrupt and nagging thought, *Am I truly myself, or just a product of an invisible force tugging me along?*

Though I received my diagnosis in 2021, I'd always had this question at the back of my mind. It didn't take a child psychologist to tell me that I was different. I'd just assumed that my difference was due to my race, my queerness, or my gender deviance, not my very thoughts and impulses. But the signs had been there all along. My parents had often told me I was blanking out. My high school friends, even today, call me "the crazy one." The slur *retarded*, far more common in the 1990s, was hurled at me so often that I had reimagined it with pride, like being a "goof." Early in our relationship, my partner—who would eventually become my wife—once told me she knew I couldn't express myself the way most people did. One day, she realized that if she wanted to be with me, she would have to trust in what I said rather than how I said it.

And then, of course, there was my queer, gender-bendy self. The inflexible autism narrative took this from me too. The way I'd always walked on my tiptoes like I was on a fashion runway, feminine and proud, was no longer a sign of queerness but of early autism. So too with the many gestures, postures, eccentricities, and brightly coloured styles I had come to understand as queer; they were now the waving red flags of neurodivergence. My indifference to my own gender pronouns, my lifelong ambivalences, my slips in and out of different selves—all of these were things I'd once associated with games, with role play, with feminine and androgynous Japanese characters I loved and wanted to become. As I imagined it, the autism narrative turned all this into a "lack of social-intentional functionality." And like queerness and video game addiction, autism too has been seen as an epidemic among young people, always on the rise.

It is possible too that when I was young, my autism was confused with all the ways people saw me as an Asian kid obsessed with video games. Asians, gamers, and autistic people are not the same, but there's something eerily similar in the way Asians—particularly Asian men—are stereotyped by Western cultures that parallels the ways gamers and autistic people are stereotyped. All of these groups are cast as asocial and inscrutable peoples who lack emotions, especially empathy. Gamers, Asians, and autistics do not make eye contact. They are silent. They only relate to others through cold and calculating behaviour. They are good with math and computers but not with anything requiring physical strength, dexterity, or social skills. All three groups are cast as "special" in ways that can mean economic advantage and gifted intelligence but also suggest copying, cheating, or conniving. All are seen as having superhuman savant-like abilities to beat others at games, whether it's the card-counting advantage of Raymond in the 1988 film *Rain Man* or the domination of Asian players in the contemporary field of esports.

In the years since my diagnosis, autism has forced me to reckon with all the things that once made me a gamer. I have experienced what Yergeau calls *resonance*, a neuroqueer feeling where one's embodied actions suddenly resonate as part of a diagnosis, when a flick of the fingers turns from a video game habit of button-mashing into a self-stimulating autistic behaviour.[12] Resonance tends to happen not with ideas or relationships but with habituated bodily action. And what behaviour feels more resonant, more repetitive and obsessive, than the daily act of picking up a controller and tapping its buttons for hours at a time?

~

Race, gender, and sexuality are relational, shifting a bit from group to group, country to country. But neurodivergence feels like an always-present vapour. It can come in very hot environments, but it can also come when it's freezing, right out of my mouth. Sometimes it disappears instantly, sucked up by an overhead fan. Other times it makes freakish clouds that dot the atmosphere, signalling a change in weather. Sometimes it grows, gaining mass, until it blocks out the sun for days.

~

As a parent with a child myself, I find that most parents love their children but fear the way their children might blur distinctions: inside and outside, girls and boys, cops and robbers, us and them. Neurodiverse children go even further, mixing identity with colour and texture, associating emotions and feelings with numbers and ideas, blurring their sense of family to include those who act the part and to exclude those who don't. Even as adults, those of us with autism don't just refuse traditional distinctions, we actively resist any attempts to be disciplined by them. As Yergeau argues, autistic people supposedly lack the concept not only of sexual orientation, but of *orientedness* itself.[13] We don't see clear boundaries between genders, sexualities, races, selves, and others. But why, in this troublingly separated world, would our lack of distinctions be considered a *dis*ability?

During the Philippine-American War, my ancestors, colonized by Spain and then America, were branded not as revolutionaries but as tantrum-throwing children with a tendency to "run amok." In 1899, the British writer Rudyard Kipling wrote a poem for the intended purpose of convincing the United States to colonize the Philippines. He wrote, "Take up the White Man's burden— / Have done with childish days."[14] Going to war against the "half child" Filipinos and colonizing them for nearly half a century was, in a sense, a means of proving America's adulthood to the world, of making and marking the distinctions between adult empires and childish colonies. Conquering Filipinos was the right of passage required for a still-developing country to be initiated into the world's civilizing brotherhood. Over two hundred thousand Filipinos died.

~

> Bodies are never singular, but rather haunted, strengthened, underscored by countless other bodies.
> —Eli Clare, *Exile and Pride*

Autism, queer Asian boyhood, and playing games all have one more thing in common: they are all construed as involuntary disadvantages. No one, our society around us believes, would choose to be autistic, queer, childish, a brown Asian boy in America, and a "video game addict." These are things to be hidden, shamed, closeted, dismissed, toned down, until one can pass for the norm or at least put on a convincing-enough mask. No one would choose to play video games all day with a fulfilling and stable social life waiting just outside their bedroom door. The world is always waiting for us to develop, to grow out of it, to choose change.

These days, the tight hold of the belief that video games will turn young white men violent has finally started to loosen. Today, games are becoming far more associated with diverse demographics: queer people, autistic people, and Asian peoples—all those who seem unable to grow out of their childhood. Everything that parents fear about video games today is everything that makes me who I am; it is me. Video games will turn you into me.

When I look back on my childhood, I don't wish that I had gone outside more or had more friends or "real life" experiences. Instead, I envy the child who could absorb games in a way that's becoming more difficult as I grow older. The more I age, the more I long to create worlds the way I did with my twin brother, leaping into ideas without caring whether they were brainy material or not. I envy all the coping and care and world making that was happening there in our bedroom. Because whatever was going on in there, whether it was neurotypical or not, of one thing I am assured: it was fucking *fun*. I don't remember ever laughing as loud, as hard, or feeling as free.

I remember these moments of fun now when I play *Sonic the Hedgehog* with my son and, as the pilot companion Tails, lift him to the clouds only to drop him into the instant-death void. His revenge comes tenfold in *Roblox* when he scooches me off a levitating obstacle course, and the limbs of my blocky body tumble apart, bouncing off into the endless nothing. Watching my despair, he can't hold back, and his explosive laugher startles me. It's an echo of my and my brother's laughter from many years ago: wild, uncontainable, overflowing the edges of identity, difference, and diagnosis.

If all my divergent differences are what forced me into that room with my brother, and now with my son, then perhaps I'm no worse for it. Being autistic, Asian, brown, queer, and genderqueer: we got it all right here. Come to our floating isles and play a while.

~

> An adventure's no fun if it's too easy.
> —Sonic, *Sonic Generations*

In the *Super Mario Bros.* games, I am a reddish-blue figure who can jump over things, jump on things, or jump to my own demise. As I move—always to the right—a world reveals itself. And everything that comes from that world is a potential danger. A gap. An enemy. A fireball. I become attuned to the jump button. The slightest offbeat, a pause for a split second too long, and I am falling rather than bouncing, or launching right into that fireball. I die, restart, and jump again. As I move, I reveal the smooth, soft world. With every jump I uncloak a new danger, knowing that soon I will slip, fall, or burn. But I'll be back.

When I feel exhausted by Mario's world—the dangerous, ever-gnawing dread of dodging someone else's fireballs—I turn to that other cherished video game mascot, Sonic. Leaving behind soft, slowly revealed environments, I plunge into the daunting, headlong fall of a blurred background. Rather than carefully watch for danger, I form myself into a hard, spiky surface and shoot through the world like a cannonball. In *Sonic* games, I need not fear the unknown. The unknown fears me.

My twin brother, Cameron, does not see himself on the autism spectrum. He has taken the online tests and thought back to his own behaviours, and he prefers not to put a stamp on his own unique way of being. Despite the different ways we narrate our lives, these differences have never really separated us. From our floating isles, we saw everything together, we crossed boundaries of language and imagination. For us, the world was not white and non-white, autistic and non-autistic, or queer and straight. No. Everything was Sonic-like or Mario-like. Every event was either a slow reveal or a head-thrusting craze. Even our coded babble was often just references to the secret names we sometimes gave each other: Mario and Sonic.

Because I cling to childhood, because my divergences mark me as a child, I still hold true to the Mario-like and the Sonic-like. Sometimes I move in careful, quiet ways, letting the softness of the world reveal itself with one small gesture or feeling. I look for the gaps, the frowns, the fire. Other times, I move at supersonic speeds through worlds of unabashed invention. But no matter what comes, I—like most gamers—will find some way to keep the world revealing itself. Whether it's a threatening world, or one that passes by so quickly that we feel like we've flown past it, the impulse is the same. Right joystick, mash button, jump. Keep jumping forward. Duck, roll, go with the flow, mask up, go astray, ignore the quest, find misadventure in the caverns. But don't stop moving—movement creates the worlds we invent together, and we must do all we can to keep them alive. And when you see a ball of fire coming at you, jump!

CHAPTER 2
Playing Roles

I've spent just five seconds in a chat room called "Dirty Schoolgirl RP" when I start receiving invites to private chat "plays." "Want to get pervy?" says one message. "Into nekocats?" says another.

I snub these invites, exit the chat room, and skim other room names: "Hot Springs," "Futanari Lounge and Inn," "Nekocat Daycare," and "You Are in a Mansion Rooming with an Opposite-Sex Roommate What Will It Turn Into."

I enter a "Bar and Grill," unsure what I'm looking for. Panda_girl and Daughter_of_hades098 post flirtatious sentences full of *quirked brows* and *faint giggles*. I can feel them longing for something: a role to play against their own, a muse to convey their other—rather than their *inner*—selves.

After an hour of lurking, I find a post that charms me into yet another role:

> Rose Lunaria: *Sits silent, with a herding pressure in her heart.*

Though brief, the sentence catches me in its gravity. I scan their profile:

> Name: Lunaria
> Special: fire type
> Sexuality: bi
> Personality: bubbly very childish and is chill until u annoy her then it burns
> *Can turn into fire-breathing dragon

These profiles, in erotic chat room land, are not merely meant to offer an identity, or to clarify boundaries, or to entice a response. They help us, the responder, decide what role we want to play, which of our characters might excite and prod theirs. Should I play a character to charm them up and earn their "bubbly" self? Or should I play a character who will provoke them and feel how "it burns"?

I launch an opening salvo into the chat room:

> You could recognize someone creeping open the tavern door, holding their bracelet's silver chain to keep those crystal charms from announcing a new presence. From the small purview beneath a sun hat, finds a table and, kicking legs up, sifts through a newspaper kept rolled up in a left sleeve, letting the sweat-mixed print rub off on fingers.

This is the first time in two years I've entered a role-play chat room. Though the medium has transformed time and again since I was eleven, the exhilarating high I get from spinning a post and the elation from partnering up with an anonymous writer to clash words and imaginary bodies remain palpable.

> Rose Lunaria: *Cheeks sunken with the thoughtfully casual pucker of glossy, venom-stung lips, silent, eyes squinting down as if she couldn't quite see words to describe her.*

A shot in my direction pushes me deeper into my role. Game on.

~

I started chat room role-playing in the mid-nineties, a weird time to be a kid, when the dial-up internet was barely useable and the information superhighway, as it was called, didn't refer to Wikipedia or Google, but to Yahoo!, America Online, and MTV.com. You could make a webpage on GeoCities or Angelfire for free, spend an afternoon learning HTML, write your thoughts in zany fonts and colours, then put up a counter on your website and proudly watch it tick up (sometimes into the dozens!). Every minute online was precious, since surfing the web took time to connect, cost a good amount of money, and only one person could do it at a time. (If someone needed to use the phone or was expecting a call, forget it.) The internet came at an especially good time for kids like me who were socially challenged and had lumbering brown and effeminate bodies that did not take well to real-life social situations. When my parents went to sleep or were at work, I spent my days reaching out to complete strangers in a realm of shared imagination.

The mid-nineties were also weird for me because I was living in Portland, Oregon, the whitest big city in the United States, a city full of people who proudly called themselves weird. Portland had the oft-floated claim of containing both the largest number of churches per capita and the largest number of strip clubs. My twin brother, Cameron, and I passed two strip clubs every morning when we walked to our Christian church, which doubled as our elementary school. Portland's odd pairing of erotic stimulation and religious purgation was everywhere. Movie theatres were riddled with films about heaven and angels (*City of Angels*, *What Dreams May Come*, *Michael*, *Angels in the Outfield*), while Portland's nightly attraction was the longest-running film and live performance of *The Rocky Horror Picture Show*, which in 2020 continued to play all throughout COVID to an empty theatre.

My sexual awakening in a city that was both intensely religious and enchantingly erotic was, in short, unconventional. No school, parent, or mentor felt it necessary to teach me, a fat brown boy in a white city, about sex. (It wasn't like I'd be having any, anyway.) The first time I recall anyone ever mentioning sex was when I was sitting at my family's dinner table, minding my business, and my mother looked at me in revulsion and said, "We don't masturbate at the dinner table." I had no idea what masturbation was, and I thought it had more to do with my left hand serving myself mac and cheese rather than my right hand, which was securely inside my pants. What was this thing called "masturbation"? My mother couldn't be referring to that clandestine stroking habit that I—the first person in human history—had invented, could she?

When the internet first came to our homes and webpages took eons to load, we kids didn't all immediately start looking up pornography, as many might assume. But make no mistake, I did use the internet to masturbate. A lot. It just never involved pictures. It involved chat rooms full of young role-players like myself, still learning to feel themselves out.

~

Imagination is collective work. It extends from games just as it emerges from legends, storytellers, bibles. It begins by moving someone, then it moves around. A father sees his son playing with an imaginary friend and feels called upon to either acknowledge the imaginary being or deny it. Either way, a whole world is built from that moment—collectively built. A world of play and love, or of discipline and shame.

In my youth, I lived so deeply within my imagination that pretend places felt more real than the people in front of me. Coming home from church, filled with the words of Bible studies and the pulpit, I often imagined hell. All day. All the time. In vivid, waking nightmares. I pondered all the ways I might be tortured there. Some were funny, like never being able to masturbate in a room full of naked people. Others were visceral, like when I saw an oil fire at a church potluck and spent a sleepless night imagining myself roasting alive.

Once, on a visit to an outdoor shrine of religious sculptures (the National Sanctuary of Our Sorrowful Mother, or "the Grotto,") I asked my father about hell. With every holy visage of Carrara marble, I heard the cries of those who suffered in eternal damnation. My father could see how tormented I was and tried to comfort me. He said hell was not a place of fire and demons. That was just the cartoon version. Hell was isolation and darkness, a place without God, without anyone. And yes, with eternal punishment. He quoted Scripture to prove it.

My father's imagining of hell was far worse than the hell of fire and brimstone. At least in my cartoonish hell, I could suffer with others. But to be in total silence and darkness forever, secluded and numb, was beyond anything my imagination could conjure. And all it took to be forever isolated in darkness was a single trespass, a single touch.

Whether for the lack of being desired or the fear of sin, erotic physical contact was off the table for my entire adolescence. So be it. There were other ways to feel touched.

~

The realm of chat room role play (or "chat RP") was born with the internet, but it descended from the elder realms of improvised live-action role-playing (LARP) and the written form of fan fiction. Like chat RP, these forms were seen as derivative, juvenile, and a tinge erotic. Though known writers would sometimes get involved in LARP and fan fiction communities, it was usually only in secret. (W.H. Auden was a known annoyance to the *Lord of the Rings* Role Play Society at Harvard for being too "in character" and continually calling himself Gimli.)[15] In the early nineties, text-based role play first emerged online in the form of multi-user domains (MUDs) where users could log into "object-oriented" chat rooms like LambdaMOO and play with shared virtual spaces whose descriptions would be stored in an online server. Writers like Julian Dibbell and Lisa Nakamura documented the early days of LambdaMOO, noting how its object-oriented spaces very often led to the erotic objectifications of the virtual body.[16]

Taken as a mode of collaborative writing, modern chat RP fuses the erotic anonymity of "playing" with strangers—each cosplaying dreamy, sparkly eyed video game characters—with conventions from science fiction and fantasy. The result is a language of suggestive yet otherworldly intimacies. Everyone *smirks, gazes, purrs, gestures toward* something, *shakes* or *cants* their head, *takes a drag, swigs,* or *chugs* their drink, *swifts hair* from their eyes, *sticks out* their tongue, and *stares blankly*, all while *glancing out the window*. Strangers *hug, sit on top of each other, nibble on arms*, and defy decorum by *putting their feet upon each other's knees*. When no one responds to your posts, you basically play with yourself. You *feel hungry, chew the inside of your cheek*, or *sup in silence*. It's no coincidence that when engaging in self-play, posts are often about your character's appetite. You've got a big one, and you're in a room full of hungry denizens.

~

In early 1997, one of my sister's forlorn lovers broke into our house and stole our Super Nintendo, plus my parents' golf clubs. Without a gaming system, I didn't know what to do with myself. One dull afternoon, while idly playing solitaire on my parents' work computer, I made a few curious clicks, and a crunching sound came from our speaker. Then, the screen brightened into a blue background, framing the square of a white text box. I had discovered a new world of games, one that only required text, connection, and imagination. Cast from my Nintendo at eleven years old, I found the role-play chat room. There, I met a handful of other young chatters, all with cartoon personas and pansexual appetites.

~

1997 was a crucial year for chat RP. The Japanese role-playing game *Final Fantasy VII* was released that January, elevating character-driven stories in video games while also containing horrendously (and often hilariously) translated dialogue. The game's fantastical universe compelled young adolescents like myself to go into online chat rooms to seek interpretations of the game's eco-terrorist characters, biopunk style, and enigmatic dialogue. The game's creator, SquareSoft, even instituted a corporation-wide ban on creating more content for the game known as "no one can open the box," since players themselves were so invested in creating their own storylines for the game. And indeed, we loved making the game's sci-fi/fantasy world our own.

The golden age of chat room role-playing was also mechanical in nature. In December 1996, the internet service provider America Online (AOL) rid users of arbitrary hourly allotments and introduced unlimited usage, allowing eleven-year-old me to cruise on the internet without accumulating steep charges for my parents. Included in this unleashing of infinite playtime was the AOL chat room service, which allowed users to create and manage their own rooms. Guilds emerged in the thousands, some favouring the game dynamics of dice rolls and experience points, while others promoted experimentation, creativity, and the sacred bond between character and writer.

Final Fantasy VII's multigenre world, combined with boundless time in chat rooms, made chat RP a space of unrestricted imagination, a floating isle that became unapologetically character focused. The writer at the keyboard was known as a *mun*, meaning "mundane," and was only referred to via their character (e.g., Rose Lunaria's mun). This convention split the real self of the mun from the performed self of the role, making it possible for characters to take part in naughty, sinful acts that their muns—perhaps good Christian boys like myself—would never dream of doing in real life. To role-play with someone meant playing along with this fantasy. Written gestures like *eyes rounded like those of owls* or *soft voice, arms folding* did not need to mention the character's name or even their pronouns. Some characters simply had no name, no gender, no pronoun, and most of us never noticed.

For those who went to chat RP to act out our fantasies, chat rooms offered space and time to bond with our character, to dwell with them long enough to respect their actions, to attune to their psychological imprints, and to play them against other settings and people. Public chat rooms acted as springboards to attract like-minded role-players who, after parlaying with a potential buddy, would then organize private chats within whatever genre they fancied. Likewise, public chat rooms were often chaotic meeting grounds with names like "All Creatures Tavern," "Outcast Orphanage," "Mental Hospital," or "Monsters Academy," all of which merged genres of sci-fi, fantasy, myth, and anime, creating aberrant worlds of experimentation that tested characters against the truly out-of-their-world.

I began role-playing in "Inns" and "Taverns," but I was quickly drawn into the world of *Final Fantasy VII*. I role-played the game's characters before I played the game itself, as I didn't own a PlayStation and had to wait for the game's PC release in 1998. Through chat RP, I came to understand *Final Fantasy VII* as a world where cyberpunk rebels fight an evil corporation named Shinra whose depletion of the planet's resources threatens to kill every human being living on it.

At first, I preferred role-playing as the game's mysterious, self-inventing, and cross-dressing main character, Cloud Strife, a mercenary and excommunicated member of an elite warrior unit. For games scholar Colin Milburn, Cloud's sustained popularity as one of gaming's most famous characters comes from his peculiar mode of self-reflective role play. Players cannot really identify with Cloud because not even Cloud is really Cloud—he is a liar and loser playing the role of "Cloud" to become, as he later admits, "the master of my own illusory world."[17] As Milburn writes, it is through Cloud's separation of his selves into roles that the player can understand themselves: "Playing the role of 'Cloud' is literally the means by which Cloud works through failure to become better than himself. We, as players of Cloud, are invited to take the same initiative."[18]

Eventually, I did play *Final Fantasy VII*, and I did fall in love with one of its characters—not Cloud, but Reno, a beautiful red-haired secret agent who sports a red ponytail and fights with an electric cattle prod. In the *Final Fantasy VII* story, Reno is introduced as a Javert-type fanatically obsessed with hunting down Cloud, though he often prioritizes small things like not stepping on church flowers. He is leader of the Turks, a black-ops paramilitary wing of Shinra whose responsibilities range from protecting the Shinra president to finding and killing eco-terrorists like Cloud and his compatriots. Though his youthful hubris is signalled by his untucked shirt and ponytail, Reno is quite menacing. In one scene, he hangs from a helicopter, giving instructions to the machine gunner. In another, he electrocutes a man with his blue-fizzled cattle prod. In another, he presses a button that causes the destruction and death of an entire city sector.

As Cloud's nemesis and foil, Reno also offers a mode of self-reflective role play. After some brutal confrontations with Reno, the player begins to learn of his double-sided personality, his ability to see his militaristic position as a mere role. The first indication is a boyish encounter where you (as Cloud) stumble upon Reno asking another Turk, "Who do you like?," meaning *Who are you attracted to?* Only after goading his friend does Reno spot you and instruct his minion, "Don't go easy on them, not even the girls."

Reno's truly quirky self comes out during a side quest to Wutai, a popular vacation spot colonized by Shinra that closely resembles an island in the Pacific like Okinawa. The islandic space and warm breeze shifts Reno from a menacing black-ops agent into a tourist looking for his next salt-rimmed margarita. When the player finds Reno and his fellow Turks sunbathing on the Wutai Village beach, Reno forbids his agents from fighting because they are "off-duty." Later, when Shinra soldiers beg Reno to help them fight, he chastises them, saying, "Lookin' at you is making me sober." Then he gives a line that was to be repeated in role-play communities for decades: "Don't misunderstand. A pro isn't someone who sacrifices himself for his job. That's just a fool."

I still remember the first time I read this line, one still commonplace on *Final Fantasy* community forums today. As a middle-school kid, my "job" was not fighting eco-terrorists, but performing my role as a straight, religious, white-passing young man. Replace the word *job* with any other role based on gender, whiteness, religion, or neuronormativity, and Reno is expressing a philosophical statement about how to live in a world that expects you to always perform a role: your "job." Reno is a pro at playing the many roles people expect of him, but he never gives himself to them. That is the way of fools.

~

> When it comes to sex, perhaps the body in question
> is not the physical one at all, but its psychic double,
> the bodylike self-representation we carry around in
> our heads—and that whether we present that body to
> another as a meat puppet or a word puppet is not nearly
> as significant a distinction as one might have thought.
> —Julian Dibbell, *My Tiny Life*

Reno, my cynical, red-haired, ponytailed, flirtatious *charrie* ("character"), guided me through every early sexual experience. The first time I had a truly life-giving sexual encounter, the first time I successfully flirted with someone, the first time I had sex, I was role-playing as Reno. I must have had cybersex a hundred times as Reno before my "real self" ever held another person's hand.

I remember well the day I lost my virtual virginity as Reno. My fellow guild members and I were hanging around the Shinra offices, listening to music (lyrics we muns would type into the chat). It got late, and characters began to leave ("gtg byebye!"), all except one, ElenaXFF7X. Soon, ElenaXFF7X and I were alone, drinking whiskey, singing, teasing, watching rain patter against the gigantic office windows. I knew nothing about ElenaXFF7X's mun, had never done the whole A/S/L? ("Age/sex/location?") thing. But I remember cybering with ElenaXFF7X that night better than I remember my first kiss or my first date. Clothing *drifted off*, breath *heaved*, hips *thrusted*, mouths *tongued*, ponytails *tangled*, and in the end one of us was *scooped up* into the other's arms.

Like many first romances, my first time was far more meaningful for me than for her. I grew too attached and became jealous when she would sit on someone else's lap and purr—though everyone sat in each other's laps and purred.

After ElenaXFF7X, I gained sexual experience with more game characters and learned how to type with one hand. Meanwhile, in "real life," away from keyboard, I was beginning to learn and understand a very specific type of manhood that I was expected to perform at all times. I was once asked to keep score for a girls' volleyball game, and for some reason I felt this intense pressure to catcall them as they played (I did, and they never let me keep score again). I was scolded in the first grade when a girl tried to impress me by doing a cartwheel, and I asked her to do it again, having never seen a girl's underwear before. The first time I was called into the principal's office in school was after I commented "Nice ass" to a boy pissing in a neighbouring urinal. (I thought *ass* meant *penis*, and I was trying to give a thoughtful compliment.) In every case, I came to understand that my words were sinful, though, having had no sex education from anyone, I didn't understand why. In time, I learned to never talk about bodies or sex at all, and to hide the feminine parts of myself: my natural dark eye lines, my red lips. I began to bite my lips before going to class, stopping the blood flow so they would turn from red to white.

In chat RP, I could keep my lips red. I could express any erotic phrase, refer to any body part, and be as gender weird as I wanted. I could touch and be touched without fear of retribution, so long as the character's mun gave permission. As Reno, my little ponytailed redhead, I felt intentional, natural, unmasked, and I felt the erotic power of written words. But then, away from keyboard, I again felt uncomfortable, queer, exhausted, as if working myself to death in an agonizing and nefarious job.

Reno was my release, my alter ego, my untucked, smooth-talking agent of destruction. Like many gamers who grew up selecting the same character repeatedly (as I also did with Princess Peach, Chun-Li, and Kitana), I eventually had to question the gendered and sexual meanings of my actions. Was I playing Reno because I wanted to *be* him, or because I wanted to be *with* him?

~

> In human consciousness eroticism is that within man
> which calls his being in question.
> —Georges Bataille, *Eroticism*

The queer theorist Judith Butler famously argued that gender is "performative."[19] Not performative as in we're performing gender as mere actors, but as in the gestures and utterances of gender produce how we imagine gender itself. In so doing, they compel others to reiterate the same norms, habits, looks, and attitudes of their own assigned gender.

I've always been drawn to the term *performative* not despite, but precisely *because* it makes gender sound a lot like the performance of an actor. From an early age, I was able to think of gender as a character assigned to me, as a role I undertook. Thinking this way gave me power over merely "acting like a man." Instead, I knowingly and (often ironically) "acted" like a man, performing the part of a man in a sustained drag performance, masking through masculinity. It was not through queer theory or even sex ed that I learned to do this, but through the imaginative and interactive play of chat RP.

At eleven years old, I had no language to understand gender and sexuality. Yet I was still searching for a different type of gender performativity, perhaps androgyny. The problem was, I did not want to be seen as ugly. I still wanted to attract people. In chat RP I could be sexy and desirable and still be queer, androgynous, and obsessed with video games. But, away from keyboard, I was fat, brown, and effeminate, and nobody found me the least bit attractive. Why would I do anything to further restrict my chances of ever knowing what it was like to kiss someone, away from keyboard?

Queer theory is great for thinking about how society reproduces gender and sexual norms and how this caters to long-held stereotypes about race, class, and nation. But queer theory, for the most part, seems to avoid dealing with the simple fact that much of our gender performativity is merely about trying to get laid. We're animals, keen for love as well as lovemaking, and many of us would happily change our behaviours (and our gender performances) if it would get someone to kiss us, touch us, scoop us up, or give us stuff. Gender is sometimes just about seeing someone you want to have sex with and adjusting yourself accordingly—that is, according to their manner of dress, their gender signals, their "vibes." The times I can recall performing at my most masculine were when I was longing to make out with someone who was attracted to masculinity. And the same for when I performed at my most feminine, or my most androgynous, or my most catty, or my most bratty, or my most overblown, geeky, game-loving self.

There is something about erotic sensation that puts us instantly into role-play mode. We become the baby girl to their sugar daddy, the student to their teacher, the sub to their dom, the princess to their valiant knight, the Romeo to their Juliet, the Kirk to their Spock, the elite socialite Daisy to their enigmatic Gatsby, the Reno to their Elena. We don't just play gender, nor do we just play *with* gender. We play gender *for* each other. And we do so especially when we're horny. Yes, the identities we inhabit can feel empowering, meaningful, and restorative. But sometimes we want to give as much as we receive. All it takes is meeting the right person for our once-sacred identities to transmorph into utterly profane roles.

~

> Get over here!
> —Scorpion, *Mortal Kombat*

I first watched porn in a basement with a group of church boys, just after we spent an hour slicing off each other's blood-drenched limbs in *Mortal Kombat 11*. While our parents ate dessert, we kids hobbled around a screen, taking turns brutally impaling, defacing, and ripping into each other's bodies. After we had gawked at the game's freakishly exaggerated violence for some time, one boy asked, "You guys wanna see something *really* crazy?" He threw in a pornographic video cassette. My twin brother and I tried to protect our souls by only looking at the screen through our fingers. Our other friends dared each other not to be the first to "bust a nut."

I don't recall anything about the porn from that night, but I do remember the elaborate brutality of playing *Mortal Kombat II* for the first time. I remember the game's operatic violence of splattered plasma, grey matter, and squirting eyeballs. I remember the demonic Scorpion performing a "spine rip fatality," a move that is often credited with creating the ESRB organization that assigns age and content ratings to all video games in the US today. Mostly, I remember hearing that implicitly erotic line at the end of every match: "FINISH HIM!" or "FINISH HER!" This line manifested our dark sides through awe-inspiring violence as well as unexpected intimacy. To be "finished" was to cross the barriers between life and death, brutality and kindness, hate and love.

In the first *Mortal Kombat*, after the announcer commands the player to "FINISH HIM!" or "FINISH HER!" the player can violently impale their opponent in a spectacle of gore (a "fatality"), or they can do nothing and let their opponent live (the loser simply falls and passes out). But in *Mortal Kombat II*, the winner can choose from a number of finishing acts, from transforming their enemy into a baby (a "babality") to performing acts of kindness and goodwill. In these "friendship finishers," players can give opponents an autographed headshot, deliver a birthday present, blow bubbles, make a rainbow, paint a picture, cook dinner, grow flowers, or break out in a disco dance.

The night of my first porno was easily forgettable next to the things I did when I was directed to "finish" my friends. Between the lustful groans of the porn star and the commands from Scorpion to "Get over here!" I learned the intense pleasures of what it meant to embrace mere mortality.

~

> What comes out of a person is what defiles them.
> For it is from within, out of a person's heart, that evil thoughts come.
> —Mark 7:20–23, the Bible

After two years of role-playing online, and after many years of playing *Mortal Kombat 11*, my straitjacketed role of a religious boy began to loosen. I was the grandson of two hardline protestant preachers, one of whom (the white one) had written twelve workbooks on Christianity and an exegesis on church history entitled *Christ-Centered Servant-Team Leadership*. We went to church at least once a day, sometimes two or three times. There was little room for error, humour, or otherworldly love. Yet, somehow, one day, the truths of religion—and truth's absences—started to reveal themselves like threads poking out of a pressed uniform.

The first thread emerged when I was baptized at thirteen. I expected a new self, with new sensations, new eyes, and new powers to think and feel. But as I emerged from the cubby bath with the preacher's fingers pinching my nose, I just felt wet. Perverse thoughts continued to come, and I felt no closer to the divine.

On its own, I could have dealt with this strange absence of the Holy Spirit. But what followed was far more difficult to absorb: how the church elders, my family, and my peers pushed me to perform the feelings of renewal that I most definitely did not feel. "How do you feel?" church members asked, holding my hands, ready to embrace me upon my answer, which should have been "renewed," "blessed," or "saved." But I refused to perform this role that included, so soon after my baptismal, telling a lie. "I feel okay," was all I could muster. It was the truth, and yet the looks on their faces told me this truth was somehow a betrayal.

My refusal to perform my role of "the baptized" dismayed those around me. Perhaps I wasn't ready. Perhaps I didn't truly hold Jesus in my heart. For weeks, I wavered back and forth between these attitudes. At times I thought the absence of God was my own fault, that I hadn't been sincere enough in my desire to be baptized. Other times, I felt the pressure in my bones to perform a role that everyone wanted me to play, but one that would have been a sin worthy of damnation. For years, the promise of saying those words and the warmth they could bring hung above me: "I feel God within me, and I know I am saved."

In a way, after the baptism, I did feel different. I could see threads poking out all around me, and the more I felt pressured into the role of a religious boy, the more I began to pull at those threads. One day in church I noticed how all the congregation members had Bibles sitting in front of them in the pew pockets, yet when the preacher quoted from the Bible, I was the only one looking up the quotes. Mostly, I found these quotes to be either taken completely out of context or just plain erroneous. But nobody else bothered to look them up, and sometimes my pew neighbor would tell me to stop reading from the Bible and *listen* to the sermon. Why even have all those Bibles in front of us, if it was so taboo to actually pick one up and read it?

Unwittingly, I pursued a path that many atheists and agnostics credit for their profound loss of faith: I read the Bible. Not just the parts preachers read, not just the red-coloured words of Jesus Christ, but the entire book. I finished it before Christian summer camp, thinking it would restore my love for God and my faith in his word. It had the opposite effect. There was so much violence, so many covenants and rules nobody took seriously, and the entire book was so draped with exaggerations and lunacy it was easy to get lost in its enigmatic parables and totally outdated commands. I was astonished at how many of the Bible's most emphasized lessons were not about sexuality at all, but about things like usury, avarice, pride, and greed. Why, when I was taught Biblical parables in school, did the sins of sex and lust seem the *only* important ones to heed? Yet, according to the Bible, I was just as deserving of hell were I gay as if I were to lend someone a dollar for the pop machine and charge him a dime as interest.

Reading the Bible destroyed my faith more than any person, desire, or video game. I was convinced that the people who claimed to follow the Bible had never actually read it, and again I felt an immense distance between myself and the roles I was meant to play. I had once been a pro at playing the role of a good preacher's grandson. But doing so now felt like being an agent for an evil corporation. And this job didn't even grant me a wage—only pain.

~

> Gender is Queer. By which I mean irredeemably strange, ungraspable, out of sync ... even when it is played quite straight.
> —Kathryn Bond Stockton, *Gender(s)*

A year after my baptismal, I could no longer play the role of religious boy. I began pulling apart the costume. I was impenitent, with a world burning inside me. I didn't care if it was the fires of truth and justice, or the flames of hell.

At the same time, I began to see how the lifetime role of preacher's son had been tearing my father apart. In 1997, his brother Daniel, who I knew as Uncle Dan, died of complications from AIDS. I was not told how he died, or what it meant for our religious family, or for my uncle's soul. My father was the inheritor of his father's religious legacy, a role that surmounted his role as a brother in mourning. By all accounts of my father's Christianity, Uncle Dan would most certainly have been sent to hell. I heard many quoted Scriptures proving this at the time, though I had ceased taking Scripture as fact.

~

With my uncle's death, my father's role as a preacher's son became unbearable, unbendable, and self-destructive. I was eleven, just logging in to the chat RP phenomenon, when my father began to drink more, and his presence became a storm of anger and grief that raged for years. My brother and I started hiding in our rooms as soon as we saw his headlights flash from the driveway. He began to lose every job he had, until he became the janitor of our middle school. Then, his despair from failing to live up to the roles of fatherhood, brotherhood, and religion turned inward into the omnivorous flames of self-hate, threatening to consume anyone and anything. My mother went into retreat, flying away to Las Vegas, bringing my brother and me with her.

Our uncle's death caused my brother and me to both see our role of religious boy no longer as a fun role-playing fantasy, but as a paralyzing nightmare. We fled to our floating isle chat rooms, which helped clarify the roles we had to play when we were away from keyboard. We may have been mundane, but we both came to the decision that we would rather be true people than good people. To commit ourselves to never telling a lie, to saying what we thought, to having no filter, was our way of rebelling against religious hypocrisy. And the biggest lie was that our roles in the church were anything more than that—roles we merged into. My role as a religious boy had become less important, less meaningful, than my online self. Given a choice, I would skip church and turn away from God just to play as a ruthless cattle prod–wielding maniac who, between battles, liked to ask his underlings, "So ... who do you like?"

~

Today, chat RP has all but vanished into the ether of virtual, visual role play. After a decade of growing into a thriving writing community, chat RP met an early demise in 2004, with the release of the hugely successful massive multiplayer online role-playing game (MMORPG) *World of Warcraft*. Almost overnight, role-players abandoned chat rooms for the three-dimensional virtual world. Guilds and storylines went from hundreds of members to dozens to none. Even the treasured chat RP comic, *Elf Only Inn* (2002–08), took a year of absence, only to return focused solely on MMORPGs like *World of Warcraft*.

Today, after over a decade of wandering in the wilderness of online fragmentation, chat RP has had small re-emergences on smartphones with apps like Amino and Discord combining chats with hashtag (#) and mention (@) mechanics, and in the private realms of erotic artificial intelligence. But these spaces feel ephemeral and are continually being restricted and censored by smartphone policies banning eroticism and sex.

Over two decades after chat RP's heyday, there is still very little (if any) awareness that it ever existed. In the circles of literary scholars, magazine writers, fiction authors, and effete critics, chat RP is virtually unheard of. Perhaps this is because chat RP produced no consumer products and had no archive or audience, other than other role-players. As an improvised practice, chat RP was too transient to capture. Users remained anonymous, and their written words lasted only until they reached the chat room's loading limit before transpiring into white space. Even while writing this, I found it impossible to locate any of my old chat room hangouts, transcripts, guild webpages, or fellow role-players. It's as if the white space at the top of every chat room didn't only erase our written words, but forever imprisoned our characters—and with them, our past selves—into the isolation of a forgotten time.

~

For myself and many in my gaming generation, chat RP will be remembered as the way we grew into our own roles and our own bodies. The bond between myself (as mun) and my character was unexpectedly intimate: Losing myself in my character did not mean knowing them from head to toe, but submitting myself to their will, letting myself slip into them (or "bleed," as role-playing scholars put it).

The act of role-playing lies somewhere between transition and drag, between taking identity seriously and making fun of it. Together we transform well-known characters from *Lord of the Rings*, *Star Wars*, or *Final Fantasy* into queer avatars from which we enact fantasies that have no other platform for expression. When others come along to play, new spheres of intimacy open up. Our desires are not merely staged, but recreated. The roles I played in chat RP were not about identity, empowerment, pride, community, getting to heaven, or even "being seen," but about testing (and teasing) the meanings of those "real world" roles. Only by seeing them clearly—their restrictions and their possibilities—could I decide which I could take on and which I needed to leave behind.

Role play, not religion, moulded and scrutinized my conduct. It placed me in unique situations, each one deserving of its own ethical reflections, and taught me how to handle my desires as well as my failures. Sometimes, when I found a partner to play with, their anonymity could transform me, compel me to react to their gazes, teases, and touches, all while carrying on a conversation "out of character" reflecting upon our characters' actions. Deprived of any sex education from my school or church, I learned through chat RP how to ask for consent, how to create dialogue with others to make agreements for both our characters and ourselves.

After dwelling for years within role-play chats, taking on new characters and inventing my own, I grew to envision myself as plural, cozy in my multiplicity, at ease with my own change. And, if I wasn't feeling accepted by those in the real world, I could always enter a *Final Fantasy VII* chat room, sit on some stranger's lap, smirk, bite the inside of my cheek, and purr.

CHAPTER 3
War and the Terror of Teenagers

> Teenagers are the most unloved group in our nation. Teenagers are often feared precisely because they are often exposing the hypocrisy of parents and of the world around them. And no group of teenagers is more feared than a pack of teenage boys.
> —bell hooks, *The Will to Change*

I had just turned sixteen and was living in Las Vegas on September 11, 2001, when a television cart was wheeled into my high school lunchroom, and we watched the second tower of the World Trade Center fall. In the days following, I don't remember feeling the things that most people say they felt: rage, an all-consuming desire for revenge, the national fervour of televised patriotic static. I do remember other things: the jocks at school coming out full force with their racism, grown-ass adults using new and old racial epithets to describe anyone from the Middle East, the intense buying out of guns and ammunition throughout the nation.

I remember friends bringing pistols and shotguns to each other's houses. I remember trucks full of white men waving American flags who would turn the wheel to fake-hit me as I walked home from school, because I was as brown as the newly declared enemies of the state. I remember watching the display of wartime nationalism that was the relentless bombing of Afghanistan, where the US military killed more Afghani civilians within a month after 9/11 than the number we lost when the Twin Towers fell. I remember watching televised bombings of the desert at night and hearing chants of "USA!" and realizing that something deep and irreconcilable separated me from my countrymen. Vengeance and violence were to be our future indefinitely. But at sixteen, I only knew the overwhelming dread of what that vengeance would bring.

All these feelings came while I also happened to be obsessed with a new video game, one that spread across the computer screens of every teenage boy, a game whose very goal was either to kill or to become terrorists. The game, *Counter-Strike*, had just been released in 2001 after spending a year in beta. Co-developed and programmed by Minh Le, a Vietnamese Canadian refugee who had no intention of referencing the Middle East, *Counter-Strike*'s mascots of masked terrorists holding AK-47s would nevertheless become an iconic image throughout the War on Terror.

Counter-Strike is a first-person shooter (or FPS) that pits two teams against each other, terrorists and counterterrorists. Each can win by eliminating all members of the other team or by completing objectives (planting/defusing a bomb, holding/rescuing hostages, killing/saving a VIP). In the two decades since the game's release, *Counter-Strike* has been credited for forming a movement of young gamers who play team-oriented first-person shooters and have put thousands of hours into games like the *Halo* series, *Overwatch*, *Apex Legends*, and *Fortnite*.

My friends and I, all teenage boys, often played *Counter-Strike* in a Chinatown cybercafé, a space of refuge from poverty, drugs, and the desert's acrid sunlight. *Counter-Strike* wasn't just popular in our cybercafé, but in every PC room around the world. To this day, *Counter-Strike* is often credited as *the* game responsible for the sudden growth of PC rooms across the globe, connecting us with players in South Korea, Russia, Brazil, and nations within the Middle East.[20] Indeed, it wasn't uncommon to find the very people our American media villainized as unlikely members of our scrappy "terrorist" squads.

If the War on Terror invoked intense dread in the blind rush toward vengeance, *Counter-Strike* brought some understanding, control, and reflection within the constant noise of patriotic sloganeering. In *Counter-Strike*, buying guns, learning how they worked and operated, then testing them out in a room full of screaming, angry young men was no toxic masculine ragefest (or should I say, no *mere* toxic masculine ragefest). Playing *Counter-Strike* was the closest thing I had to a therapeutic experience as a teenage boy. For us, those PC rooms were a safe space, partially because anyone who wasn't a teenage boy would never feel safe there. And why would they? As bell hooks knew, everyone is afraid of teenage boys.

Counter-Strike could only show us our scarred, dried-out surfaces, not the immense worry and grief we carried with us. We were the generation who saw ten million people protest the Iraq War across the world only to see nothing change. We were they who watched the first Black US secretary of state, one of the most trusted leaders in the world, knowingly lie about the reasons for going to war and then get exposed for those lies, and still see nothing change.

Throughout the political and personal ruptures of war, playing *Counter-Strike* in a PC room and screaming rage-filled obscenities was a medicine, a release. It was a floating isle where I could control the violence happening on the ground and turn it back onto the commanders and capitalists who profited from war and death. Taking on the persona of a soldier or a terrorist, I felt like I could control the fighting. Perhaps, if I knew how to use an M3 assault rifle, I could do what scholars, journalists, and protesters could not: stop the real soldiers from firing their real guns.

But, I must say, I wasn't very good at *Counter-Strike*. Round after round, I would crumble onto the pixelated tile floor next to my downed brethren, feeling defeated, lost to the wars raging on indefinitely inside and outside my nation. In those times, just getting through the day was a struggle of either repressing or purging my anger. Sometimes the safest impulse was to turn the rage inward, to offer myself as a digital effigy. Sometimes it made more sense to blame my keyboard—by hurling it against the nearest brick wall.

~

> War is when the young and stupid are tricked by the old and bitter into killing each other.
> —Niko Bellic, *Grand Theft Auto IV*

Like many teenage boys who play shooting games, I had what many refer to as "gamer anger."

In games, there are as many words for anger as there are words for love and care in a yoga studio. There's being *on tilt*, going *toxic*, *gettin' mad*, and all the digital variations of rage: *e-rage*, *nerd rage*, *gaming rage*, *rageosaur*, and *rage quitting*. It was normal as a teen to visit a friend's house and see patched-up holes in their wall near their gaming devices or bite marks on their keyboard, or hear the "rage rattles" of their controllers—the result of something inside coming undone.

Gamer anger often comes from a confrontation with the limits of one's own skill, when we are faced with our own lack of precisional prowess with a controller or a keyboard and mouse. In multiplayer games, gamer anger arrives from feelings of cheating or bad sportsmanship. Sometimes the anger feels justified by some real or imagined element of unfairness—internet lag, bots, cheap or cheesy strategies, or just the game being badly designed. Most often, these moments of blame simply soften the blow of a loss or an in-game death. But the need to blame unfairness can also come so swiftly that feelings of anger are themselves taken as signs of unfairness, in much the way that anger is often attributed to an injustice in the world, whether or not it is warranted (and it often is). As teens during the War on Terror, often the anger we felt was justified because it came from a desire to live in a just and fair world. But being alone, literally left to our own devices, we troubled teens could not measure our loss, could not see our anger as anything but a raw emotion that sometimes caused us to break a keyboard, punch a hole in a wall, or play chicken with oncoming traffic.

We often see gamer anger as a problem to be solved rather than something we actually come to games to feel. When games are approached as a form of daily stress relief, anger seems like a disruption of the fun and pleasure we are *supposed* to be having. Our play experience—the sparse time we've set aside for "fun"—is being ruined by someone, a designer or a player who has decided to abuse our precious time, to disrupt our needed release. Our rage increases. Even when we play a game we know will spark our anger, we feel like a failure whenever our attempts to stifle that anger fail.

Our failure to repress gamer anger also had a more social and political meaning: that society's stereotypical view of us as isolated, anger-filled gun nuts on the verge of a rage-filled explosion was in fact true. Gamer anger interiorized these stereotypes, invigorated the cycles of rage and alienation, despite the fact that *no causal link* had ever been found between video games and violence, and that the reason most teenage boys who committed violence played video games was not because games were violent, but because *most teenage boys played video games*.[21] And yet, we teenage boys were always made to feel that our anger was exceptional: pathological, dangerous, threatening, as if we were always one nerd rage away from committing a school shooting. And why not believe those stereotypes? The massacres at Columbine and Virginia Tech were both blamed on video games, not on gun laws (or the lack thereof). This still occurs today, when news media attempt to give a "fair" depiction of gun violence by blaming it upon the easiest, simplest, safest, and most incredibly wrong answer: video games. Thus, our gamer anger is intensified by interiorizing this media bogeyman within ourselves. We do not understand our anger as an opportunity to reflect on social ills, to examine or call out the hypocrisy around us, but take it as a sign of our individual failure. The raging gamer is a loser in every arena of life, even the virtual one.

As a brown teenage gamer, anger was something everyone assumed I had. And the threat of letting out my anger was a measured risk of being policed, harassed, or incarcerated. Always, then, my tendency was to repress my anger, an anger that came from social injustice, from the violences of war, from feeling helpless to stop the upticking body counts of young brown men and women, boys and girls. As with many young men, my anger came as a secondary emotion that spawned from the grief I felt for not having the life I'd expected. Life was not success and growth, but the hardship of living in a cockroach-infested apartment with broken air conditioning in one-hundred-degree heat and working a minimum wage job cleaning movie theatres. Rather than show any appreciation for my cleaning up their messes, theatregoers spilled popcorn in front of me or attempted three-point shots with their extra-large drinks, only to shrug and walk away when they missed the garbage can. Life, it turned out, was an absurd joke. And the people around me eventually began to feel my rage.

~

In my detachment from the world, *Counter-Strike* served as my primary mode of connecting with others. As the first globally popular online shooter, *Counter-Strike* heralded a form of gaming that was about connection, even if that connection looked more like confrontation. When I felt anger in *Counter-Strike*, I didn't feel it alone. Success, humour, tension, anxiety, bliss, rage—I felt these emotions as a unit along with everyone on my team. Our unifying impulse was compulsory, yet the connection was powerful. We were instantly bonded by the trials we faced, the adversities we shared. And if I was playing with friends in the same physical space, as I often did, our games would last well after the rounds were over and the keyboards were out of our hands.

My crew of Las Vegas teenage boys must have been frightening to everyone around us. We were a surly hermetic unit who had a jaundiced view of the world, who mooned families through restaurant windows and tossed doughnuts at passing cars. We young malcontents, we interrupters, we photobombers of tourist opportunities, we strip-mall adolescents. We didn't express fear or anger or grief or agony—all of those emotions were bottled up. All we expressed was a cool nihilistic indifference. At Walmart, we would leap into shopping carts and knock down displays of sporting equipment. During holidays, we would throw yard ornaments at people's windows (pumpkins, stuffed reindeer). Rather than participate in sports, we once streaked naked through a baseball field while parents and referees chased us. We thought it was a goof just to be alive, so we spent our lives shocking tourists, busting balls, and raising hell. What did the adults around us know? To us, they were just hypocritical, clueless suits, about as relevant as the non-playable characters in our video games.

~

In Las Vegas, games are everywhere—on controllers, on screens, on slots, at convenience stores, at the movie theatre, at Denny's. We played games in our bedrooms while our parents played them at bars or in living rooms as they bet next month's rent on a football match. Growing up in the world's arcade, I was suspicious of the guilt and wariness I was supposed to feel about games. I was surrounded by people playing other types of games with far more imminent consequences.

One would think the ostentation of Las Vegas would work against itself. How could so many people gawk at the giant buildings, cheap buffets, and art gallery Monets around them without becoming enraged at how much money the casinos were raking in just to keep the lights on? I had the same feeling walking into the megachurches of flat-screen televisions, high-production bands, and televised sermons. At some point, the grandeur must give away the heartless extraction of the system itself. We teenage boys, too young to legally gamble, were impressed by our city's obvious exploitation, its shamelessness, its invitation to self-destruction.

It wasn't just the path to self-destruction, but the method. Of all the ways to destroy yourself or to be exploited, why this one?

In *Addiction by Design: Machine Gambling in Las Vegas*, anthropologist Natasha Dow Schüll draws on fifteen years of field research in Las Vegas interviewing gambling industry workers and elites to understand how gambling works in a city that is made from the ground up—in architecture, in design, in planning—to facilitate it. Schüll finds that Las Vegas casinos understand something fundamental: gamers are not actually playing to make money, to "win," but rather to reach a particular emotional state. Schüll calls this state the "machine zone," the collapse of one's sense of time and place through the saturation of sensory input, increasing the velocity of time "with a surplus of moments."[22] Time's elasticity comes through feelings of "just one more round," where time "stops mattering."[23] Winning need not occur for the player to feel this suspension. All they need is a sensory experience of flashing lights and buzzing sounds.

I saw this desire for the machine zone in the adults who avoided us, who saw us as a threat to their suspended fantasy. They spent all hours of the day grinding and churning on slot machines, getting so immersed in their machine zones that they couldn't keep track of the money they lost. Some were even proud of their gambling addiction because it proved they were "free" (whatever that meant). Everywhere, people loved the machines that were slowly bleeding them dry.

We called them hypocrites, but the gambling gamers were not that different from us, the video gamers. Like video games, gambling gives some sense of control over the world—in this case, control over the most important thing in our society: money. Money lost is at least gone by the gambler's choice, not because they were laid off or enduring a housing crisis or seeing the result of a bad investment (the more legal type of gambling). While we teens played *Counter-Strike* to feel control over the war machine, the adults around us gambled to feel control over their fluctuating finances. We all played for the same reason: to gain some sense of empowerment and autonomy over the futures we had lost.

Like many game makers of colour, Minh Le, the co-creator of *Counter-Strike*, has rarely discussed his ethnic background. He usually doesn't have to, as he has always gone by an internet handle: Gooseman, a cartoon character based on Clint Eastwood's cowboys from the animated space western *The Adventures of the Galaxy Rangers*. Although other designers such as Steve Swink have seen Le as an auteur who had total control in creating *Counter-Strike*, Le has preferred to shape himself as a community collaborator rather than an artist or game director.

When I interviewed Le in 2017 for the online art journal ANMLY, he was candid and reflective of how young (and "naive") he was when *Counter-Strike* was in development.[24] He made no attempt to deny the game's political importance but rather noted how its popularity happened to coincide with the War on Terror. Even though most of the terrorists in *Counter-Strike* were not Arab, the game's popularity skyrocketed as its terrorist vs. counterterrorist set-up came to mirror the wars in Iraq and Afghanistan. For Le, the collaborative project of the game often meant including popular design choices that he himself didn't understand at the time. The game's only Middle Eastern–inspired map, "de_dust," was submitted by a member of the community (Dave Johnston), and Le even rejected it numerous times for being "too ugly." He released the map despite his doubts only to watch it grow into the game's most iconic setting; today a Google Images search for "Counter-Strike" will immediately yield images of masked gun-wielders against a desert background.

Le's recollections of his time making *Counter-Strike* reflect many of the same anxieties I felt as a young gamer with Asian heritage. When I asked why it was his co-creator, Jess Cliffe, and not Le himself who provided the voices for *Counter-Strike*, Le responded that his own voice sounded too "prepubescent." When I asked why his racial background rarely came up in interviews, Le replied that he liked to "shy away from controversy," that his ethnicity was always present in his name, and that he was "very proud" of his Vietnamese heritage—he met consistently with other Vietnamese refugees and said, "We formed a close community."[25]

Le's story of making *Counter-Strike* reflects that of an artist far more interested in the international community than in the American or Canadian minority communities. For Le, counterterrorist forces against terrorist teams had come to define much of twenty-first-century global warfare, which made them ample subjects for players around the globe, especially young men. Only one of *Counter-Strike*'s team units is American, while the others belong to the French GIGN, the Israeli IDF, Germany's GSG 9, and the UK's SAS. Today, a cursory glance at the *Counter-Strike* community boards reveals the game's global breadth, with more players in Russia than in America and comparable populations in Brazil, Poland, and Germany. As journalist Albert Chan observed in Hong Kong in 2008, "If you walk into … any of the cybercafés, nine out of ten computers are running *Counter-Strike*."[26]

Counter-Strike created a culture of PC rooms and cafés that felt sacred during the War on Terror, because they were spaces where the rules *mattered*. There was no fun to be had, no purpose in playing, if not for the fact that everyone had to follow the same rules—no exceptions. In the cybercafés no referee could be bought, and no PC or keyboard was any more powerful than the one next to it. But outside these cafés, the game was rigged—the rules were being trampled upon. Hard work was met with a hard life. And despite the public unveiling of atrocities and lies, wars still raged on.

~

As with its maps, characters, and design choices, *Counter-Strike*'s unofficial mascot also came from an offbeat community project that eventually became one of the game's most recognized elements. This mascot was FPS Doug, a character from the 2004 Canadian YouTube mockumentary series *Pure Pwnage*, a gaming icon whom *The Daily Dot* in 2021 described as "Gaming Culture's Original Meme," a "screamy, hyperactive, Mountain Dew–swilling persona."[27] I first encountered the phenomenon of FPS Doug in cybercafés, when I heard fellow teens victoriously scream, "BOOM, HEADSHOT!" at the top of their lungs every time they got a kill or, well, a headshot. Soon after, I discovered the real FPS Doug on YouTube: a head-shaved, adrenalin-fuelled caricature of what the world imagines teenage gamers to be, and what we had internalized in ourselves.

Like many of our generation, FPS Doug was raised in the military machine threatening to grind us to bits. But unlike us, his zombielike addiction to rituals of violence was irrecoverable. The game that first brought FPS Doug (and the actor who played him) into shooters was not *Counter-Strike*, but *America's Army* (2002), a game created by the US military to spur recruitment and train would-be soldiers in the aftermath of 9/11. In his YouTube sketches, FPS Doug complains that he can't even keep a job at his father's gun store: "Anytime I get a gun in my hand, it just automatically points to somebody's head."[28] He says he wants to join the military but is afraid of war, because "there's no respawn points in RL [real life]." Like many, I was entranced by FPS Doug: his intense focus, his leaning so deep into the monitor that he could fall into it, his restless jumpiness, as if his torso were the heart of a machine and his arms the veins giving it pulse.

~

FPS Doug came to popularity at a transformative time for shooting games. Many today immediately identify shooting games with the *Call of Duty* series, which emerged in 2003—the same year the US invaded Iraq—and especially its *Modern Warfare* subseries: a militaristic fantasy takedown of mostly Middle Eastern–coded terrorists.

If the original sin of Hollywood was D.W. Griffith's 1915 film *The Birth of a Nation*, a virulently racist story of the rise of the Ku Klux Klan that was screened at the White House and circulated as an obvious flex of white supremacy, then the original sin of video games might be the *Call of Duty* game series. Like *The Birth of a Nation*, *Call of Duty* is a technological marvel, one of the first games to merge action hero shooting and in-depth storytelling that often reflects on present-day warfare.[29] As a member of a global military alliance, you can shoot and kill "terrorist" soldiers while they sleep or while they huddle in a corner in complete darkness, or while you bomb them from an unseeable drone. As a terrorist, you can start a bloodbath in an airport. Like *The Birth of a Nation*, *Call of Duty* has been immensely popular and easily became the bestselling shooter in the world. According to *Kotaku*, *Call of Duty* is the only game series to have claimed the title of number-one bestselling game in the US four times in a row, and it did it twice, first from 2008 to 2012 and again from 2014 to 2017.[30] The games' many scenes of American and European soldiers shooting, bombing, and torturing Middle Eastern peoples circulate everywhere. Like *The Birth of a Nation*'s scenes of minstrelsy, rape, and lynching, *Call of Duty*'s violence is poignant and terrifying because it is real—it works as an automated transmission of real anti-Arab media at a time when anti-Arab racism has been at a crux and violence toward Arabic and Middle Eastern peoples globally is not only tolerated but expected.

~

The common interests between war and play did not begin with video games. The first-ever tabletop game discovered, Tabula, dating back to at least the fifth century, was, by legend, created by a Greek soldier who sought to simulate his experience in the Trojan War. Since then, games like chess, Battleship, Go, and backgammon have all taken direct inspiration from and attempted to simulate war.

Video games inherit the traits of tabletop games by not only being *about* war, but also by being products *of* war. The two-axis joystick, the missing extension of every gamer's thumb, was invented and developed by German scientists during World War II in order to control guided missiles. The first video game, *Tennis for Two*, was created by William Higinbotham, a member of the Manhattan Project, essentially for the purposes of military propaganda.[31] The game was only ever playable once a year, on the annual "Visitor's Day" when the top-secret US Department of Defense laboratory, Brookhaven National Lab, opened to convince nearby residents that they had nothing to fear from their friendly neighbourhood Cold War weapons research facility. The first-ever game console, the Odyssey, was created by Ralph H. Baer, a defence-industry worker who developed an advanced light anti-tank weapon for use in war. The Odyssey was then developed by Sanders Associates, a defence contractor specializing in radar technology.

Even in Japanese games, the investment in American militarism has been present from the beginning. Nintendo, a company now synonymous with the term *video game*, was originally formed in the 1880s as a playing card company whose profits relied heavily on illicit gambling rings organized by Japanese crime syndicates (or yakuza), but it later survived by appealing to American troops during the US occupation after World War II.[32] Nintendo's biggest rival for two decades, Sega (an abbreviation of its original name, Service Games) was actually founded in the United States as a slot machine manufacturer serving US military bases, first in Hawai'i, then occupied Japan, then expanding to American bases in South Korea, the Philippines, and South Vietnam.[33]

In the 2000s, during the miasma of militaristic violence that coincided with the War on Terror, I had many friends and family entering US military bases as members of the marines, navy, and army who professed to spending much of their downtime on their bases playing *Call of Duty* games. My younger cousins serving in the military may never know that before the massive popularity of *Call of Duty*, shooters were less about killing terrorists and more about slaying demons (*Doom*), cosmic monsters (*Quake*), and racists (*Wolfenstein 3D*). Their biggest stars were not soldiers, but Indigenous warriors (*Turok*), Jedi rebels (*Star Wars: Dark Forces*), and spies uncovering corporate conspiracies (*System Shock, Deus Ex, Perfect Dark*). Perhaps the greatest hero of the shooter—and voted as such by *GameSpot* in 2009—is Gordon Freeman of *Half-Life*, a bespectacled scientist with a degree in theoretical physics from MIT who becomes a resistance hero in the war against an interdimensional alien empire.[34] Gordon was the adult we wanted to become, because he was once a teenager like us: young, geeky, and thrown into a world compelling him to fight.

~

FPS Doug represented a different kind of icon—not a hero we aspired to become, but a sad clown lamenting how this game genre we had come to love, the shooter, had fallen into the arms of the corporate and militarized empires it had once inspired us to fight against. The original viral video of FPS Doug begins as a mocking parody of the military-bro player but ends with a depiction of the anxieties that this player represents, with a poignant moment of gamer anger, exaggerated but nonetheless true to life. Fragged in a mess of dark-red pixels, FPS Doug asks his friend Kyle, the cameraman, to leave, too ashamed of what is about to happen to let it be captured on video: "Kyle, you better leave, man. Just go." From outside the house, we hear agonized shrieks followed by frenzied bangs. Finally, FPS Doug emerges into the open garage, thrashing his keyboard against the concrete floor, smashing it with his foot, then breaking it against the wall, wailing in anger.

This was the anger we were not supposed to see, the anger that meant loss, failure, and shame. Gamers everywhere understood the anger unleashed by FPS Doug when his high of getting a "BOOM, HEADSHOT" was stonewalled by an in-game death. It's the same anger that can come from internet lag or from someone walking in front of the screen. It's the anger of disruption, of losing the flow, of being thrown off your groove, when the brisk and sometimes breakneck rhythm of the game meets a dead end and it's too late to hit the brakes. It's the anger too of losing that casual, mockable distance between yourself and the violence occurring everywhere around you.

And yet, none of those feelings of broken rhythm had anything directly to do with war or violence, per se. The keyboard was our generation's electric guitar, something that could get crushed on a hard floor, but also something that created melody. It could impress everyone in the room or catch their attention with a single stroke. Even in those moments of losing ourselves, our keyboards offered a way back, an instrument we could use to harness our anger, transforming it through a different beat.

As a teenager in PC rooms just picking up the rhythm of *Counter-Strike*, I had a fondness for one of FPS Doug's sillier aphorisms: "I can dance all day, I can dance all day, try hitting me!" In his original viral video, FPS Doug says this while jerkily rabbit hopping back and forth, a relied-upon strategy for dodging bullets in a game. In real life, it looks plain screwy.

For myself and many in our cybercafés, "I could dance all day" was our personal gaming mantra. We likened ourselves to dancers because, like dance, games released the emotions that evaded the languages of pain and grief, which were unavailable to us. What we couldn't speak about, what couldn't be seen, came out in dance, even if it was a dance of swift fingers stammering on a keyboard. Perform your moves just right, and you have every right to declare, "BOOM, HEADSHOT!"

~

To work through their anger and isolation, young men tend to gather in spaces of ill repute. For me growing up, these places were cybercafés, parking lots, and Las Vegas punk venues like the Huntridge, the Castle, and Tremors before they were all shut down. But from the 1920s to the 1950s, young and daring men tended to convene in one of two places: pinball arcades and dance halls.

In 1930s New York City, pinball arcades were stigmatized as tantalizing spaces where young men of colour, along with Irish and Italians, would begin lifestyles of gambling, asociality, drug dependency, and gang-related violence. Though arcades were officially spaces for pinball gambling (with real cash payouts), they were often rebranded as "penny arcades," "sportlands," or family-friendly "playlands."[35] US lawmakers saw past these euphemisms and framed the arcade as a public gambling den connected to the rise of mafias and casinos. Fiorello La Guardia, New

York City mayor through much of the 1930s and 1940s, famously went on a crusade levelling pinball machines with a sledgehammer, claiming that the game machines were a "perverter of innocent children."[36] Even after pinball companies removed any gambling-related elements, the National Association of Citizens Crime Commission continued to villainize the industry for supposedly driving children to crime "to obtain funds for their craze."[37] When video games entered the arcades in the 1970s, they became part of a space already maligned as a gateway to drugs and violence.

As with cybercafés, arcades were common sites in Chinatown and other underfunded urban areas. So too were dance halls, where, from the 1920s to the 1940s, young working men went to dress up in fancy attire and swing. In major cities like Chicago and all along the West Coast, Filipinos and other men of colour frequented taxi dance halls, where they paid to dance with mostly white working-women hostesses.[38] Excluded from owning property or marrying white women, Filipinos resembled a threat to nationwide security, as well as racial white purity. Tales erupted in the press about taxi dance halls where white women were seduced by lonely Chinese, Latino, Black, and especially Filipino bachelors. The anxieties of Filipino sexuality, along with unionization and typical racial bigotry, led to anti-Filipino race riots across the West Coast of the US and Canada that attempted to cast Filipinos out by raiding dance clubs, as well as through beating, intimidation, and murder. These racisms culminated in the Tydings–McDuffie Act in 1934, which curtailed Filipino migration to fifty persons per year and declared Filipinos "aliens" ineligible for citizenship, even though they were colonial subjects, the Philippines being a US colony at the time.

No matter the time or space, anxieties brew when young men of colour engage in dance, whether it's in taxi dance halls, or in the dance halls of zoot-suiters, or in jazz and hip hop venues, or in TikTok dances that often mimic mechanical video game movements. From dance floors to arcades to cybercafés, we young dancing men of colour were long perceived as declarations of a war not fought with guns but with our own moving bodies.

~

> Dance, so conceived, does not name a fixed expression but a problem, a predicament, that bodies find themselves in the midst of, whose momentary solutions we call dancing.
> —Randy Martin, *Critical Moves*

Altercations were common in cybercafés, as was throwing down and acting beefy in the parking lot after someone had shouted, "Let's take this outside!" But once outside, realizing that we had no way of engaging in battle without our keyboards and mouses, that it felt awkward to swing our arms rather than our wrists, fights ended at the shit-talking stage, when someone eventually said, "Wait 'til the next round! I'm gonna own you!" and we all rushed back indoors, relieved.

The one time I did get into a fight over a game, however, it wasn't over a shooter game, or even at a cybercafé. It was in a casino arcade, while playing the more explicitly danceable game, *Dance Dance Revolution*, or DDR. DDR games were not dances of the fingers but of the feet, where players followed neon-coloured arrows of rapid foot combinations. Eventually, these flashy multicoloured arrows brought us into such a natural dance flow that we began to see them in our dreams, and we would wake with our feet in the air, trying to follow them. Like shooting games, dancing and rhythm games were automated forms of anger therapy for young men, a means of getting out aggression, whether played in the arcade or on dance pads at home. Dance games were also more socially acceptable than shooting games, as they caused onlookers to watch, laugh, gawk, or mock rather than clutch their children in fear. But like shooting games, dance games were also fiercely competitive, and close defeats often led to someone screaming, "Let's take this outside!"

My first fight over a game occurred in a casino parking lot where we began to throw down, one gang of young men taking off their shoes while we kept ours on (theirs were Air Jordans, ours were Goodwill sneaks).

We threw fists in the air, got pushy, but our fists never made contact with each other. There was wrestling and lots of taunting. Eventually, we found a paltry excuse to walk away. "I'm hungry, let's get some Jack in the Crack."

~

Violence was part of my adolescence, as it was for most teenage boys. I was beaten up, bullied, harassed, and there were always bruises somewhere on my torso. Police helicopters constantly followed us home with their spotlights. White nationalists, straight-edgers, and random strangers threatened us, making an example of anyone who didn't plead for their respect. At a house party, kids drew on each other and made bullet holes in the roof. (I heard the pops while I was in a bedroom with my friends watching *A Goofy Movie*.) At another party, we passed around a shotgun, and when it was my turn to hold it, I pointed it right at my brother Cameron's head. "Boom, headshot!" I said. My brother has never forgiven me for that.

One day, at the height of our rambunctiousness, my crew and I decided to bring *Counter-Strike* outside of our computers and into the suburb where my most well-off friend lived. It was the golden hour when we strode down from atop the city's mesa to play with air rifles that looked identical to real shotguns and M16s. I snuck around my friend's wealthy white neighbourhood pretending I was a terrorist, keeping my rifle tight to my chest. I opened a gate and heard a whisper and crept backward. Above, I heard the whir of a helicopter, and when I looked up at it, a spotlight hit my eyes and a whiteness eviscerated my sight. I turned back to the street and saw a dozen men. They weren't teens, but older men with badges, their guns drawn and pointed at me, all of them screaming, "FREEZE, DROP IT, HANDS IN THE AIR!" My toy gun fell, and one of the police officers threw me into a garage door. I was handcuffed and flattened against the hood of a police car. My mouth wasn't muffled, but my words just bounced off their armour until my friend emerged from his garage, hands up, his fair skin mirroring the setting sun, and I felt the hands gripping me begin to slide.

~

> We are all continually pumped with gross and inaccurate images of everyone else, and we all pump it out.
> —Barbara Cameron, "'Gee, You Don't Seem Like an Indian from the Reservation'"

Today, many shooting games take place on floating isles. The 2017 game *PlayerUnknown's Battlegrounds* (or PUBG), which in 2021 had an estimated player count of 1.2 billion (four times the number of users on Twitter), invented an entirely new type of shooter by reinventing the island map. After dropping onto an imaginary isle, the playable map area begins to shrink, while its one hundred players get squeezed together, forcing confrontation. Known today as the battle royale shooter, PUBG's innovative design has inspired a new generation of online shooters: *Fortnite*, *Call of Duty: Warzone*, and *Apex Legends*, the latter taking place on islands that inexplicably float in the sky.

The spaces of shooting games within islandic maps mirror the isolation of these games and of teenage boys. These islands are spaces of play and refuge but also of containment. They reflect society's desire to keep young men away, to isolate them into digital cages where they can let their anger run rampant until they "grow out of it." But our islands were never isolated. We were always looking down at the world and smouldering in anger. The world tolerated us, so long as we kept to our cyberspaces. Leaving that space carried dire consequences. Our choice was clear: stay in our virtual cell, or risk living in the real prison cells that were always open and waiting.

Today, many of the young cheery boys who shouted, "BOOM, HEADSHOT!" and danced with their fingers went into either the military or the prison system, and others went to drugs or suicide. My best friend, who always tried to drag me to the cybercafé so he didn't have to return to his abusive home, disappeared from our scene, became an addict, and was last seen sleeping on a street of unhoused people in Las Vegas. My other friend who was there the night I was pinned down by police, is today a police officer himself. His last words on social media before I blocked him were about moving to Detroit to "clean up the streets." I had two friends named Chris, one who brought a gun to school and had bite marks all over his game cartridges, the other who fought in the Iraq War and came back a different, quieter person.

Many more I've known still live with tragedy and violence, but they go on living. Some do not. They all lurk in my mind whenever I play these games, whenever I find connection with another player in a game. When I play *Apex Legends* and parachute onto a floating isle, I wonder if my teammates feel the same connection. Or perhaps some only feel the sting of exclusion: the women and other players who might feel anger at both the world *and* at us, we who gated off these islands for ourselves.

When society could not deal with us, we found refuge in the isolation of islands. But whatever happened on those islands that floated above the world eventually rained down upon the world. Our safe space of masculinity, anger, and rhythmic connection easily slipped into seeking blame for the anger we felt. Outside the floating isles, our daily lives consisted of constant physical and psychic violence, and of facing the world's stalwart indifference to it. Within our floating isles, our anger led many of us to begin crafting our way out, to plan our vengeance. And plan we did. No one was watching.

CHAPTER 4
Final Fantasies

On Christmas Day, 2002, when I was seventeen years old, my first girlfriend—the first girl who ever held my hand, the first to express any attraction or care toward me—died in a car wreck. She was in the passenger seat, and the driver, her new boyfriend, was high and drunk. The car hit an electric pole on the same street in Las Vegas where I once took the bus to school.

He walked away unharmed. Her name was Teal.

On the way to Teal's funeral, I stopped by the street where she died. Flowers adorned the pole, alongside a blown-up image of Teal's high school yearbook photo, the same signed photo of her I carried in my backpack, calling me "a good friend."

Teal and I never really had a breakup moment. When we were fifteen, after going out for only a short while, we realized there were other ways for a boy and a girl to cherish each other. We still hung out, sat with each other on the bus, and listened to music together (she had a feverish love affair with industrial rock, especially the band Orgy). We were both used to playing roles for everyone around us—our groups of friends, our families, our teachers. I was the angry brown boy, she the blond girl who often wore black. Together, we talked mad shit and rocked out.

But in the year before Teal died, I hadn't been a good friend. Since I started going steady with someone new, I stopped checking in on Teal, unsure of how a friendship with a girl was supposed to proceed outside of my new girlfriend's orbit. Teal cared for me, saw more in my pudgy, queer, angry self than I ever could. But I hadn't returned her care in so long.

Teal's funeral was in a massive church, standing room only. I had to peek on my toes to see the preacher give his final words. On the way home, I put on one of Teal's favourite Orgy songs, "Fiction (Dreams in Digital)." As soon as the chorus came, I pulled over and sucked back tears. I hated the flowers, the gigantic church full of kids Teal and I used to joke about, the teachers we would flip off as soon as they turned their backs. I punched the steering wheel, making loud stuttering honks, until an inner voice screamed at me to stop. How many people, I wondered, were at this funeral to assuage their guilt, to capitalize on the shock value of a young woman's corpse? They knew and loved her. Most of them knew her better than I did. But I knew her dark side: the depression and isolation and anger that she hid away far better than I could. I wasn't certain, but I felt Teal would have hated her funeral too. So often, we'd hated everything together, and that was our bond.

I decided then that when I joined Teal in death, I would leave clearer instructions. I decided too that it wouldn't be long.

~

> After you died I could not hold a funeral,
> And so my life became a funeral.
> —Han Kang, *Human Acts*

When my uncle died of advanced HIV–related illness in 1997, my response was to withdraw, first into video games, then into online chat rooms. I wasn't brought to my uncle's funeral. His life as a gay man was sanitized by my religious family. I never had the chance to become closer to him through his death, to remember all the things I admired about him (his lisp, his jokes, his joy). Video games were how I came to handle death, queerness, and my own anger. After Teal's funeral, the opposite happened. Video games had fuelled my rage at the world, but even to have rage, one must still have hope—an expectation that things can and should be better. But something in me perished. Bright rage was squelched into a bleak darkness. Every moment, I was seconds away from a breakdown; with every step, I wanted to fall to the concrete and hear my bones snap. I felt stranded in every conversation, wondering if the other person was as detached from the universe as me, if they were as tired of living in it as I was. And video games no longer soothed me. As with every other arena in my life, I was merely forcing myself to play along. But I didn't have to play this game, nor did I have to live this life.

~

There is an event in the 1997 game *Final Fantasy VII* that has often been called "the death of video game innocence." It comes just over halfway through the game, after the player has grown to know and play as Aeris, a long-haired flower girl and the most reliable healer of the player's band of heroes. After the player (as Cloud) fails to defeat his evil rival, Sephiroth, Aeris leaves the party to take him on herself. As in many video games, the player is tasked with rescuing the young maiden. And after smashing through enemies, the player finds Aeris in a small sanctuary, ready to be saved. But the game doesn't allow you to save her. Just as you approach, Sephiroth descends from darkness and impales her with his long Masamune sword. Aeris falls, lifeless.

Aeris's death is not just that of a character. Over the past thirty hours of gameplay, Aeris has become your friend, and you have seen her joy, anger, and sadness. She has also been your healer, whom you have entrusted to cure your bodies and to create wards of protection. You feel her loss on many levels: as a companion, as a healer, as an apprentice whom you have invested many hours in training and levelling up. Her loss doesn't only feel shocking but, like all losses of a loved one, *unfair*. How could a game just steal this person away from you?

With the death of Aeris, it's not guilt that haunts the player, but a sense of existential dread. In the game world of *Final Fantasy VII*, the planet is already dying; the life force of the world is getting sucked up, humongous monsters are emerging everywhere and destroying entire cities, and a meteor is hurtling toward the planet that will kill most of its population. Aeris is just the first to go. Even Sephiroth says as much just after he kills her: "Do not worry. Soon the girl will become part of the Planet's energy."

You, as Cloud, respond, "Shut up. The cycle of nature and your stupid plan don't mean a thing. Aeris is gone. Aeris will no longer talk, no longer laugh, cry...... or get angry...... what about us...... what are WE supposed to do? What about my pain? My fingers are tingling. My mouth is dry. My eyes are burning!"

Aeris was a symbol of something sacred and fragile within us. And her death, as Cloud voices it, is beyond our understanding. His reaction rejects the purpose of death that I saw at every funeral, every memorial. Death is only cheapened when it is given a higher purpose, to *become part of the Planet's energy*. Death is a loss to the world. A real, painful, burning, and deeply unfair loss. And like any major loss, it forces us to face our own being.

"What are WE supposed to do?"

~

> I'm not afraid to die. I just don't want to be there when
> it happens.
> —Andy Warhol

After Teal's funeral, I became more outspoken about my longing for death. I would jokingly tell friends, "I'm only planning to live long enough to play the new *Final Fantasy*. If it sucks, I won't be waiting for the next." It was never clear to my friends or to myself whether these jokes were just banter or serious cries for help.

One night, at a gaming party in my friend's trailer home, after all my friends had passed out on bunk beds, I thought deeply about my own death. As far back as I could remember, self-hate had always been there, and along with it, a profound and unexplainable emptiness. I felt a constant pain and a desire to escape everything. As I sat in that dark room with my friends' sleeping bodies beside me, I knew I had to make up some greater reason for these thoughts, or else they would kill me.

I thought of the games I played and the melancholy characters at their centre—Cloud or *Final Fantasy VIII*'s Squall—young men adrift, severed from the world around them, carrying an almost elegant indifference to their own survival in it. Scarred by war and shaped by abuse, these men at least gave something to our world: their own stories, the comfort of knowing we are not alone. If I was truly waiting for the next *Final Fantasy* game before I died, then perhaps *Final Fantasy* too explained my suicidal ideation—that only artworks like *Final Fantasy* were worth living for.

That night, I held on to the only explanation for my despair that made sense: I was destined for art, in whatever form it might take. These unrelenting thoughts of harming myself were not a sign of failure or madness, but a key, an initiation into the bohemian realm of tortured artists, of poetry, music, and storytelling, that promised, if nothing else, that I wouldn't be alone.

I knew no artists and had no artists in my family. But this was how I imagined an artist might feel. As an artist, it didn't matter that I hated myself, that I always would hate myself, because wasn't that just something all artists did? Did it matter, in the end, whether I was even a good or bad artist? So long as I had this thing called *art*, it didn't matter if I created the shitty or the beautiful, the read or the unheard of. At least I would find some greater reason for all of this pain.

So, what kind of tortured, self-loathing artist would I be? I was a decent musician for my age. I had played piano, saxophone, and guitar.

But I didn't like playing with others in bands or in concerts. Well, I also had a deep passion for writing and creating worlds out of the video games I played. But I had no talent for writing, and no one ever wanted to read the stories I wrote.

Clearly, whichever path I took would take a lot of work. It would mean devoting myself entirely to that art and nothing else.

I took a coin out of my pocket and flipped it in the air. Heads: writer. Tails: musician. The coin landed. Okay. *From now on, I am a writer*, I decided. *And nothing else.*

~

I began to envision myself as a writer by penning stories of the shared worlds that my brother and I had created, thickening our role-play characters into people who were more like our teenage selves—people wrecked by anger, disappointment, and loss.

I went to open mic nights to share poetry. I read every book I could on literature and writing and spent all my time improving my art. I wrote relentlessly. Within months I'd written my first novel, a cyberpunk, *Final Fantasy*–inspired story about a tower in the middle of a Philippine jungle that housed mythical and possessive spirits. Immediately after finishing this, I began my second novel, a series of intertwined stories about friends I knew in Las Vegas who after high school had become sex workers, pushers, addicts, penniless derelicts. Once done, I began a third novel: a "lavapunk" story about an island being sold off and terraformed by a big tech company. My fourth novel (*four*—why?!) was a prose-poetry hybrid story that took place in an underground slum full of clones who were born and bred only to support those who lived in the "upper levels" (basically, a poetic reimagining of *Final Fantasy VII*). All these novels were joined by dozens of short stories, novellas, and poems, many inspired by games. Only a few of these writings were read by anyone other than myself. None were ever published.

I remember just finishing one of these novels—I cannot remember which—when I got the phone call from my mother telling me my brother had been in a car accident. He was travelling with a group of people I'd never met, going near a hundred miles per hour on the freeway, when a tire blew out. The car flew off road and rolled, and Cameron, in an attempt to help, took the steering wheel from the passenger side, injuring his spine.

I don't recall even attempting to reach out to my brother. I had switched all my community college courses from math to English and was overloading on credits, hoping to transfer to a big university, take writing courses, and graduate as soon as possible. When I wasn't studying, I was writing like mad. Sometimes, my brother would call me, asking if I wanted to play *Super Smash Bros.* or *Halo*. But I always refused. My brother was a part of the simulated life I needed to leave behind.

~

The *Final Fantasy* series as a whole has never relented from delivering harsh truths. Even the series name, *Final Fantasy*, might seem like a morose title for a game series that is currently in its sixteenth instalment. Part of an anthology series, each *Final Fantasy* game contains its own universe, which disappears after the story ends. While the games do have recurring mechanics (levelling up and party-based combat), creatures (Chocobos), names (Cid, Biggs, Wedge), and myths (magic and crystals), their worlds are always on the brink of a final end. The first *Final Fantasy* game was named as such because it was, according to the developer Hironobu Sakaguchi, his last-ditch effort to make a successful game before he "quit the games industry [to] go back to university." The game would have been his "final" one, had it not sold well.[39]

The first *Final Fantasy* game begins in a collapsing universe with the opening lines, "The world lies shrouded in darkness. The winds die. The seas rage. The earth decays." Made by only seven people at a relatively unknown company, SquareSoft, *Final Fantasy* expressed the designers' anxieties of failure, of seeing their dreams as artists and storytellers vanish in the demands of a meaningless corporate system. For many players, the game's world felt gripping and uncanny because it reflected their own.

Today, the *Final Fantasy* series has sold over 190 million copies and become crucial in any discussion of games that feature psychological depth, social awareness, and complex world building. Many *Final Fantasy* games take over forty hours to complete, feature a huge cast of characters, and contain over a hundred thousand words of readable dialogue. *Final Fantasy* games are the Victorian novels of video games.

While the first *Final Fantasy* game, released in 1987, was groundbreaking in its role creation and world building, *Final Fantasy II*, released a year later, deepened the player's emotional involvement by asking them to face death. You, the player, take on the roles of three orphans whose parents were killed by an evil empire just before the orphans too are killed by this empire—slain in cold blood. But then you're resurrected and, of course, you have every reason to join the rebels fighting the empire. People guide you along the way: Josef, Minwu, Cid, Ricard. All of them, like your own family and friends, die. With each death, the player mourns and finds the strength to carry on, burdened with becoming the hope for which they sacrificed their lives.

Final Fantasy III gives players more friends to mourn: Desch, who sacrifices himself in a firepit, and Aria, who tosses herself in front of an arrow. *Final Fantasy IV*, known today as an early breakthrough in video game storytelling, ramps up the tears. Nearly every character except the main one, Cecil, ends up dying or disappearing. Even when characters supposedly don't die, it's implied that they *do*, since *Final Fantasy* games were known for having references to death and grief sanitized when they were released in North America. These worlds were so full of danger and decay that if someone disappeared, we assumed the worst. We'd probably never see them again.

It is difficult to express how the deaths in these games impacted players at the time, including myself. The characters who died were, after all, mostly represented by pixels on a screen. But it was deeply troubling to play as Galuf, the wise fighter in *Final Fantasy V*, and throw everything you had at the evil warlock Exdeath only to watch your life force slowly deplete to zero. Or, in *Final Fantasy VI*, to play as Celes, a woman who betrays her empire, her family, and her friends, then joins a band of rebels, only to lose—to lose so completely and catastrophically that, in order to teach her a lesson, the evil empire devastates the world, killing or disappearing everyone you have come to know in the game. As Celes, you wake up a year later, stranded on a desert island, next to your mentor, Cid, a father figure who has kept you alive. Now, you must keep him alive by catching fish and caring for his wounds. But even in this, you fail. Cid sickens beyond your help. He dies too, and you are left without guidance or hope. In despair, you return to a cliff where many have leapt to their death. You jump, just as determined as they were for a release, a "final" end. But somehow, you wash ashore, still breathing. The world denies you even the quick bite of death.

These are just pixels, you tell yourself. It's just a video game.

When I was young, I could feel the remorse and loss of living in a desolate world, one that left you sick and stranded. I too was on that solitary island, and I too had given up hope. But I had those pixels.

~

When I first played these early *Final Fantasy* games, I was quite late to the party. My entry into their realms was prompted by my second-ever girlfriend, Kristy, who urged me to play them with her. Like me, Kristy grew up struggling with poverty and loss, things she found expressed in role-playing games. But unlike me, Kristy wasn't interested in stories about innocent flower girls like Aeris, the damsels in distress who beckoned boys toward heroic pursuits. Kristy wanted stories steeped in the grandeur of empires. Stories of power, guilt, trauma, and the childhood innocence that was quickly fading from our grasp.

I met Kristy in keyboarding class, the only place in all of high school where I didn't feel like a total loser. I was the fastest typer, and I knew how to use this new untamed search engine called Google. When the teacher left the room, I showed everyone how to rig the computers to play *Quake II*. For two hours a week, among the clattering of keys, I was the guy to know and was often asked for help with homework or how to perform functions on Excel sheets—a glimpse of a life without shame. Eventually, my prestige led me to help Kristy. I soon realized she was better with computers than me, but she lacked my boastful arrogance.

Kristy's half-white and half-Filipino lineage mirrored my own racial background. Our shared heritage, gender androgyny, passion for punk music, and love for video games formed an unbreakable bond. She lived in a rough neighbourhood of Las Vegas where, at least once a month, the echoes of drive-by shootings pierced the air, prompting her to craft tales for her younger siblings that downplayed the danger outside as mere fireworks displays.

Kristy had six brothers and sisters, and I saw daily how much work she did for them: food preparation, fixing furniture and computers, aiding with homework, ensuring they took their medications. Her dedication was unwavering and often interrupted our budding romance. Her high grades and ability to play every role—parent, tutor, fixer, sister, star student—gave her purpose, but also an overbearing sense of responsibility. She often dreamed of escaping these roles but knew she never would, never could, so long as her family needed her.

We often played games on Kristy's family TV, creating a captivating after-dinner ritual in which one person played while her six siblings, her parents, and any random visitors all assumed the role of astute commentators. This approach to playing games, often known as the "player two" view, was both astounding and nerve-racking. I remember watching Kristy's brother play *Animal Crossing* while her family gave deft commentary on the game's forms of budgeting, resource management, and labour exploitation, which they dissected from the game's crafting mechanic. Once, during the New Year's Eve countdown to 2005, we skipped out on watching the famed Las Vegas fireworks to instead bask in the prismatic light of *Animal Crossing*.

~

The first role-playing game Kristy and I completed together was *Final Fantasy IV*, her favourite game of the series. She made me play all the important parts, tossing me the controller while she tried not to spoil the plot or recite lines of dialogue.

Final Fantasy IV focuses on the story of Cecil, the captain of an imperial army who has committed unspeakable atrocities. Regretting his life as a soldier, Cecil walks the earth plagued by guilt over the innocent lives he has ended and the still-living people he has maimed. Though he knows he doesn't deserve it, he finds forgiveness in a town that was once decimated by his army. His chance for redemption comes in two five-year-old twin mages, Palom and Porom. At first, Palom and Porom follow Cecil only to spy on him—and perhaps to kill him. Yet over time, they come to see his inner light and his desire to change. They declare to their city of mourners that the person who massacred their loved ones deserves forgiveness. Redemption, voiced through the children, seems possible. Palom and Porom join Cecil's quest, with his promising to protect them.

When we came to a scene where Cecil and our party of rebels were fleeing a castle, Kristy tossed me the controller. "You'll have to play this part," she said. After a gruelling boss battle, our party entered a corridor. Kristy leapt behind me and shielded her eyes. It was a trap: the doors on either side locked, and the stone corridor walls began to squeeze inward with loud *crunch* sounds. Palom and Porom exchanged looks. *Crunch*. The walls tightened around us. The twins leapt to the walls and placed their small arms against the moving rock. Together, they shouted, "BREAK!" and suddenly they were gone—petrified into motionless statues holding back the tide of stone.

Kristy was crying. My eyes reddened, and I tried to hold back tears. My still-living party members tried casting spells on Palom and Porom. I tried to action-button them awake. The twins' final act was to save me, Cecil, the man who had massacred their village. My forgiveness was their last hope. Now, their stone bodies were sanctified into statues, monuments of memory.

Of all the games I played with Kristy, I have always remembered this moment with the twins from *Final Fantasy IV*. Over time, their tragic demise took on an unexpected allure, a beautiful and memorable finality. They were only five, yet their deaths promised that perhaps my own death might be similar. Each died along with their best friend, their twin. Neither would ever miss the other, neither would have to grieve the other. There was a freedom, I thought, in making that choice.

To be so young and have something so straightforward to die for—that was also strangely enviable. The twins had a clear purpose. There was an evil that could be defeated through their final act. Perhaps this was the real fantasy.

~

> The point of literature isn't to just understand the world, but to end it.
> —Solmaz Sharif

The twins' death in *Final Fantasy IV* is the only time I remember seeing Kristy cry. Perhaps it was the only time I cried in front of her. This ability of games to unlock our emotional selves was apparent in every gamer I knew, whenever we talked about the games that made us who we were. For this reason, I never separated my love for games from my love for literature and writing, and I was always absorbed in both.

Both reading and video games are known as common pastimes for autistic people. I have encountered many on autism forums who claim that they either read or played games every waking moment when they were young, and that, like me and my brother, they spent nights daydreaming about the worlds of books and games. I've grown to recognize myself in these narratives of young people who learned to function with only one hand because the other was always carrying a controller or a book; who seemingly survived for years on cereal and granola alone; who could get absorbed so deeply into novels and games that they could recall the events, names, and maps of a game's inner world far better than their own "real world."

Reading, writing, and games give many neurodiverse people a way of learning about the world around us, of discovering the social traits and expectations that we cannot figure out ourselves. By being "in character," by embodying a literary protagonist or playing a role, we become more socially savvy. Eventually, we turn our social selves into work, and every social situation becomes a test. Sometimes, we'll do anything to get through them. Other times, we treat socializing as a sport, a way of practising the arts that once eluded us. We are always working to suss out *their* opinions, to understand *their* desires, to fulfill *their* social expectations. We morph, mask, put on a role catered to *them*—only minutely and hesitantly ourselves.

But in books, games, and writing, I could create a space where *I* truly existed, a place where *they* couldn't reach. In these realms, I was more than just someone trying to please those around me. I was the creator, the world, and all the characters in it. And in writing these worlds, I could translate my anger and restlessness into something greater. The more I dwelt within these worlds, the more I wrote about them. I wrote furiously, page after page feeding the uncaring flame.

~

> Any consideration of what the novel is today, and any true understanding of what narrative aesthetics are doing in general, is impossible if we do not also understand the work video games are doing.
> —Eric Hayot, "Video Games & the Novel"

One year after Teal's death, I had shape-shifted into a despairing, self-loathing artist. This was my typical day: after working at one of the many jobs I hated (movie theatre usher, knife salesman, warehouse stocker, typer, survey taker), I would return to my apartment below a freeway where I lived with four guys and other random in-and-out visitors.

I would turn on the kitchen light, let cockroaches scurry into the cabinets, grab a cluster of beer bottles from the refrigerator, then collapse onto a mattress I had found in the dumpster. Because our air conditioning was always broken, I would position two fans to blow straight into my face and then drink myself to sleep. In the morning, I would tilt every bottle in front of me until I found one with some weight, and I'd sip myself awake.

I usually didn't eat for most of the day. Some days, I didn't eat at all. If others around me were eating, I would joke that I was on a "liquid diet," meaning my only calories were from alcohol. Once, I tested my resolve by starving myself for five days straight, until my tongue, out of desperation, started to impulsively lick my teeth as if it could eat them. When I did eat again, I spat most of the chewed food into napkins that formed a nimbus cloud next to my plate. Sometimes I stabbed myself with forks and knives, right in my belly fat, wishing I could slice it off. I only stopped when I saw spots of blood pinching through my skin. Eventually, I thought, I would take it further. I would be lithe in the afterlife.

I mention all this because, on the surface, I was an achieving academic, blazing my way from community college to university, acing all my courses even when I overloaded on them year-round. When I encountered friends from high school, they commented on how good I looked, my sudden thinness taken as a sign of health and self-control. My body withered, but my mind was on a constant adrenalin high. Whenever I wasn't in class, I was in the library, the only place with air conditioning where I could read and write in peace.

My first writing course at the University of Nevada, Las Vegas (UNLV), was a mixture of ambitious MFA graduate students and undergraduate wannabe authors like myself. It was a pummelling introduction to shared writing. As one student pointed out, bringing a short story to a writing circle was like bringing a dove to a committee of critics and letting each one pass the bird around, each bending its form, cracking a different bone, breaking flesh until it fit into their idea of an "MFA story."

What you had at the end resembled something beautiful, avant-garde. But to you, it was just a mangled bird carcass.

The second thing I learned in my first fiction writing course was that video games were a taboo subject signalling thoughtlessness and immature storytelling. Thus, my desire to talk about games alongside my stories marked me as an outsider and an idiot. Not only did I write stories about my experiences being Filipino, androgynous, and neurodivergent (though I didn't know it at the time), but I also declared proudly that I found more inspiration from *Final Fantasy* games than from Carver, Hemingway, or Cheever. I soon learned that there was no faster way to lose the respect of your peers, to doom your dove, then to say, "My short story was inspired by a video game."

Historically, writers have always had to hide their less-respected influences. During the domination of Christianity in Europe, writers and poets hid their paganistic Greek and Roman forebears, just as scientists had to hide their denial of Scripture. During the Victorian age, many authors tried to downplay the inspiration that came from colonialism, drugs, and sex. Today, in an age when literature has come to replace the divine, to say that one's main source of inspiration is video games has a heretical imprint. Book reviewers often save their most vicious prose for comparing books to video games, such as when book critic Maureen Corrigan from National Public Radio lambasted Chang-Rae Lee's novel *On Such a Full Sea* as a literary failure, calling it a "video game of a novel."[40]

As I quickly learned, any comparison of a story to a video game instantly makes the room cringe; it is an insult of the highest order. A writer can discuss the influences of nature, plays, music, cinema—anything but a video game.

~

> Technologies are always used to tell stories, that is in fact their fundamental feature.
> —Ken Liu

One day in our writing class, we had a very special guest: Wole Soyinka, the only Black African author ever to win the Nobel Prize in Literature—a telling fact that is still true to this day. Ever since I had discovered Soyinka's name on the UNLV faculty list, he had been a hero of mine. I had read his plays and essays hoping to one day meet him, as he was rarely on campus (he was often either in prison in Nigeria or in hiding). Even when he was absent, our writing classes felt elevated just for being within his orbit.

The class was eager to talk to Soyinka but gave a collective groan when they realized whose short story happened to be assigned for that day: mine. Our resident Nobel laureate was going to read a story inspired by video games.

To my classmates' credit, my story was incredibly weird. It was about a man without any passion or awareness—your usual "sim." One day, this man absent-mindedly trips and falls into a mall fountain. When he gets up, shivering his way out of the water, he sees that the mall is entirely empty of people. There's one other strange difference: it is full of eggs. So many eggs litter the floor that he cannot take a step forward without possibly breaking one. What will he do? How will he go on?

Perhaps this story was genius; more likely it was terrible. Certainly, for the students and the professor, it was not the story they wanted to discuss. Not on the day Wole Soyinka came to class.

Soyinka's hair was far greyer in person than in his author photos, which reminded us that he was real and that he had been through hell. When it came time to speak about my story, he gave no evaluative comments but asked how my imagination worked, where my ideas came from, and how I'd come to write with such strange grammar and diction. I answered as honestly as I could: Sometimes I learned from literature, sometimes from the things in my life, and sometimes ... from video games. The professor tried to divert the conversation, to get Soyinka to give us his "best tips for writing," but Soyinka kept prying.

"What games?"

"Mostly *Final Fantasy* and other role-playing games. Some of the writing in them is in broken English, but it's interesting."

"Interesting."

The professor kept trying to redirect the conversation, but we continued. Me, a self-loathing anorexic gamer, and the incomparable Wole Soyinka, chatting about the *Final Fantasy* series. Though Soyinka didn't know much about video games, he did not assume they were immature or anathema for a writer. His ignorance of games only made them more thought-provoking.

By the end of class, the rest of the room was stewing. How could our one day with the star of the MFA program be taken up solely with talk of video games? But I didn't care if they hated me or if they thought my writing was dull and uninspired. My story did not need their critique, their tips, their judgment, their publications. Wole Soyinka thought my dove looked cool just as it was.

~

> So much of the work of oppression is about policing the imagination.
> —Saidiya Hartman, "Storytelling While Black & Female"

Despite my momentary victory with Soyinka, the closer I came to graduation, the more I doubted myself as an artist and regretted choosing this art of writing.

I had written four novels, and not a single person had read any of them. Before even picking up one of my short stories, most had already passed judgment. I was a young brown man, awkward, unsociable, feminine, poor, working in warehouses, and obsessed with video games. How could anything worth reading ever come from my hands?

My frustration mounted. Perhaps video games were the reason for my failure. Despite Soyinka's encouragement, the nagging voice that said games were the creative opposite to literature began to amplify. With every rejection letter, every manuscript that collected dust, every unreturned email, I felt that my last-ditch effort to persevere, to choose life over death, was, in fact, my final act.

I threw in one last shot and applied for a dozen graduate schools, in both MFA and English literature programs. If I could not be an artist, I could at least continue to train as one. Despite having near-perfect grades, I didn't get into a single graduate school.

If I wasn't a writer, then what was the point? It was either writing or nothing.

What was I supposed to do?

~

Even in the most sanitized, cartoonish video games, death still runs rampant. One only needs to be in a room with a kid playing *Super Mario Bros.* to hear it: "I *died* again!" "I'm gonna *kill* that Goomba!" "Why do I keep *dying*?"

In writing courses, I was taught not to write about death. The last thing a writing group wanted to hear, I was told, was another sob story about the death of a grandparent, or a pet, or a childhood friend. For my writing mentors, references to death were cheap tricks to gain a reader's sympathy. But for me, death wasn't a trope. Death was everything I needed to reflect upon and write about.

Games fixate not just on the loss of a life, but on the loss of entire worlds and realities. Often, a game will allow the player to shift from the "real world" to a dark realm where most everyone is dead—a world populated by monsters, a world of darkness and decay. In the 1991 game *The Legend of Zelda: A Link to the Past*, this is the Dark World, a desolate place that mirrors the real world. In the game's 1998 follow-up, *The Legend of Zelda: Ocarina of Time*, the Dark World is not just a mirror world, but the future. In the Light World you are a forest child riding horses and meeting princesses, but in the future, when you are a teenager, the world is covered in darkness, and most everyone you knew is dead or enslaved. The Dark World is not a foreign realm; it is the future awaiting all of us.

Games feature the deaths of loved ones, of entire worlds, and, most commonly, of yourself. In *Final Fantasy x*, you begin in a beautifully dynamic world only to see it get obliterated, along with you. Though you've perished, you wake up a thousand years in the future as a resurrected spirit. Going back in time isn't an option. Everyone you ever knew is dead, and few people even remember their names, their city, their civilization. You have survived, but only to defeat the monster who destroyed your world. After that, your purpose will be fulfilled, and all the wandering ghosts will forever disappear from this world, including you.

In *Final Fantasy x*, you don't witness a friend or innocent flower girl perish. *You* are the innocent person edging closer to death. The only way to save the world, to lift the "veil of darkness," is to leave it. Your death is the only way to move forward, a justice to the world. You will be mourned by those who go on living, but the planet cannot heal until you are gone. With your final breath, a fresh start.

~

A month before graduating college, I began burning bridges. I cut everyone out: my parents, my friends, my twin brother. I gave away all my belongings: my car, my games, my manuscripts. I became an arsonist of my own life. I wanted to destroy them both: the simulated life I had been given, and the life of the artist that had given me false hope.

Days before graduation, I snuck around my campus in the dead of night and slipped a story into every copy of the UNLV literary magazine I could find. It was my first autobiography, a story of sitting in their workshops, of dealing with their elitist student-run journal. It was about the misogynistic and racist writing in every MFA class that sought only to mimic lionized white male authors. Later, I would hear that someone had published an editorial response to my story, but I never read it. They were all dead to me, and I would soon be dead to them.

My last bridge to burn was the one linking myself to my girlfriend, Kristy. It was a difficult break because we never argued, and we'd supported each other through our hardest, darkest moments. For four years, we had grown up together, lost our virginity together, driven our first cars together. I couldn't explain why we needed to break up, because I didn't really know. I loved her, and she loved me enough to want to start a family with me. But—I *hated* "me." And I didn't want her, or anyone else, to be there when I finally decided to do something about it.

I didn't attend my graduation; I was already on the road. I left Las Vegas, heading north. I accepted my world veiled in darkness. I stopped battling the monsters. I went alone to that solitary island where I would watch the world ravage itself apart.

CHAPTER 5
Would You Like to Continue?

I'm sitting in the passenger seat of a banged-up truck approaching the Sierra Nevada mountains near Reno when the driver points forward with a weathered, wrinkled finger. "There's going to be a tornado there, around the next hill," he says. "I can feel it in the air. The high and low pressure."

Sure enough, around a hill of dried yellow grass, there it is: a twister, humongous and encircled by torn and tossing foliage.

The driver pulls over, the tornado only miles away. He walks around the truck and opens my door. "I am sky-fucking-high right now," he tells me. "The low and high pressure mean there's gonna be a bigger storm once we get to the mountains. That means snow, loads of it. You gotta drive."

The driver was a seasoned traveller I'd found on Craigslist just the day before. We made a deal: deliver me from Salt Lake City, and the gas is on me. I'd expected some odd scenarios, but I was new to this augury magic of low and high pressure. And I'd never driven in snow before.

The driver's seat smells of cigarettes. I find my controls—the interface that will navigate me through the oncoming storm. "I've never driven stick shift," I say, but the man doesn't seem to hear me, his mind captivated and unnerved. I say again, "*I don't know how to drive stick.*" The man caves into his seat, staring in frozen awe at the tornado steadily creeping toward us.

I take a cue from the driving games I grew up with: *Gran Turismo, Daytona USA, Need for Speed*. I press buttons. I try, fail, try, and fail. Eventually I learn there is an all-important joystick that has to be pressed with care and given constant attention. Later, I learn it is called the "clutch."

After an hour of starting and stalling, I'm driving in a snowstorm with no visibility beyond a blanket of white static. I'm still learning to shift gears, and I can't stop now. What if I can't start the engine again, and we freeze to death? I feel the truck's wheels slipping. I glance over the ledge and see the drop—a deep, foggy nothingness, dragging me toward it. A voice whispers, "*Dive in.*"

Is this it? Is this how it ends, finally?

Ahead of me, a rectangular shape emerges through the snow: the back of a semitruck. I remember how, in racing games, tailing another car gives you a speed boost. I don't know why this is, but I stay behind the truck, hiding in its shadow. With the truck guiding us, we break through the storm and reach yellow grass again.

For days, I think back to that pull, the gravity drawing me toward the edge. One fact weighs upon me: I believed I was going to die, and I didn't pray, plead, or cry. I saw the end and had no wish to be saved.

~

In June 2005, when I was nineteen years old, I gave up everything I owned, including my car, and moved to Seattle, Washington, in the hopes that a drastic change—a new setting, a new city—would illuminate me with some reason to stay alive.

For ten tractionless months in Seattle I worked as a part-time temp mindlessly processing data entry forms in local hospitals. I read books in dark cafés blaring hardcore screamo punk. My depression felt literal: my life was reduced, my future stalled, my body weakened—everything seemed to press down. In practice, depression meant unending masturbation, each day a piranhic jab at my self-esteem that consisted of waking, looking up porn, fucking myself again, and watching porn again. Entire months snuck by in this rut: death by a thousand smuts. But besides touching myself, there was one other thing my inertia permitted me to do: play lots and lots of video games.

For those ten months, shuttered inside an underground apartment infested with black mould, I played *Halo*, *World of Warcraft*, and many other games. But there was one that I woke up to every day and went to sleep with every night. This was the 2002 open-world game *The Elder Scrolls III: Morrowind*. *Morrowind* was no heroic, Arthurian fantasy. *Morrowind* was a drab, dreary, dangerous world, just like the world I was living in, the world I longed to leave.

~

Morrowind takes place on the island of Vvardenfell, where every city and environment has been shaped in some way by Red Mountain, an active volcano at the island's centre. Most of Vvardenfell is desolate, filled with burned, deformed trees, edged rock surfaces, and storms of blinding ash. One could search Vvardenfell for hours and find no grassy meadow, no pristine lake, no grove of pine trees, no verdant landscape, no lush foliage, no sun-reflecting ocean. *Morrowind* lacks the picturesque, prelapsarian beauty typical of fantasy settings. Instead, one finds harsh extremes of dreary and dreadful, of dark rain clouds and intensely bright haze, of desolate Ashlands and foggy moors of wild overgrowth. And when the island's palette isn't a dozen variations of dirt brown, it's often gradations of grey—grey clouds, grey trees, grey rock. Sometimes the entire screen might look like an asphalt parking lot. The creatures around Vvardenfell are also variants of the same brown, black, and grey colours, their diseased and infectious bodies as drab as their names: mudcrab, cave rat, ash ghoul, wild guar, and Lame Corprus. And in case you're thinking of trying to escape this godforsaken island, the ocean surrounding you is plagued with two kinds of creatures: slaughterfish and terrifying spear-wielding mermen called Dreugh.

Because *Morrowind* takes place on a single island, the player remains within the game's guardrails without needing to hit invisible walls. The island landscape, as in many games, promises that players can eventually explore every inch of land. The island is whole, and every bit feels intentional, held together like an epic poem, one that according to its developers took "close to one hundred man-years to create."[41] Just over the crest of any hill is entirely new scenery, a new time signature, a new mood. At the game's beginning you move sluggishly slow, forcing you to notice the care poured into the game's smallest details. Your first-person view is low to the earth, as if your eyes have been transplanted into your waist. This makes the terrain intense, seen in extreme close-up, so that every rock, tree, and mushroom seems to scroll up over the horizon while you glide steadily, drifting over the muck.

Morrowind begins on a prison ship pulling into port. Then, after a brief accounting by a local census taker, you are left to roam. With no home and no clear direction, you become itinerant, wandering from guild to guild, hostel to hostel. You are protector of nothing, kin to no one; you are just a prisoner tossed off a boat and are subsequently treated like scum by everyone around you. You may join a guild and build from the bottom up, but you'll always be an outlander.

There isn't much destiny to be gained in *Morrowind*, few epic battles, and no dragons to slay. To play *Morrowind* is mostly just to pace around its desolate landscape, running errands to slightly improve your status. Though few of the locals see how violent, desolate, and ugly the island truly is, it's strikingly obvious to you. You are the travelling upset, an enigma, there only to mill about and witness a world that was dead and broken long before you stepped into it. You have no purpose, and you don't need one. You can sleep anywhere, eat whatever is around, and if you piss someone off or step off a ledge, well, death isn't that big a deal.

~

> For writers it is always said that the first twenty years of life contain the whole of experience—the rest is observation.
> —Graham Greene, *The Comedians*

I was twenty years old when, after ten months of playing an itinerant wanderer in *Morrowind*, I went itinerant myself. I gave away my possessions again (video games included) and found a group of campers to drive me from Seattle to Utah. When we stopped in Salt Lake City, I ditched them. For the next six months I had no home, no car, and no job. I would sleep anywhere, eat whatever was around, and if I pissed someone off or stepped off a ledge, well, no big deal.

I had experimented with homelessness before, when I'd bus into downtown Seattle to panhandle and get to know the city's wayward youth. We called each other "street brothers," "street sisters," and "street parents." I found unexpected community in my street kin, as well as a constant desperation, as many of our discussions turned to the best places to score medications, to dumpster dive, to piss and shit, to steal, to evade security and police. The street families helped each other, but they also didn't want to fall victim to each other's addictions, spirals, desperations. I'd never spent the night with them. Having a bed to return to only a bus ride away will always be preferred to sleeping out in the cold.

After ten months in Seattle, I was tired of merely cosplaying at being unhoused. I felt strangely at home with the queer, poor, frustrated, marginalized youth who were antagonized by every city cop, security officer, and landowner. I too felt isolated and hated, but this somehow felt appropriate, given the state of the world. We were all exiled from our families and communities, some by force, some by our own refusal, and some because we knew that leaving was the only way.

One would never think of homelessness as an empowering experience, but in a way it can be, particularly when the weather is suitable and you've got your health and youth. I was homeless at twenty years old, when my body didn't cramp up from sleeping on a bench. I felt a rush of power when I went dumpster diving, thieved snacks, picked plums or pears from trees, ordered coffee at a restaurant only to eat someone's leftover food, or just went hungry for a couple of nights and survived just fine. Every nutrient I got into my body felt like levelling up in *Morrowind*. My survival skills gained a permanent boost.

At first, there was a gamelike thrill in beginning every day not knowing how I would eat or where I would sleep. Sometimes I walked until my body collapsed below an awning or on a patch of grass in a park. But mostly, being young and new to unhoused living, I would find somewhere to stay: a couch, a bunch of blankets on some student's floor, in the back of someone's car, or I would use my credit card for a ten-dollar spot in a bunk bed.

The feelings of open-world empowerment that came with homelessness lasted maybe a month. In Salt Lake City and later in San Francisco, I learned quickly that there are other things that drive you indoors besides the cold, and most of them came from outside the street community: violence and theft from passersby, the constant harassment from cops. And while I no longer had a home or a car, unlike my street families around me, I still had an active credit card.

~

For most of *Morrowind*, journeying through the island of Vvardenfell feels like slogging through an overgrown swamp. Vines spread across rocks, walls, and city homes. Everything intertwines, everything melds, everything rots. Enormous mushrooms propagate the land, feasting on the decaying bodies of dead creatures and travellers.

Swamps are not conducive to settlement, and few of the people on Vvardenfell seem to be there by choice. Villages contain creole populations of settlers, exiles, outcasts, and rogues, while smugglers and thieves reside in caverns nearby. Still, these villages become fondly remembered homesteads once you venture into ancient ruins full of demonic lords or try to debate the power-hungry slaveowners of the great houses who claim the right to own people as a long-standing cultural tradition. While *Morrowind* is awash in vampires, flying beasts, and necromancers, the powerful houses of *Morrowind* are its most monstrous inhabitants. Try to talk to a slave to get their point of view, and you'll find it just as dismal. Mention the words "Go free?" to them, and they come back with the phrase "No. There is no hope for us."

Morrowind's enslaved peoples come in all types but are mostly reptilian or feline humanoids who cross the swampy boundaries of human and non-human. Like the amphibious creatures of mythical bogs, Vvardenfell's hybrid beings transgress distinctions of animal/human, flesh/machine, and living/dead. *Morrowind* doesn't just expose you to these parahuman types, you yourself might be one—you might be a Khajiit, a feline humanoid assumed to be a thief; or a Dunmer, a dark elf assumed to be a terrorist; or an Argonian, a reptile humanoid assumed to belong in chains. But no matter what type of person you are, or whatever type you encounter, in *Morrowind*, all life is cheap. You can kill almost any character in the game in broad daylight, in the middle of town, without any punishment, so long as you taunt or annoy them enough to attack you first. For those you can't taunt, like imperial guards, you can kill them in a single blow and then merely pay a fine of about forty gold. So, life isn't technically worthless—it's about the same price as a silver plate or a chained helmet.

When I'd lived in Seattle, I zombied from job to job, café to café, street to street, and the more I saw, the more I despised the rushing corporatism of the city, the unavowed racism of its seemingly progressive residents. But in *Morrowind*, I found a world that never hesitated to expose the realities of race, class, religion, environmental decay, and death. If they trust you, many of the game's characters will repeat the worst stereotypes about the game's other races. Some are passive-aggressive in their racism, while others, like the dark elves, are straight-up xenophobic.

From the moment you step off the boat and onto the island of Vvardenfell, the complex violences of the real world are there. The slave trade, the drug trade, and the sex trade are all in full force throughout the game, and its worst victims (as well as its most comfortable benefactors) are determined by gender, race, and wealth. In one eye-opening mission, you are tasked to escort a slave, Rabinna, to a different city, where a man awaits her for sex. But when you arrive, the man throws punches at her with the intent to kill her. If you take him down first and Rabinna survives, she will tell you that he attacked her not out of hate or lust, but greed; she is holding drugs inside her stomach, and he simply needed to get them out.

Clearly, *Morrowind* is no escapist Tolkienian fantasy. Its borders between good and evil are as fuzzy as the cattails lining a riverbank, its cruelty as infectious as tendrils creeping through mud. Evil is the world, and in my most despairing moments, *Morrowind* was a safe and comforting place. Unlike the real world, *Morrowind* never denied the brutal bullshit of its world. In *Morrowind*, the earth is cruel, people are cruel, and you too are among them. And that cruelty, heavy as it is to bear, will never lift—no new god, no prophesied leader, can transform a swamp. The more you try, the more dead bodies you'll leave in your path—more feed for the island's giant fungi. Of all the cruel people in Vvardenfell, you may be the worst. Surely, even this accursed isle would be a better place without you in it.

Go free?

No. There is no hope for us.

~

> The challenge of modernity is to live without illusions
> and without becoming disillusioned.
> —Antonio Gramsci, *Letters from Prison*

The first time I gave up my possessions and moved to Seattle, it was in a final effort to find a reason to live. The second time I gave up my possessions, I also gave up hope. Wandering from city to city without direction or home, I was no longer interested in last resorts. I was done messing around with death. This was to be the last summer I would see, the last sun to grace my skin. The more I thought about it, the more I felt the great weight of work, failure, and grief begin to lift.

In Seattle I'd played with all the ways I could end my life: a gun, suffocating in a car, an overdose, starvation, hanging. I saw the movie *Pi* and the image of a drill pressed to the back of my skull lingered in my mind. When spring came, I decided, I would stop wandering Vvardenfell and start roaming the real world. The end of exploring the game would inspire a new ending: to roam until death took me. Somehow this felt more like destiny, more honest and respectful to those who had raised me. In *Morrowind*, you often encounter death just by walking around; a creature attacks you, you get poisoned, you fall into a pit of lava, you drown while scavenging a shipwreck. I too would give myself to the elements, to whatever end fate determined. Such an end would be easier on those I loved, freeing them from blame through a death of natural causes, an end sanitized by randomness. No one would weep and wonder what they did wrong.

Giving myself permission to die followed a strange game logic. In games you die while aiming for something, while on a mission. Death comes with the straightforward choice to play: go out, go on the move, and eventually, you'll perish.

~

I meet Peter while eyeing a bowl of fruit-flavoured condoms in San Francisco's Green Tortoise Hostel. Peter is from New Zealand and can't believe how the city's cafés are full of people at all times of the day, people spilling into the streets nursing lukewarm Americanos. "Work is not work here," he tells me.

I think Peter might be a virgin when I see him sneaking a peek at a couple having sex in our room of co-ed bunk beds. When the woman on top catches him spying, she throws her panties into his glasses.

I like Peter, but when he mentions he's heading to Los Angeles, I lie and tell him I'm going to Seattle. Perhaps I could travel with him, but I'm on a different mission.

~

I hardly remember my time in Los Angeles, or even how I got there. Twenty years later, it is a frozen chunk in my cold-storage memory.

At some point, my family found me in Los Angeles. I may have logged into a hostel computer or some random person's laptop and seen my mother, sister, and brother bugging my friends, asking if they'd seen me. The fog of memory is thick here, but at some point, somehow, my sister convinced me to meet her in Palm Springs. She was going for a work training course and may have tempted me with the idea of a shared room and a private shower.

My sister had a harder life than me. Not merely because she was darker than me—a mixture of Black, Filipina, and Indigenous (Kānaka Maoli)—but also because she never met her father, because she was one of two Black girls she knew growing up, because she was the first-born and was expected to take care of my twin brother and me while also receiving the worst of our mother's militaristic demands. My sister's troubles arrived in her teens: she was homeless, in and out of jail, on and off drugs, and she had a child when she was sixteen. My own suicidal intentions felt middle class and tame compared to the challenges she faced throughout her life. Perhaps this was what pulled me to Palm Springs to meet her.

If my sister was checking in on me, if *she* felt the need to save me while building a new life, who was I to deny her? I told myself this was still part of the plan, just a brief detour to tell my family goodbye.

~

> People see fogs, not because there are fogs, but because poets and painters have taught them the mysterious loveliness of such effects.
> —Oscar Wilde, *The Decay of Lying*

In cinema, fog captures the horror of nightmares and the fantasy of dreams. Fog is the coupling of adventure with the incontinent terror of being hunted by whatever may be lurking in the haze.

In video games, fog has a much more practical use. It is added not just for atmospheric effect, but to save computer memory by reducing frame rates and draw distances. Nearly all first-person games from the 1990s and early 2000s used fog to conceal enemies, landscapes, and structures. For players let loose in a sprawling open-world game like *Morrowind*, the practical limitations of game fog create a pared-down landscape that reduces the limitless possibilities of the game space to a few visible options: go to that hazy-looking human-made structure over there, or go toward those tall things that could be either trees or monsters, or wander directly into the fog and find a pond, a cavern, or a cliff's edge. Once you arrive at a new place, the fog reveals more shaded objects. There are no binoculars or telescopes; the only way to know a thing is to move toward it. Every step is discovery.

Morrowind's constant and unending fog feels purgatorial. It makes the game's otherwise drab, mud-coloured creatures appear like mythical beasts. At the same time, the fog works to cover up so much that you begin to feel a sublime emptiness in the landscape, a poetic silence in the nothingness a mere stone's throw away. As you move, mountains unfold, flowing upward like a giant bubble gaining lift, before expanding into scattered hilltops. Your movement wakes up the hibernating landscape. And don't you want to stick around just a bit longer to see what else the fog might reveal?

In a despairing world, the fog teaches a mode of survival. It does not give hope but keeps you going, promising nothing but mere possibility, gesturing toward the uncharted horizon. The fog asks not, "Would you like to continue?" but "What the heck is that gigantic marshmallow-looking thing over there?"

~

Like the fog of games, the fog of memory also has a practical use. It keeps our most devastating, traumatic moments silhouetted in a haze of disbelief that renders the past unimaginable. It makes survival possible by turning our sharpest pains into soft, fluffy curves.

Some shades of memory are unapproachable and will always remain in the fog. I hardly remember it, but somehow, in Palm Springs, my sister convinced me to return to Las Vegas, because it was my mother's birthday, and I would be her gift: the wayward son returned.

I surprised my mother at a happy hour, but I could hardly make eye contact. I knew how it felt to become unanchored by someone else's absence, and I didn't want to see what my absence had done to her. *Don't put this on yourself*, I wanted to plead. *It's not your fault*.

For a month I remained in Las Vegas, sleeping on a couch at my brother Cameron's "party house," which brings its own haze of memory—offering and being offered drinks every morning, afternoon, and night, waking up at a nearby park or on the front patio, seeing dried blood in the bathroom and wondering who hadn't cleaned up after themselves. I substituted the fog of travel with the fog of drink. I wanted to prove to my family that it was going to be one or the other. And the longer I stayed, the worse I got. Of course, being the loud-mouthed dramatic one of the family, I couldn't know how this made them feel, or that my brother was going through his own inner crisis.

During high school, Cameron and I had both enrolled in the Marines' Junior Reserve Officers' Training Corps. We were those kids who wore full military uniforms to school, polished our boots, and practised military drills during sporting events. While I had only joined the Junior Corps to avoid taking physical education courses—to save myself from being bullied in locker rooms—Cameron was a more serious soldier who dreamt of joining the US Marines and fighting terrorists in Iraq. But by the time high school was over, the lies about WMDs and all the systemic abuses of Iraqi prisoners and civilians had convinced my brother otherwise. The revelations of the Iraq War broke his patriotism, as well as his trust in family and friends who continued to support the war.

If I had opened up to my brother at the time, I might have found that he too was adrift in the fog, looking for a way to leave this world honourably. His plan was more commonplace than my own: to go to war and sacrifice himself for his country. I was always confused by this, since our family was from two colonized spaces, the Philippines and Hawai'i, and because, well, after having thrown off the crucifixes of our grandparents, choosing to fight now for a Christian country against an Islamic enemy seemed an odd choice. But I began to understand that it wasn't love of country that my brother was seeking. Like me, he sought an easy way out and a purpose his loved ones would remember. He too longed to exit the game.

~

One morning I awoke on my brother's front lawn, still drunk from tequila, and realized I couldn't do this here, leaving someone else to clean up my mess.

I texted my brother while he was at work. *I'm leaving again*, I told him. *I found someone on Craigslist to give me a ride east. Thank you for hosting me.*

My brother didn't try to stop me. He only asked that I wait until he got home so he could say goodbye. When he arrived, he told me he had just quit his job at the movie theatre and was leaving all his possessions to his roommates (yes, even his video games). "I'm going with you," he said. "Now we can travel the country together!"

He had called my bluff. We were back again on our floating isles: role-playing, wearing masks, pretending that this was just an adventure.

Our father had left the United States a year earlier to teach English in South Korea, so we "borrowed" his grey Ford sedan and departed for a new floating isle. This one was not too different from the isles we had once created in TALK story nights, in our own language. Now, our isle was the open world.

~

> The world is a mist. And then the world is
> minute and vast and clear.
> —Elizabeth Bishop, "Sandpiper"

When I recall the next four months of wandering North America with my brother, I mostly remember the good times—the close calls, the meandering nights, the hikes, the random sex with a random person in a hostel bunk bed. But our first week travelling together in the deserts of Arizona has always been sealed off by the fog of memory: a complete whiteout. When I try to access these memories, I experience heavy breathing, forehead sweat. I go into auto-rehearsed trauma responses: counting from one to ten, wiggling my toes and fingers, grounding myself on a table or chair, breathing through the pain. Still, the fog refuses to lift. Perhaps the fog that covers these memories is different, a pollution haze created by the industrial factories demanding we remain productive, persevere, and forget. This fog, heavy as a mercury cloud, feels hazardous. I have written poetry about these moments in Arizona. I have talked to friends and therapists about it. But even the memories of writing those words and having those conversations is blocked—a secondary fog concealing everything in a protective blanket.

So, I have had to rely almost entirely on my brother's recollections of these events. As soon as I ask him about it, I feel nauseous, disordered, my brain screaming like a prisoner in a cell. He takes me through it, walks me through his own haze of memory, comparing his shadows to my silhouettes.

At some point near Flagstaff, Cameron caught me trying to sneak off. Perhaps it was at a restaurant, or maybe a rest stop. Perhaps I was asking a trucker if I could get a ride to anywhere but here. Perhaps I was just walking away into the desert. After he caught me, he asked what I was doing. I couldn't tell him.

Later, in the car, I did some strange things. Maybe I punched the dashboard. Maybe I clawed the windows or my own face. Whatever I did, I frightened my brother enough for him to pull over. I fled into the desert. I hurt myself. Maybe I smashed rocks against my head or ate dirt. Cameron tried to stop me, and I attacked him. I screamed at him all the things I'd never intended for him to know: I wanted to die. I didn't want to be saved. I wasn't supposed to sleep in a car. I was meant to sleep on the street. I wasn't supposed to be watched over. I was meant to disappear. It was the greatest kindness I could do for him, for our mother, for our sister. I had a plan to keep everyone away, to exit this life as quickly and quietly as I possibly could without hurting anyone. And he was fucking it all up!

I beat him. He started hitting me back. I told him I would kill him if he followed me into the desert.

I don't know what my brother did to calm me down. Perhaps I walked away and he just waited for me to return. Perhaps he told me that he had similar feelings, that *he* in fact needed me to save *him*—which was true, but something I wouldn't understand until many years later. Perhaps we just beat each other until we were close enough to see death and turn away. Perhaps exhaustion took us down.

Whatever happened in that moment, it was the first time in my life that I was honest with anybody about my suicidal thoughts, the first time I voiced them out loud to anyone, including myself. But once exposed to the Arizona sun, those thoughts were no longer an unfathomable, unknowable thing. They were just a thing, like any other thing. And things, once approached through the fog, have texture—they can be seen and touched and carried and put into your inventory.

I recall none of our time in Arizona. But because I am alive now, I know that somehow I got back into the car with my brother, and he continued to drive.

~

> in childhood, I thought
> that pain meant
> I was not loved.
> It meant I loved.
> —Louise Glück, "First Memory"

When I read poetry, I am reminded that the fog of memory doesn't just obscure the past. Poetry's abbreviated space might give little to documents and archives, but it gives to the imagination. We see shapes in the mist, intermittently visible impressions of ourselves. The fog of memory isn't just time passing; it is the survival instinct of our present kicking in, reimagining the past, telling us who we are now.

Through memory's haze, I recall seeing the white hippies of Northern New Mexico bowing with palms pressed at the Indigenous women selling them hand-braided bracelets. I remember poking at tarantula holes in the Texas desert with a long stick until a fuzzy leg stuck to its end. I recall the plantations of Louisiana and the smell of rotten flowers inside houses built to hold enslaved people. I recall wandering through New Orleans only one year after Hurricane Katrina had flooded the poorest parts of the city and telling a wise weathered traveller that driving through the United States was like following the chemtrails of death, where the racist, classist, world-ending bullshit was plain to see. And the traveller told me, "You've been living your whole life on a dime. Now, it's a nickel. Imagine how you'll see the world when it's a quarter." And I imagined.

~

In the academic discipline of travel studies, many authors have made many hair-splitting arguments separating the joys of travel from the trials of spiritual pilgrimage. The most popular theories in the field consider the "sensescapes" that travellers encounter, the "wanderlust" of romanticized youth, and the way "leisure" is always dependent on conceptions of work in postmodern capitalism. Perhaps, for the majority of modern tourists, this is true. But these theories never grasped why I and many other disillusioned, marginalized, and self-harming people might give away all that we own and pick up for the road.

Morrowind offers travel not as leisure but as pilgrimage, as dealing with loss grounded in the motives of spiritual desolation and rejuvenation. At times, *Morrowind*'s fog gives the island of Vvardenfell an ethereal beauty. It is the haze of sunlight in the early morning, but it lasts all day; it is the mist on the lake, but it lasts.

Throughout the fantasy world of Tamriel, Vvardenfell is known as a sacred place, a temple preserve led by holy guides, mages, and chiefs. Many of its wanderers are pilgrims looking for a shrine: a crude slab of stone that announces a birthplace or a battle. The player is not given much information about these pilgrims or what occurred in their lives that made them seek a particular shrine. And, considering how uninvitingly treacherous the landscape is, it seems that all of Vvardenfell's pilgrims have taken great risks in travelling there alone. So, they rely on wandering strangers, like the player, who could just as easily help them as rob and murder them. Many pilgrims are kidnapped and held for ransom, and even after you rescue them, any of the island's deadly winged creatures could attack them, ending their spiritual journeys.

~

In Nashville, I start speaking at open mic nights again. I recite a poem inspired by *Morrowind* that has since been lost. An older man, another wise travelling elder, approaches me as I am leaving the stage. I brace, thinking he's going to tell me how awful my poems are, or how I shouldn't be writing about video games, or how I'm proof that fat young brown boys shouldn't write poetry. Instead, he extends his hand. "I just wanted to say good job," he says. Doubtful there was anything noteworthy in my words, I still clasp his hand, swallow my suspicions, and shake back.

In Atlanta, my brother and I feel out of place, finding few Asians, few brown dudes in a predominantly Black and white city. We visit the Martin Luther King Jr. memorial, Ebenezer Baptist Church, and a jazz festival. Then, in the city's most popular drinking area, we find groups of white men and women strolling, joking, snacking on deconstructed chicken and waffles.

While hiking the Appalachian Trail near Asheville, my brother catches me when, head in the clouds, I walk too close to a cliff's edge. I am trying to regain balance, windmilling my arms as I slip toward the sunny conifers in the valley below, when Cameron grabs my wrist and throws me back to the grass.

"Bitch-ass cliff," I say, catching my breath.

"Newbie wannabe cliff!" Cameron shouts.

"Get a life, cliff!"

"Or better yet, learn to take my brother's life better!"

~

At the base of Red Mountain's lava pools, the stronghold of Molag Mar provides pilgrims rest and protection before they embark upon Vvardenfell's most dangerous paths. Its hostels are full of volunteer escorts who warn travellers of the ravines, ridges, and diseased creatures awaiting them. "If you get in trouble," an escort tells me, "you're on your own."

The landscape outside of Molag Mar is volcanic rock covered with an overlay of cinders. I walk the pilgrimage route to Mount Assarnibibi, marching within the Foyadas, the "fire-rivers" in the native Ashlander language—deep, ash-dark ravines created by lava flow. When the ash storm blackens my vision, I find a cave and fight herds of powerful skeletal monsters. I am high-levelled at this point in the game and make quick work of the diseased creatures. Deeper in the cave, I find a dead pilgrim, his body contorted like a rag doll, holding a low-level axe and wearing common clothing. He has nothing worth looting.

I push the option "dispose of corpse," and the pilgrim's body disappears. The man's desire to cleanse his soul, to find forgiveness, to receive spiritual blessing—disposed of. How did such a weak and ill-equipped person end up here?

And then, I get it. The pilgrims of *Morrowind* are not walking toward a new beginning, but to their final end. As with my own travels, their pilgrimage is just an excuse. Under their smiles, their hopes, and their mantras, their search is not for restoration but for the bright avenue of freedom from this life. Pilgrimage just provides the kindest way to do it. They will be known as heroes and martyrs whose deaths mean transcendence to a better place. Their pilgrimage is a way of disappearing forever; it too is a suicide.

~

After visiting the museums in Washington, DC, my brother and I are low on funds, so we spend less time in hostels and more nights sleeping in parking lots. One night, after brief stops at the witch-burning field in Salem and the underwhelmingly tiny Walden Pond, we drive through a lightning storm and pull over to sleep in a rock-filled parking lot.

I awake to vibrations. The coins in our cupholders jitter. A horn screams, and a light in the distance strikes us. I try to remember where I've parked. I recall the bumps I thought were large rocks but could have been the rails of a train track.

I struggle to find the keys as the train's whistle grows louder, its light beaming straight at us. As my brother begins to wake, I think of all the characters we played together—Sonic and Tails, Peach and Mario, and the twins of *Final Fantasy IV* who died together so they would never have to go through life mourning each other. The train's horn blares and I brace for impact, grabbing the wheel, closing my eyes. Is this how it ends, finally?

The train whizzes past us, inches away from our car. A rush of wind thrusts against the passenger side, rattling us. I brace for an impact that never comes. Instead, we sit and watch tonnages of metal thunder past us in the dark.

I didn't pray. Again, I saw the end, and I didn't wish to be saved. But this time, I also didn't feel any regret, any sadness for opening my eyes and remaining on this planet. I look at my brother, breath still heaving.

The train would have been the best way to go—two corpses, disposed of. An unfortunate accident unworthy of speculation. And yet, we are still here. For some reason, still here.

~

> You like to dance close to the fire, don't you?
> —Morrowind

Stranger moments emerge through the fog of our trip around North America. After wandering through Montreal, Toronto, and Detroit, we picked up a Chicago-style pizza in Chicago and left it, foil-wrapped, in our trunk for weeks while we wandered through the Badlands, Yellowstone, Zion, Portland, and Seattle. Then, at the Canadian border to Vancouver, customs officers searched our vehicle and found the decayed, fungal mass of spoiled cheese. They gagged, dry heaved, and chose vengeance: they forced us to take off our shirts and do jumping jacks while they laughed at our wobbling rolls of fat.

Too many times to remember, my brother and I confronted suspicious police officers and citizens. We were migratory, unemployed, and unhoused brown men with overcharged credit cards sleeping in parking lots. The more beat-up our car got and the less we tended to shower, the worse the stares, the guarded responses, the harassment. Soon, we grew tired of travelling North America altogether.

With our funds depleted, my brother moved to South Korea to teach English with our father. There, he quickly found friends, a mixed community of immigrant wanderers and local outcasts. These exiles were not fleeing the horrors of war but the quiet devastations of their homeland: youth-killing gun violence, poverty without a social net, a lack of adequate and universal health care, and a political class propped up by religious extremists. They fled a war machine that had, for decades, routinely sent soldiers to police the world and sold bombs to countries while shrugging off civilian death tolls, passing on the use of that enduring Cold War euphemism "collateral damage." After once having aspired to offer his life for our generation's call to war, my brother found a strange solace in the margins of another country: not just an outsider, but an ex-patriot.

With my brother abroad, I chose to stay in Seattle for no other reason than I was used to it and knew someone who would give me a couch to sleep on. But little time passed in Seattle before I was back to my restless, insomniac self. This time, I found a team of adrenalin junkies to run antics with me. We smeared coagulated pig's blood in a suburb's city square. We drew chalk murder outlines on sidewalks. We broke into construction sites to play with the equipment and try to drive the vehicles—forklifts, bulldozers, dump trucks, whatever we could jack.

One night, we broke into a construction site on an overpass above a freeway, and we climbed inside a crane. We found the keys in the passenger seat. As soon as I turned the engine, the vehicle started plodding forward. But there was no brake—at least, nothing at my feet. I looked out the window. We were about to go over, and I saw the headlights of the cars on the freeway below me, a thin stream of sparkling white.

My friend pulled the keys out, and the engine sputtered, dead. We sat in silence. Again, the snowstorm. Again, the train. Again, the street light that killed Teal. Again, the HIV that killed my uncle. Again, the cancer that killed my grandmother. Again, the pilgrims and their disposable corpses. Here we were. Still alive, but still waiting for the end.

~

I replay *Morrowind* every couple of years, but I have never completed the game. I have never ventured far enough into Red Mountain to battle the mad god Dagoth Ur. Whenever I pass Red Mountain's Ghostgate, I open up my map and realize there are still so many places I have never been. Then I open my journal and remember all the promises I made to pilgrims to find their loved ones, or to transport their sacred items to a dock in case they perished (and perish they did). I remember the letters I picked up from the dead, the pilgrims cut open by skeletons or kidnapped or enslaved or killed by a diseased creature. I think about how they never had a chance to stare into this mountain, to feel renewed by it, and to turn away.

At twenty-one, after giving up everything, trying to end my life, and then travelling in a big circle around North America, my pilgrimage still did not end. Something remained broken—something deeper and submerged. I felt done with death, but something continued to drive me toward it. The only way I knew to survive it was to outrun it. There are always more quests, more updates, more isles to explore, more secrets to discover. And in my bleakest times, when I yearned to disappear, I still wanted to know: What could that be—that grey silhouette, that strange shadow, that unknown figure, resting gently in the fog?

CHAPTER 6

Pleasures of the Open World

In January 2007, after nearly a year drifting in a self-destructive pilgrimage around North America, I joined the tide of whitewashed-up expats and floundered into the Pacific Ocean, beaching ashore in a new, unfamiliar world.

I followed my twin brother (who had followed my father) to Gimhae, a small South Korean town near Busan. For eight to ten hours a day, my brother, father, and I taught English to elementary school students and spent the rest of the day planning the next day's classes. Fascinating as the country was, we rarely left our main corridor of hagwons (private schools), noraebangs (karaoke rooms), and chimaek (fried chicken and beer) restaurants. We never received vacation days, but we were close enough to Busan to take weekend ferries to Japan.

My days in Korea were hemmed in by regimentation. But my nights were steeped in reckless abandon, meaningless make-out sessions, and getting blackout drunk before downing M-80 energy drinks the next morning to teach six-year-olds. All the while there remained the familiar sanctuary of a famous Korean export: PC rooms, or PC bangs. With at least two on every block, PC rooms were an intermittent retreat for my brother and me: our daily lunch breaks, our escape from the heat and humidity, our cheap accommodation on nights when our sensations were so dulled by drink that we couldn't hear the percussive keyboard clacks. Within those dark smoke-filled caverns, we escaped to a place not of anger and warfare, but of an easy, nostalgic solace. The perfect place to gasp for air.

~

For many gamers, Korea and Japan represent two homelands of gamer culture, Japan for having birthed Nintendo, Pokémon, and most game genres, and Korea for having popularized new ways of playing games through massive esports stadiums, social games like *MapleStory*, and the global rise of PC rooms.

PC rooms emerged in Korea in the 1980s, before the rise of the internet. The first electronic cafés opened near universities as places where students could use high-end computers to do homework for a stunningly low price.[42] Under the guise of study spaces, PC rooms eventually became underground gaming centres known mostly for American-made video games like *StarCraft* and *World of Warcraft*, before giving way almost entirely to American military shooters like *Counter-Strike*. Of course, as twenty-year-old gamers using PC rooms to sober up, my brother and I did not see the imperial histories that helped create them. The popularity of PC rooms rose through *Counter-Strike*, a game known for American militarism during the War on Terror co-created by Minh Le, a Canadian Vietnamese refugee, within a genre created by *Doom*, a game that itself was co-created by John Romero, an Indigenous game maker of Mexican, Yaqui, and Cherokee descent. We, like the YouTube and Twitch streamers of today, did not play these games to confront overlapping histories of capitalism, empire, and settler colonialism. We just came to play and forget about our day.

When my brother and I returned to PC rooms in 2007, something had changed. In the decade following 9/11, many first-person shooters were seeking to overthrow their reputation as training grounds for US militarism and Islamophobia. Game makers were refusing to play into the weaponization of the genre that convinced players to support unprecedented defence spending and the bombing of unknown people in foreign lands. Shooters were becoming more critical (*Spec Ops: The Line*), non-combative (*Portal*), and parodic (*Borderlands*). *Counter-Strike* had changed too: no longer was I trying to merely outgun, outaim, and outshoot my opponents. Now, I was trying to balance on metal-grated catwalks, to vault over rooftops, to parkour down bridge-long playground slides, and to rocket-launch my virtual body into a gigantic rock pit. By 2007, *Counter-Strike* had turned into a carnival of freewheeling user-made worlds that upended the serious and competitive aura that had defined the genre. Many of the new community-made maps were on floating islands filled with zombies, easily breakable glass floors, obstacle courses, viruses, natural disasters, and role-play adventures in magical high schools.

One of the most popular user-made modes in *Counter-Strike* featured neither guns nor acts of killing and would go on to influence any game that featured first-person movement. This was called "surf," a sub-genre in *Counter-Strike* that exploited a small movement mechanic: once you hit a steep slope, you begin to slide on it. Press forward, and you can't stop. Combine this with a game map made entirely of slopes, and you can whizz through the open air, blazing through the still-processing ramps. Jump at the right time, and your teeth-gnashing fear of falling soon eases into a pleasurable drift above a boundless world.

~

There is a picture I took of myself in Fukuoka's circular Canal City Mall that has been lost to time. I was travelling in Japan alone, entranced by the neon lights of kanji and kana, the 1980s-looking vending machines, and the tinkles and chimes of pachinko parlours. In the mall I met a futuristic robot made of yellow blocks whose sponged rear end shined the mall's glossy floors. With my small yellow Kodak, I took a selfie with the robot's touch-screen face. Standing there in my thin blue yukata, I enticed other robots to join in—a penguin, a puppy, and, of course, a pink cat. I extended my arm as far back as I could to capture them and myself—the kawaii posse.

In the year I spent living and travelling in Korea and Japan, I saw everything and perceived nothing. Games to me were always Asian, were always linked to Asia. And living there felt like a homecoming: the cosplay, the anime, the delicate movements of pachinko and Korean drinking games that felt like the delicate sensitivity of using a mouse or a joystick. Here, crowds of impressed onlookers could truly appreciate a man playing *Dance Dance Revolution* on expert.

The pleasure of travelling in Korea and Japan was often so intense, so distracting that I forgot what had brought me overseas in the first place: anger, self-destruction, the convulsive impulse to flee my place in the world. But the excitements of Asia drove me to a new identity: Westerner, gamer, explorer, brown and drunk miscreant stumbling from one neon-cloud city to another. This was a particularly vapid form of pleasure, what the theorist Roland Barthes called a "form of drift" that secures one's identity and social world—a pleasure that puts us right back in our place.[43]

For Barthes, pleasure stimulates both socially and sexually, reproducing (with slight variations) one's very identity and social world. Pleasure is not necessarily about buying into propaganda or ideology but about drifting in a secure space, secure with the self and thus deludedly content with the power we hold over others. In his travels to Japan in the late 1960s—far before video games were a thing—Barthes perceived an enormity of pleasurable glittering objects or "signs," which for most tourists would create a fantasy of "lovingly gazing toward an Oriental essence."[44] Like my own wanderings in Korea and Japan, Barthes found examples of this "loving gaze" in games like pachinko, in exotic foods and imagery, and in the pleasures of play.

What is it about travelling to the Far East that induces such pleasure? Past the buildings full of consumerist figurines, anime pillows, and postcards touting our favourite video game characters, is there any larger purpose for us?

~

While *Counter-Strike* games were exploring floating islands of playgrounds and surf slides, other shooting games were attempting to combine the ample pleasures of travel with the militaristic pleasures of battlefield domination. These were hybrid shooter / open-world games, often set in the Global South and almost all featuring white male protagonists compelled to kill thousands of enemies and to save brown locals, all while participating in tourist fantasies that include hunting game, water sports, and hang-gliding. The German-developed game *Crysis* (2007) sees the player investigating a space-alien structure just off the Eastern Philippines coast, while the Polish-developed game *Dead Island* (2011) includes battling zombies in an island resort located off the coast of Papua New Guinea. The Swedish-developed game *Just Cause 2* (2010), which takes place on a tropical island in Southeast Asia, wears its racial politics blatantly in its stereotypical brown, moustached despot and by tracking players' progress through the amount of "chaos" they have inflicted, ending with the explosion of an atomic bomb reminiscent of atomic testing throughout the Pacific. Many of these games, riddled with American militarism and racist caricature, invite players to bring security and order to Third World chaos, an aspartame pleasure enhanced by the game's exotic locales, tourist adventures, and militaristic acts of headshotting brown men while scoring with scantily clad brown women.

One of the first of these exotic open-world shooters was 2004's *Far Cry*, the first in the *Far Cry* series of games that have today sold over fifty million units worldwide. The first *Far Cry* game was an engineering spectacle, one of the first shooting games to successfully dispel the fog that had obscured vision in games like *Morrowind* or squeezed shooting ranges into small maps in *Counter-Strike*. For the first time, players could drop into a gigantic map filled with mountainous terrain, hazardous coasts, and military bases poking through jungle trees, and see *everything*. The open world was no longer filled with wonder and mystery but with heads that could be spotted miles away, through a sniper's scope.

In *Far Cry*, the player controls Jack Carver, a former United States Army Special Forces soldier who wields a military backpack and a Hawaiian shirt and seems capable of speaking only through cheesy action-film dialogue. *Far Cry* takes place on an unnamed Southeast Asian archipelago. This is not to inform the player about Asian history but to showcase Crytek studio's new game engine (CryEngine), which specialized in players seeing far distances without extra loading times and in keeping the entire game world alive in real time, a place of clear skies. Even so, the game features ancient temples and Japanese colonial-era outposts, remnants of imperial violence that often disturb the pleasures of the travel space. As you traverse these landscapes, you create dead bodies everywhere you go—more skeletons to join the unexplained colonial remains around you.

Like in *Far Cry*, my own travels in South Korea and Japan often stumbled across colonization and militarism. In Seoul's Itaewon bar district, I got lost looking for a dance club and happened upon the US military base, surrounded by nationalist propaganda as well as posters and graffiti recalling stories of rape, assault, and disappeared sex workers throughout the Korean peninsula. In Japan, the neon disco light fests ceased at the remains of Nagasaki, the peace memorials, and the relatively unknown firebombing museum in Tokyo that commemorates the hundred thousand dead and the one million left homeless after US bombs decimated the city. Through the loving gaze of video game tourism, these places were inescapable eyesores, reminders of the violence I was running from, the anger and hopelessness that brought me here. My commitment to inebriation, to bumbling through Asian cities, could not help but bump into apparitions of my homeland, and of myself.

~

> I came to expect despair every time I set foot in my own country, and I was never disappointed.
> —Nina Simone

After eight months of living in Korea and travelling to Japan and later China, my excursions were interrupted by an unexpected event: after two years of nothing but rejections, I was finally accepted into a graduate school program.

"Don't let them change you," my brother told me as I left our shared apartment. It was the last time we would live in the same city. He would soon move to Seoul, where he would sink new roots for the next thirteen years.

The first lesson I learned as a graduate student in the University of Washington's English program was that I was much poorer than I realized. The first meeting of my graduate student cohort was an introductory brunch. I didn't know what brunch was, had never had it, and wasn't at all prepared for how expensive an avocado toast could be. Once I saw the prices, I refused to order anything besides an overpriced drip coffee. Then, when a family at a nearby table stood up to leave, I asked them, "Excuse me, do you mind if I take your leftovers?" Eating someone's leftovers was common in twenty-four-hour Las Vegas diners, where we east side punks would order coffee and wait for someone to leave their food behind. But in graduate school at a top research university, asking to finish a stranger's meal, I learned, was not a common thing. The mixture of shock and dismay on the faces of my cohort never left me.

Unlike my cohort, I had spent two years in community college. Most of them had never stepped foot inside one. Unlike them, it had taken me three tries to get into this graduate school, when for them, this was their middle choice after failing to get into the Ivy Leagues. Unlike them, I went thirty thousand dollars into debt my first year, while they had scholarships, fellowships, and teaching assistantships to offset tuition. Unlike them, I had been so desperate to get into the University of Washington that I had moved from Las Vegas to Seattle years prior so

I could qualify for in-state tuition. They had never been to Seattle and were afraid of the "street brothers" and "street sisters" inhabiting it.

I nearly left graduate school that first year, after my supervisor told me he had personally denied my application in the previous years. I had only gotten in, he told me, because of "persistence." Someone else on the committee had felt pity for me. He, on the other hand, hated my work and thought my writing was beyond repair. He told me—quite bluntly, as he was a German specialist—that I simply did not belong in graduate school.

I felt defiant. Like any challenge in a video game, I would fall, get hit by a fireball, but in the end, I would persist. Perhaps I would do so just to defy them, to prove that I could do it.

Now, years later, I tend to agree with my supervisor's assessment. I did not belong in graduate school. It was never my place. Every year, as soon as the academic year ended, I would get out of Seattle, max out my credit cards on a plane ticket, and return to my self-imposed exile in Asia. Gradually, year after year, I strayed from touristic pleasures, heading instead toward the dark void of its possible disturbances. If I didn't belong in North American academia, then let me become one with the outside. Let me be a contagion and invite the disturbances in.

~

The plan is to travel until the pain runs you over. But Bangkok was the worst place to start. It's just too easy here, in the land of smiles.

This was the first line I wrote while travelling in Southeast Asia in 2008, the line that would later become the opening of my first published novel, *Stamped: an anti-travel novel*, released a decade later in 2018. Looking back on this line now, seventeen years after I wrote it, it seems obvious that going overseas was for me a form of self-destruction, slightly more grand and adventurous than wandering North America. I took every risk, wandered every dark alley. Despite all the attractions, I was still fed and fuelled by the yearning to go out in a blaze of travel glory.

Whenever I landed in a new city, I walked just as I gamed, leaving my memories, my self, far behind. Over time, I became so skilled at travelling alone that the act itself began to feel like home. I could look at the tallest towers of a city and clock the distance between myself and them, as well as the hills between us. I had never heard of Google Maps, but in my mind I was always that white dot in a video game traversing a strange geography. And with all the time in the world, nowhere was unwalkable.

When I arrived in Bangkok's backpacker district of Khao San Road, I walked the entire night, through the old Chinatown, the business districts, the bridges and beaches, the temples and schools. I saw the infamous sex districts, the tourist "rest and recreation" zones that were too remnants of colonial power. Since the Vietnam War, American military personnel had helped carve and reimagine Thailand as a sex tourism destination for US servicemen, marking Asian women's bodies as the cost of entry into the realm of global peace.[45] In the 2000s, I saw clubs where sex workers wore colourful cowboy hats and waved American flags while surrounded by statues of bald eagles and posters promising "LBFMS"—American military lingo for "Little Brown Fucking Machines."

These moments disrupted the pleasure of walking and often caused nausea and intense sickness. In those moments, I kept going—pacing without direction, disturbed at what I saw but unable to turn away.

~

After the first *Far Cry*, the game director of *Far Cry 2*, Clint Hocking, sought to give its sequel greater political complexity than any other first-person shooter. With the ambition to make *Far Cry 2* a hyperrealist tale about present-day colonial power set in Africa, Hocking sent research teams to Kenya and Tanzania and based story elements on literary works like Joseph Conrad's *Heart of Darkness* and Frederick Forsyth's *The Day of The Jackal* and *The Dogs of War*. Hocking's determination made 2008's *Far Cry 2* a shooter with unprecedented complexity and a narrative that challenged human rights discourse by representing international actors as pleasure-seeking diamond hoarders and war criminals.

Playing *Far Cry 2* feels nothing like the pleasurable tourist drift of the first *Far Cry*. In the game's opening sequence, the player (who can choose from a wide selection of races and nationalities) wakes up in a hut, having contracted malaria. Sickness is not merely dressing for the story—symptoms of malaria will hit the player in real time, making them slow, energy drained, blind. Even the game's touristic aspects only harm and aggravate: the map is difficult to read as it jumbles in your lap while you drive, you are forced to spend time fixing cars before driving them, and the only currency in the game is rough diamonds, which makes buying anything other than guns extremely difficult. Plus, soldiers and mercenaries are continually hunting you, and—unless you can somehow make sense of the game's labyrinthine plot—you have no idea why.

In games, one of the most dreaded disruptions of fun is when the player gets stuck in a "death loop." Death looping occurs when the game saves a player's progress just before their death, when they are cornered by enemies, have low health, or are weakened by poison. The *dis*pleasure of playing *Far Cry 2* emerges through this death loop, since nearly every save point in the game can become a trap, leading to hours of repetitive death. After saving, the player is tasked to drive across the free and open game world where military outposts threaten them at every turn, making every minute feel like a gamble. This makes the game not merely challenging but also unfair. With every respawn, the player can get stuck, condemned to repeat the loop, their fun dismantled by an aggravating, seemingly unfair problem: death.

~

Laos was the second country I visited on the infamous "Banana Pancake Trail" that reaches through Thailand, Laos, Vietnam, and Cambodia. My first impression of Laos was of a sleepy, laid-back paradise of four-dollar motel beds, shiny glasses of coconut shakes, and free plates of green curry from Buddhist wats. I spent days by the Mekong River, watching its burly brown creep. Every now and then a local tried to sell me cigarettes or condoms or Viagra. Sometimes I fed stray cats.

In the UNESCO World Heritage city of Luang Prabang, I fell ill. According to my guidebook, malaria was common in Laos, and I should go to one of the many medical clinics for tourists. I did not go. Instead, I spent a day half paralyzed on a sweat-dampened mattress, my bones aching, my vision fading. Hallucinatory dreams told me I had a high fever, though I had no thermometer.

It took years to discover that I did not catch malaria on that trip. It was hepatitis A, a disease found in feces. At some point on my Southeast Asian pleasure cruise, I ate traces of virus-loaded shit.

When the worst of the disease passed, I left my room and saw street animals around me: dogs, cats, roosters, chickens. Unlike the robots at the Japanese mall, these creatures were all indifferent to me. I had come to their home seeking adventure but found only an illness that would leave permanent traces in my body. Their languishing eyes were clear: I had nothing to offer them.

~

> One of the great features of this journey will have been: my almost daily bad migraines: fatigue, absence of siesta, food, or more subtly: big change in routine, or even: more serious resistances: *revulsions?*
> —Roland Barthes, *Travels in China*

Far Cry 2's aggravations with disease and death offer no pleasurable drift, but something more akin to Roland Barthes's conception of *bliss*. Unlike the easy feelings of pleasure, bliss "imposes a state of loss" and unsettles the player's "historical, cultural, psychological assumptions."[46] Unlike pleasure, bliss comes not in the form of a drift but of stress and discomfort.

Bliss is a narrative rupture short-circuiting one's sense of self by overloading the imagination. Socially, bliss invokes a crisis of dissolution, of losing oneself within the intensity of the experience, even if that experience is simply tedium. The blissful experience of *Far Cry 2* unsettles the security of an imagined exotic world ready for the player's violent intervention. It also asks an important question about war and violence—namely, how did we come to expect war and violence to be a pleasurable experience? Why might it seem so aggravating, so *unfair*, to experience acts of violence as themselves violent?

Far Cry 2 takes place during a civil war run by Western mercenaries, international aid organizations, and NGOs, who all become increasingly more violent as the trade in blood diamonds begins to dry. When the player contracts malaria in the game's opening, the game's antagonist reveals himself: the Jackal, an American arms dealer whom the player has been tasked with assassinating. The Jackal ridicules the player's human rights language that calls him a "destabilizing influence" because he is "in clear violation of the Joint Signatory Framework." "It's not sick to arm people," the Jackal says. "It's sick to bombard their crooks and dictators in protection of our interests, and they call it 'international justice' … The drone is the oppressor. The AK-47 is the great equalizer. I empower these people." Since the player of *Far Cry 2* is not by default American, the Jackal represents the most American presence in the game, a villain who criticizes the international lack of force by providing force himself.

Rather than encouraging the player to become stronger, to save civilians, or to impress local women, the main goals of *Far Cry 2* are to kill the Jackal for money and escape the war-torn country. This assassination narrative is not only told through cutscenes but through interactivity so that the realism of the story corresponds to the action of the game. As games journalist Tom Bissell writes, the act of killing in *Far Cry 2* does not give pleasure but guilt, remorse, and disappointment. After Bissell listens to the blood-freezing screams of a man he set aflame with a Molotov cocktail, he feels "a kind of horridly unreciprocated intimacy with the man I had just burned to death."[47] He concludes that *Far Cry 2* is "virtually alone amongst shooters," as the game "may reward your murderous actions but you never feel as though it approves of them."[48] *Far Cry 2* makes acts of violence *feel* violent, whether you're committing them, trapped in their death loops, or falling from a cliff after being unable to read a torn-up tourist map.

~

> War is my home.
> —The Jackal, *Far Cry 2*

In Hanoi, each of the six beds inside my hostel dorm was occupied by a young American travelling alone, harrowed by guilt over a war of unimaginable brutality, a war rarely taught with any depth in US schools, yet one we felt in every street of the city, in its very air.

We hid our faces as we lined up for confession at the war museum, aptly named in its brochure the Museum of American Imperial Aggression. Inside, we saw the death tolls from every village stretching through Indochina. We found images of people deformed by Agent Orange, napalm, and phosphorous bombs. Then, pictures of children born in contaminated lands, some who had confused an unexploded ordnance with a children's toy, with brutal consequences. Outside the museum, people with missing limbs held signs that both condemned us ("Agent Orange did this") and offered redemption ("I Love America!" "I Want to be Americanized!").

The young travellers I met in Vietnam were totally unlike the carefree expats in Korea, Japan, and Thailand. Here, in a land devastated by the bombs our taxes paid for, sent by the politicians we voted for, we young Americans followed the aftermath of our nation's atrocities. In Cambodia, a country America had bombed with more tonnage than was used by the Allies in all of World War II, our pilgrimage laboured through unclaimed dog tags, death-toll statistics, schools converted to prisons converted to photo opportunities. On the outskirts of Phnom Penh, we saw American tourists emerge from the fields of death and genocide feeling victorious for having faced death—the death that our country felt (and continues to feel) no responsibility for.

We young people travelling alone found little pleasure in this cruise through dark tourist sites. Sent adrift upon the shock waves of empire, we searched not for ourselves, but the bliss of our own destruction. We tinged everything with danger—we catwalked from one rooftop bar to another, we bolted across ten lanes of unpredictable traffic, we rented motorbikes though we'd never driven one before, we careened across freeways, marching into a quick and blurry end. The thought of an end like this calmed our agitated bodies. We would catch ourselves daydreaming only to wake to the nightmare of our own heartbeats. Free, for a moment, from our histories, from ourselves.

But who was this *we*? This *our*? Who were we broken and marginalized youth who had infiltrated America's crime scenes, who needed to make the violence of our empire so palpable, and who wished to die in that place where our bombs had taken so many lives? We unnamed, unacknowledged American exiles visiting sites of unnamed and unacknowledged American bloodshed.

We travelled to clear up the fog. We felt our way through the "malaise," what scholar Natalia Duong describes as America's refusal to take responsibility for its war crimes in Asia through the uncertainty of disease and death itself. As Duong writes, "the inability to verify a specific and singular result of Agent Orange exposure has also been cited as the main obstacle in securing definitive legal reparations from the US government and chemical manufacturing companies."[49] The fog over American wars is diffuse, making death unlocatable, unblamable, unseen. Who were we to march through death worlds created by us but that most of our compatriots refused to see? What did it mean for us to visit gravesites overfilled with people who had silenced themselves and young people who hadn't, and to say on behalf of our nation, "We were here. We did this. We invaded your home, because our home is war itself."

We were all the Jackal, selling arms, relentlessly jiggling the pot of war, mocking the international actors, the NGOs, the protesters, who all professed love for peace but could do nothing to stop us. We were the

Jackal, but we were also the ill, death-looping mercenary sent to kill him. Could the violence that broke us also be the same violence that brings us ecstasy, joy, pleasure? Was there any possibility of this *us* ever forgiving *us* enough to stop trying to destroy *us*?

~

> How many of these gentle people have I helped to kill
> just by paying my taxes?
> —June Jordan

I did not plan on staying in graduate school after receiving my master's degree. But in 2008, the Great Recession had me thinking otherwise. By then, my dead-end temp jobs were replaced by a teaching assistantship, which had me being called "professor" by students only a couple years younger than me. Plus, I no longer needed to pay tuition. As the opportunities to live and work in Asia dried up fast due to the recession, I decided to carry on with this academic side quest, and plod toward a PhD.

After two summers travelling through East and Southeast Asia, I decided that if I were to get a PhD, my studies would be tethered to my travels, aimed toward understanding the historic and present resonances of American empire in Asia. I taught courses in ethnic studies and pursued Asian American studies, a field devoted to the knowledge of imperial violence in Asia and to understanding how our complicity with US empire could be drawn from our own identities, whether from immigration stories that encourage American exceptionalism or from performing as quiet and high-achieving model minorities.

Within new areas of study, I grew determined to find "my people," whoever they were. I joined and eventually went on to lead an Asian American studies research collective, a group of students from different disciplines dedicated to the social impact of Asian American studies. We invited scholars and artists from across North America and, in 2011, we were able to reboot the Seattle Asian American Film Festival, still in operation today.

The field of Asian American studies, enclosed and abstract as it may have been, helped me to see my own yearning for death as a collective feeling akin to the feelings of travellers I met in Cambodia and Vietnam. I found a new cohort: young budding scholars who, like myself, had devoted their early careers to understanding that thing we lacked in ourselves, the thing broken and unfinished inside us. Graduate education was a way to confront this brokenness, to connect with others within and outside our nation who were nevertheless victims to it. This connection, wrought through our own self-loathing, was a different way out: a refusal to participate in the imperial war machine that embroiled us all.

For us travellers, players, and readers, death was once the only form of resistance we could envision from our small and isolated isles. But the more networks we saw for resistance and revolution, the more our paths toward self-destruction seemed like only one of many ways to escape it. We didn't hate ourselves—not truly. Just the parts of ourselves that had so easily accepted the status quo, the parts that could see bombs fall on TV in the morning, then spend the afternoon playing games launching explosives at brown villagers, and see nothing wrong.

Asian American history taught me that we did not deserve our own hate. It was far easier to continue on with our own racisms than to try to change—to do endless work on ourselves and, in all likelihood, still get it wrong. So, I spent my summers travelling in Asia, and though this increased the gargantuan student debt I would have by the end of my PhD—nearly fifty thousand dollars—travel was part of my education, and my survival. Being there, bearing witness, facing those parts of myself, was my blissful break.

~

In 2009, I spent three months taking trains through India, photographing roaming street cattle and watching the largest slums I'd ever seen pass by, fenced off from the largest golf courses I'd ever seen.

Near the Pakistan border in the holy city of Amritsar, while sitting in a crowded temple serving dal, I met an American traveller so deeply traumatized by growing up Christian that she swore to never step foot in a Christian country again. South Korea, the Philippines, and Singapore were all off her travel list. She was on vacation from her teaching job in Malaysia, "a Muslim country," she noted, attempting to provoke the sense of fear most Americans might have. And it worked. I felt that pinch, a fragility in my emotional undercurrent. I, an American raised during the War on Terror, had that spark of fear in just the thought of visiting a "Muslim country."

The traveller sensed my fear. "Malaysia," she said. "Indonesia. Do they seem like scary places?"

~

> White men are saving brown women from brown men.
> —Gayatri Chakravorty Spivak, "Can the Subaltern Speak?"

Travel gave proof to the histories I absorbed in textbooks. But video games helped me understand my own nation—how we made war permanent, how we normalized violence, how we continued to convince ourselves, generation after generation, to intervene, to invest, to invade.

In 2012, *Far Cry 3* became the first game in the *Far Cry* series to top sales charts and is today heralded as a classic among games where players blow up entire villages. While critics admired *Far Cry 2*, designers like Jeffrey Yohalem, the lead writer of *Far Cry 3*, found the game's attempts to make violence feel violent too aggravating to play. In response, Yohalem sought to make *Far Cry 3* a less realistic game, one that smoothed out the violence, making the act of repeatedly shooting and killing brown locals a more pleasurable thrill ride.[50]

In *Far Cry 3*, the player controls a privileged white traveller from Southern California, Jason "Bro" Brody. After refusing to pay for prostitutes in a Bangkok nightclub, Jason and his similarly gullible white friends are persuaded to parachute over a tropical island in Malaysia, where they are captured by pirates whose local Malay leader inexplicably speaks with a Hispanic accent. The game is filled with shocking human rights atrocities, from setting fire to a man in a box, to sex trafficking and rape, to forced army recruitment of children, all challenging the player to push forward, to shoot and kill scores more. Along the way, the player is rewarded with Indigenous "tataus" that give new skills, as well as the affections of a local warrior goddess named Citra, who drugs the player into hallucinatory fantasies while riding him topless. Unlike *Far Cry 2*, these atrocities and sexual fantasies are not meant to disturb the player but to align with the pleasures of military domination: rescuing brown women by killing brown men.

Though *Far Cry 3* has abysmal racial representations and worse politics, it continues to be regarded as an innovative step forward in shooting games. As with many mundanely imperialist games, *Far Cry 3*'s repetitive violence often gets dismissed as a misunderstood form of parody. But by signalling guiltlessness, racist parodies can have worse effects than a straightforwardly racist game. Were games like *Far Cry 3* explicitly racist and colonial, players would feel unable to enjoy a game created by careless, bigoted designers. But here, within the floating isle of parody, the act of killing remains the same but *feels good*—a pleasurable surf within an automatic, unthinking drift.

~

Who would I have become, had I absorbed the dehumanizing fears that so many shooter games like *Far Cry 3* spoon-fed into me?

Had I trusted American media, I never would have sat on the wooden planks of a Malacca harbour, annealed by a sun docked on the sea sky. Had I bought into the Islamophobia doled out upon my generation, I never would have been in Jakarta, listening to the imams' songs coming from three mosques at the same time, merging with the music of jackhammers, buses, and people jabbering on their cellphones. I never would have gone into that club in Bandung and seen the youthful transgender warias dancing with veiled women and gay men who enticed me to join them with a kiss.

In Malaysia, I found a Muslim country completely unlike those in the games I played: a place of many cultures, languages, and racial backgrounds. In Indonesia, I found that the country with the largest Muslim population in the world was also a place where queerness grew from beauty salons, nightclubs, and convenience store patios. Travel brought me to face my own country's violence, but it also introduced a new form of self-destruction, one that spared my life but destroyed all the things about myself I needed to let go—my bigotry, my ignorance, my complicity, my ego, and my deepest fears. The death loop was painful but not endless. And it promised change.

~

By the time I played *Far Cry 4* in 2014, I had travelled to nearly every country in Asia and was no longer held captive by the series' attempts to isolate Asia into remote isles of violence, terror, and death. But in *Far Cry 4* you aren't just *in* Asia, you are Asian yourself.

Far Cry 4 gave me my own Asian American identity in the protagonist Ajay Ghale, a returned son who arrives in Kyrat (a fictional country modelled on Nepal) to bury his mother's ashes but ends up helping rebels vanquish a despot from Hong Kong. While *Far Cry 3*'s imperial propaganda was masked in satire, *Far Cry 4* used a more contemporary tactic: employing the diversity of its main character to make the act of killing fun again. As with parody, diversity too can offer a militaristic experience without consequence, the same violent acts made pleasurable through the stylish filters of social justice. By encouraging players to identify with a brown American man, *Far Cry 4* pushes them along a redemptive narrative that marks their acts of killing other brown men as necessary to rescuing other brown brethren. Indeed, as a mixed Filipino/Chinese/white player, I was constantly reminded of my own debts to my homeland by the various rebel leaders who pressured and pleaded for me to avenge my family against the overseas (Hong Konger) imperialist. Yet, like clockwork, there I was again, killing brown people with my newly obtained weapons and skills. There I was, occupying the role of a killer whose darker skin welcomed me to wreak havoc, assured that any ethical quandaries were safe in developer hands.

~

>Your peeping is no witness.
>—Fady Joudah

By the time I arrived in non-virtual Nepal, I had been travelling for a decade, from 2006 to 2016. By then, I could see the patterns in every travel sphere. In every major city I had visited, there was a club filled with white backpackers wearing elephant-patterned pyjama pants and holding two-dollar cocktails. In every city stood grand statues and temples covered in white bird shit. In every hostel, rats congregated on the rooftops at night, but in the morning, the sun shone through each thatched roof, leaking light into red-veined eyes.

I felt claustrophobic in Kathmandu's narrow alleys. I thought I would see gorgeous mountains like in *Far Cry 4*, but for the first week I barely saw farther than a couple blocks. As I walked the streets, the rear-view mirrors of motorbikes scathed my arms. Around every corner it was "What do you want? Hash? Girl? Trek?" until *hash*, *girl*, and *trek* all meant the same thing: *What are you really doing here, brown American man?*

After that first week, I resigned myself to the city. Perhaps I would never see the Himalayas. I would never get that photo opportunity, would never pretend I was taming the landscape. After so many bouts of wanderlust, I had grown immune to the pleasures of travel, its syrupy optimism promising thrill without consequence.

Over the years, my travels had become less reckless, less death-defying, less of an addictive adrenalin rush. Somewhere along the way, my stringent desire for my own destruction began to wane. I had seen so much of death, met so many travellers and local people in mourning. We learned to grieve differently—by connecting the deaths of our friends and family with deaths that occurred overseas, the deaths that our country, our tax dollars, our indifference, were partially responsible for. In light of our shared histories, we gave death new meaning. We no longer wanted to join the dead but to share their names, memorialized for all to see.

And now, there was this *we*: travellers and scholars who sought to confront themselves, we wanderers in mourning. Over the years, I would remember them and group their names with those whom they mourned. I would not just carry their names with me. I would let them carry me, whisk me away through an open sky, toward a future where I—no, *we*—could escape the loops of death and venture on.

CHAPTER 7
Game-Sensing the System

I arrived in Nanjing, my new home, in January 2014, during a winter storm. With my guitar slung over her shoulder, a student volunteer helped carve out a path in the snow leading to my on-campus apartment. I followed, wheeling two giant suitcases, one weighed down by my large gaming computer, the other by my monitor. I lunged up the stairway to my apartment door. Inside, it was freezing. The water seeping from the bathroom sink crept through crystals of ice. The student tried to guide me through every appliance. We turned on the heater, which spewed cold air in a loud roar.

"You need to pay money on the electricity." The student said, tapping the meter. "Be careful, it will run out soon."

The meter read 230.

After the student left, I sat in bed, waiting until the air blasting from the vents felt warm. I did squats to keep my body temperature up, as I'd learned from survival television shows. I put on six layers of clothing, each one tinged with icicles from the high humidity.

The meter read 20. Somehow, in only an hour, nearly all my electricity had drained away.

In a mad rush I turned off the lights, unplugged the refrigerator, the water heater, anything with a cord.

When I returned, the meter read 10.

The heater was sapping the electricity, and soon it would shut down. I had no SIM card, no phone, no way to call for help. I began to curse the Chinese way of doing things—the senseless, idiotic, communist system!

I sat staring at the ceiling heater above my bed, waiting for the moment it sputtered out and I froze to death. It wheezed as the temperature gauge began to lower. Finally, the meter read 0. An execution. With a tired longing, the system slowly died.

In the morning, I awoke with purple lips and red ears, but I was still breathing. My luggage was in bed with me with blankets on top, a traveller's cocoon. I had survived the night.

At a glacier's pace, I dressed myself with blankets still furled around me. On my way out, I looked at the meter. In the morning light, I saw a small button on its side, where the student had tapped.

I pushed the button, and the 0 turned to 15000. The heater purred awake.

The system was working fine. I just hadn't yet figured it out.

~

In 2013, after six years of graduate school and seven years of travelling recklessly around North America and Asia, I grew tired of finding ways to destroy myself. And I was tired of merely pretending to live in the floating isles of games. I began to merge the two worlds, to understand how games could reimagine the world I had inherited—its everyday violences, its hypocrisies, its bureaucratic complications that name us, assess us, reject us, and, in the end, push us to hate ourselves to the point of death.

Relieved of the urge to destroy myself, I began to wonder why I had been so determined to do so in the first place. What kind of violent, messed-up system was I born into? How had it worked on me so well, doing exactly what it was built to do: demand the utmost obedience, on pain of depression, poverty, and death? And could I, or anyone, ever hope to escape it?

~

When I graduated with my PhD in December 2013, I made quick plans to escape the United States forever. I had put up with a permanent war in the Middle East, police slaying young Black citizens, and a recession caused by elite bankers while injured people paid thousands of dollars for an ambulance ride.

I began to search for other systems. I applied to hundreds of academic teaching jobs until I landed a low-paid professorship in Nanjing, China, teaching ten classes a year. My supervisor warned me that if I accepted the position, I would never be coming back to the US. No one would want to hire me. Once you accept an academic job outside of America, you're forever tainted as a failed academic and regarded with suspicion, desperation, and otherness. I didn't care. I was nearly fifty thousand dollars in debt, and I refused to give another portion of my money or time to the US empire. Taint me, I'm gone.

I had travelled to China before on three separate trips—once to the North, once to the middle, and once to the South. But living in Nanjing as an American immigrant forced a system change, a total flux in the genre, one in which I—as both brown and American—was always under suspicion.

This new system revealed itself slowly, in code. I soon learned that in Nanjing, a "suburb" was more crowded than any American city I had ever lived in. Some phrases, like wú jiǔ bùchéng xí, meaning "without alcohol, you can't have a banquet," were held as a sacred truth among Chinese colleagues. The 1911 revolution of Sun Yat-sen, whose grave was a tourist attraction in Nanjing, was here referred to as the "bourgeois revolution." If a student ever took a selfie without including others, they were considered selfish and disgusting. Whenever students told ghost stories—"Don't go to that hilltop, it's haunted!"—what they really meant was *That's where we go to have sex. Don't interrupt us.*

And then there was the way my students and friends in Nanjing played video games. Some played to learn English, some to bond with classmates in games like *League of Legends,* while others played in their own quiet way to defy their parents, their heterosexual, nationalist upbringing, and the Chinese state itself. Many games were obtained illegally, smuggled through China's "Great Firewall." Two of my best friends in China, nicknamed Sunshine and Winter, took me into arcades to play games, then to cafés to blabber about the games we played. Sunshine and Winter were an inseparable couple who lived together and slept in the same bed, yet didn't identify outwardly as lesbians due to the fear of harassment and repercussions from the state. But in arcades, they could dance, touch, and fall into each other's arms.

In Nanjing, video games were not nationalist, militarist, or associated with male toxicity in the way they had always been in the US. But this did not mean they were good, either. In fact, video games were still considered contaminants: corrupting, overly sexual, queer, radical, scandalous, as well as imperial, bourgeois products from the foreign powers of America and Japan. From 2000 to 2015, the Chinese Communist Party banned gaming consoles, making exceptions only when console companies joined partnerships with Chinese companies. Even games made within China had to go through widespread content monitoring. Through these policies, the Chinese state successfully branded video games as uncontainable threats circulating in suspicious underground networks of moral degeneracy. Even so, they couldn't stop the youth from playing them. Today, China is responsible for around 25 percent of the entire consumer market of video games, surpassing the US as the largest single nation of game players and buyers.[51]

When I moved to Nanjing in 2014, games were still banned, censored, and vilified, marking the playing of games as itself a radical act. Due to the state's protectionism, games were rendered politically meaningful and subversive works of art that had the power to reveal the flaws in the system around us. While North America was awakening to the ways games weren't entirely male and straight—known later as the infamous Gamergate scandal—in Nanjing, I played games with queer friends who revealed to me something that should have been obvious all along: despite their reputation in North America, for most of the world, video games have always been radical. As well, the vast majority of players, like the vast majority of the world, have always been non-white, non-American, and non-Western. These games that we from the West held dear, it turned out, were never really about us.

~

Video games inherit many artistic traditions, but their ability to reveal the flaws and inequalities of our systemic worlds comes directly from tabletop games, ranging from the hierarchical royal structure found in chess (where the masses are literal "pawns") to games that simulate colonization and war, like Battleship, Risk, and Settlers of Catan.

Few tabletop games are better known for detailing the deep, systemic troubles of our status quo than the long-beloved game Monopoly. As a family-oriented game, Monopoly has always been difficult to explain. Be the first to buy up land and build hotels on that land. Force other players to mortgage their homes or desperately sell them for half their value. Keep overcharging them for rent until they have no more assets to pay their bank loans and end up in debtor's prison without any ability to support their family—a family that likely has the same needs as the very family playing Monopoly.

Though Monopoly's origins are often credited to Charles Darrow, who sold it to Parker Brothers in the early 1930s, the game was actually patented much earlier, in 1903, by a left-wing feminist named Elizabeth Magie, who appropriately called it the Landlord's Game, creating distance between the players (likely renters) and the role they played (the landlord). Magie saw the Landlord's Game as a progressive pedagogical tool, a "practical demonstration of the present system of land-grabbing with all its usual outcomes and consequences."[52] Though it was nearly identical to Monopoly today, the Landlord's Game also featured a poorhouse, a public park, and a secondary set of rules: an entirely different game where the wealth generated from one player's actions (random rolls of the dice) brought income to *everyone*. Over time, only the rules of the monopolist found their way into the homes of middle-class families, who would use the game not as a demonstration of capitalism's ills but as a training ground to best take advantage of them.

Games always hover somewhere between critical investigation and mindless indoctrination. Even though Monopoly has departed far from its origins as the Landlord's Game, Monopoly today is just as much a means of training young minds to be land-grabbing capitalists. But so too can Monopoly provide an insightful lesson on the consequences of capitalism: the well-being of one person being prioritized over a community of people who end up in dire poverty. Monopoly exhibits the way mere chance—a rough roll of the dice—can completely upend someone's future by determining the total control and gentrification of land by a sole entity—or, just as easily, demolish real-life friendships at the table where Monopoly is played. Moreover, the very act of creating a monopoly, even in a nation as capitalism-fevered as the United States, is still an actual *crime*, though its convicted perpetrators always seem to have a Get Out of Jail Free card.

Monopoly is perhaps the most telling example of the systemic lessons that games teach: by embodying the system's own mindset, we can come to understand its processes and injustices. The threat of games is not in telling us who we are, but in telling us how the systems around us operate, revealing their hypocrisies, our own complicities, and how *we* are in fact produced through that system. In moments when I felt trapped within an obscure, soul-crushing structure, video games demystified this system, taught me not just how to avoid getting sucked into it but how to see its wider structures, its underground sewers and unlocked gates, and find other ways out.

~

There is a common phrase gamers use for how we attune to a game system: *game sense*. While a player's mechanical skills with a game can be instant (getting a headshot, jumping at precise moments), game sense can only grow with time, through understanding the many crucial events that must occur in order to win. In fighting games, a skilled player might charge in with combo after combo. But a player with good game sense will be able to predict where that opponent will be five or six moves afterward, as well as the ultimate charge they might be getting, the stage drop-offs, the pressured space between them and their opponent, and how to exploit their opponent's fight patterns to parry, rush, and combo right back. In team-based shooters like *Counter-Strike*, game sense means an awareness of where your team is, the types of fights or defences they are engaged in, and how you can best add value to the group through better positioning, by lying in wait or by doing nothing at all.

While lessons in capitalism are common in analog games like Monopoly and in digital games like *SimCity* or *The Sims*, video games have also used game sense to provide crucial demonstrations of the systems of racial belonging. Even as their representations of race have oscillated from horrendously offensive to thoughtfully empowered, they reveal the ways race works across the globe—its rules, its processes, its price to play. A game series that famously oscillates between these representations is *Mass Effect*, a role-playing space opera that tasks the player with managing a multialien, multigendered, multiply queered military unit working for a confederation of planets. Though games journalists often celebrate the *Mass Effect* series for its diverse representations, especially in gender and sex, none of this changes the fact that the player's main goals are to work within a rogue military faction, helping to commit genocide (in the original *Mass Effect*) and establish human supremacy (in *Mass Effect 2*).

As the captain of a rambunctious spacefaring squad, the player must deploy a series of escalating tactics to keep their team of multiracial aliens in line while also exploiting their capabilities for violence. In a particularly revealing scene, the player is dispatched to an enemy planet where they must convince their squadmate, Wrex, to follow a plan that will result in the continued forced sterilization of his entire race, constituting an act of genocide. If the player selects the wrong dialogue choices, Wrex—who belongs to the strong but quick-tempered Krogan race—will grow incensed and end up killed by a human squadmate. However, if the player successfully shows Wrex how his interests in his own race are minor concerns in the grand scheme of things, Wrex will remain in the squad and oversee the continued genocide of his own people. As the leader of a multicultural team, players of *Mass Effect* are meant to demonstrate tolerance and multicultural acceptance, but only with the presumption that it will reward them with their squadmate's specialized labour.

By mapping out the ways that systems of multicultural acceptance can still go awry, *Mass Effect* stages a playable demonstration of *colour washing*, a term similar to pinkwashing (using queer politics to cover up corporate scandal or state violence) or greenwashing (using environmentally friendly publicity to do the same) that captures how diversity and cultural tolerance are deployed to wash out the violence of capitalism, militarism, and colonial empire. *Mass Effect* teaches us that even when media and institutions give us empowered queer and marginalized identities, no amount of empowerment can erase our roles in furthering imperial and colonial violence. In fact, they can make us even more complicit.

~

> I read somewhere that pilots see better,
> in part, because they are asked to.
> —Pavneet Singh, "Letter 6"

After years of backpacking, hostelling, and Banana-Pancaking around, I began to lose the grounding of who I was and the systems I belonged to. I had become like the weary expats I had met sipping coconut shakes near sluggish bodies of water. A self-exiled and self-proclaimed travel expert, I could enter a new space and note all the settings, props, and glances dictating how I would identify and who I would choose to be.

But while making a new home in Nanjing, there was no easy in-and-out pattern I could rely on, no returning to a North American norm. For the first time, I had to fundamentally attune myself to a new system and find ways to live well within it.

My first goal was to figure out how to present my messy neuroqueer, mixed-race, mixed-up personhood in a way that was sensitive to systemic pressures and true to myself. To the white expatriates, I was often expected to play the role of their straitlaced Asian sidekick, encouraging their debauchery in foreign lands, ready to co-sign their white supremacist bullshit, their "logic" against the Chinese state that merely repeated clichéd depictions of "the Orient." For Chinese colleagues, introducing myself as mixed race was a choice between different negative connotations, whether I used the term 混血儿, which could suggest I was a half-white bastard child, or 杂种, which was closer to "impure." Introducing myself as Filipino was another can of wriggling worms. The first character in the word for Filipino, 菲, literally translates to "poor and unworthy." Literal translations aren't always meaningful, but the views of Filipino workers seemed to suggest otherwise. If brown skin was seen in China, as in much of the Global North, as a mark of poverty and disgust, then white or lighter skin was treasured as a collective ideal. My female students often told me, repeating their parents, that even if a potential husband had the "three ugly traits" of greed, anger, and ignorance, their light skin could make up for it. They would still make an adequate spouse, because their children would also be light.

Adjusting to this new system did not, of course, mean passing as white or lightening my skin, but finding ways to remain proud and still troublemaking, to disrupt the system's injustices in whatever way I could. Learning how to do this—that is, developing enough game sense to play well—would, like in any game, take time.

~

In the 2015 game *Massive Chalice* I play an immortal ruler tasked with breeding superhuman warriors into even more powerful superhuman warriors. To do this, I matchmake the strong, adroit, and resilient and distribute their children to kingdoms whose plebeian populations will serve to protect their bloodlines. Because of their racial stock, my newly bred scions possess a unique power over the masses and are heralded as demigods.

In *Massive Chalice*, I'm put in the shoes of a medieval eugenicist tasked with creating a super race in order to keep out an invasive force—the Cadence—from taking over my kingdoms. My subjects are sorted not just by wealth and citizenship, but by fertility and "chance for children." The racist logic of eugenics is never named in *Massive Chalice*, and by remaining unspoken, it becomes a rational outcome in the face of a persistent existential threat. Of course, as the trusted ruler of a kingdom, it is your duty to protect the realm. Of course, part of that duty includes training the best military defence. Of course, part of that training is selecting the strongest soldiers. Of course, those soldiers, if matched well, will breed even stronger soldiers. Of course, part of this breeding entails sterilization of weaker populations and the creation of a bloodline regarded as superhuman, Übermensch. The words *eugenics, racism,* and *genocide* never need rear their ugly heads. Instead they come slowly, drawing you in, until you realize you're making "rational decisions" that would also be considered human rights atrocities. Do you go on with this system? You wouldn't fail your kingdom, would you?

Massive Chalice attunes us to the ways racism and white supremacy operate without ever being named as such. White supremacy insists on a sacred "breed" of people whose culture, personality, and class interests are best matched, best fit for the nation. In *Massive Chalice* the populace celebrates the divine offspring of its elite, even when you marry a nineteen-year-old to an elder. When matched well, these subjects reproduce just fine, a superhuman race capable of generating offspring like ever-flowing child mills. But try to match a same-sex couple, and those genetic traits are lost forever. Within these racist systems, queer sex becomes a greater threat when it's undertaken by the elite class, while love across classes (and asexual love) threatens state control. According to the system's logic, any transgressions among race, sex, and class risk the livelihoods of everyone in the kingdom. You, as the ruler of this kingdom, must mete out the consequences.

~

> Everything has value only when ranked against something else; everyone has value only when ranked against someone else.
> —McKenzie Wark, *Gamer Theory*

Game sense is rarely learned alone but takes frequent communication with teammates, spectators, and friends. I learned how to navigate Nanjing's obscure systems of seeing race and identity by befriending other people of colour—particularly one spunky, talkative Indian British woman named Raks. Like me, Raks had travelled through many Asian countries and had become an expert at attuning herself to every new context. We often met up at girls-drink-free cocktail nights. Raks would slip me free drinks and tell me stories, like the time when, after three years of teaching English in Nanjing, she discovered her school had been paying the white teachers more and had been telling parents that she was half Latina and half white rather than Indian. Nearly fluent in Mandarin, Raks took it upon herself to wear henna and to discuss her cultural traditions in class, taking time to find the right words to communicate her heritage without merely casting all Chinese as racist and bigoted, as some white teachers were accustomed to doing.

Raks taught me the best words in Chinese to term myself, to present my part-Filipino, part-Chinese, part-white heritages without trying to downplay any or make them seem exotic. Having students write about how racism was handed down, generation after generation, in their own lives, opened many doors. Some strategies, like telling friends that Bruno Mars was Filipino, seemed juvenile but went a long way (except when I was then asked to karaoke a Bruno Mars song). Among fizzy pink cocktails, Raks and I strategized, shared stories and challenges, and invited others along to share theirs. Late nights, we danced in nightclubs with the brown and Black people of the city—we empire's minorities, letting loose with Arab, Indian, Filipino, and African migrants. Together we came out of our personas, celebrating living another day within this strange system that might someday be our own.

~

The Palestinian activist and scholar Edward Said wrote that the "other" was not merely something to be rejected or eradicated, but something to be separated, "controlled, contained, and otherwise govern[ed]."[53] Said defined *otherness* not as a type of identity, alterity, or racial difference but as an active role against the system who does the othering, who attempts to keep its others passive, obedient, silent.

The 2013 game *Papers, Please* by famed game maker Lucas Pope attunes us to the violences of nationalist othering by revealing the overlapping practices of border security with state-enforced racism. In the role of an immigration officer, the player navigates the bureaucracy of a seemingly benevolent state institution. But through mundane and minute practices, the player becomes discriminatory and predatory toward exploitable populations of refugees, political exiles, and queer and trans immigrants. In *Papers, Please*, everyday decisions about restricting vulnerable groups into a country are layered with choices about finances, the well-being of family and friends, and the always-dangling possibility of political imprisonment.

Papers, Please demonstrates the cruelty of a system that publicizes its own human rights fantasies yet enacts prejudice, negligence, and violence through sets of repeated gestures: checking passports, stamping, comparing, scanning, checking for visual authenticity, all with a burgeoning paranoia for terrorism and the gnawing fear that if you don't meet your quota, your children will starve. Yet, even as you are meant to process each migrant through rigorous and exacting puzzles, with daily rule changes and new types of documentation to consider, every spry sprite who tries to pass through the immigration checkpoint has a story. Some claim to come for shopping, some to take a vacation, some to visit family, some to seek refuge. Eventually, the game reveals not only the corruption of the system itself, but the corruption of repeated puzzle playing—the "banality of evil" that replaces the personhood of the migrant with the mysteries withheld in their documents. After so many hours of gameplay, the player begins to focus solely on solving these puzzles—that is, on discovering the flaws in passports, visas, immigration letters. Find a smuggler, a trans person, a terrorist, a member of a restricted group, and you've won the puzzle. They go away—refused, beaten, imprisoned, disappeared—and the next puzzle begins.

~

One day, while I was looking for ways to better analyze the system in China, the system came to analyze me. It came in the form of a young woman, a "new friend" brought to class by my student monitor—the student responsible for both helping professors and reporting their political messaging to "the Party." After listening to my class with a full smile and perked ears, this new friend stood up and approached.

She introduced herself with an Anglo name, Mary. She told me, as if it were a common thing, that she was a military informant for the Communist Party. And then she invited me to tea.

I had enough game sense in China by then to know that being invited to tea (hē chá, 喝茶) is a euphemism for being questioned by the authorities, a phrase meant to put a face onto the Communist Party's tactics of intimidation. Being invited to tea was no laughing matter. My colleagues had told me stories of two American professors who had been asked to tea after breaking the "Three Ts" policy of talking in any way about Tibet, Tiananmen Square, or Taiwan. Both of these American professors were promptly deported.

As Mary walked next to me on the school's gravel path, rocking about in high heels that were clearly a nuisance for her, my mind raced through a torrent of fears—fear of harassment, fear of financial insecurity, fear of jail time, fear of deportation. Frankly, I enjoyed living in China, and I did not want to leave.

Mary took me to an empty tea house, where we ordered lunch (no actual tea). She sat across from me, her white bubble-patterned jacket sharpening the glare from the droning elliptical lights above us. "I'm going to ask you a list of questions," she said. Behind her, I saw a black-suited waiter lotioning up his hands, rubbing them methodically. Perhaps, I thought, that handsome man will strangle me to death.

Mary's first question was about Taiwan. She claimed I had told my class that Taiwan was a country, not a province, and that I was publishing research and organizing meetings on Taiwanese independence. "Why do you tell lies about Taiwan?" she asked. "We should make sure you know the objective truth."

Had I been like some of the white teachers, I probably would have responded with counter-arguments. I probably would have contended about what "objective truth" really meant. I may have even said, "But Taiwan *is* a country," and been promptly deported for insurrection. But after living in Nanjing for months—slowly honing my game sense alongside a community of brown immigrants—I knew that arguing wouldn't help anyone. Instead, I played the fool.

"Why would I say Taiwan is a country?" "What does it mean to report someone?" "I thought guo in Chinese meant 'province', or 'place.' Does it mean 'country' too?" "I've been to Taiwan—it has a beautiful *country*side!"

When my ignorance didn't seem convincing, I went with an age-old traveller's tactic: responding to every point with "How?" or "Why?" or "Really?!" until they've either exhausted themselves with explanation or assumed that I was just another lost tourist.

"Have you participated in the Sunflower Student Movement in Taiwan?"

"What is that?"

"Do you plan on visiting Hong Kong soon?"

"Why? Is Hong Kong a nice place to go? I've heard it's expensive."

Satisfied that she had successfully intimidated me, or at least confused me, Mary ordered dessert. While spooning sugar onto my coconut pudding, she switched to a new tactic, transforming from a fierce interrogator into a demure honeypot. She told me in a confiding, vulnerable voice, that she did not really like the Communist Party. She'd had to join because of her parents. All she really wanted out of life was to attend a Justin Bieber concert. And by the way, she thought I looked just like her other favourite singer, Bruno Mars.

That evening, as I reeled from the confusion of that encounter, I received the first of many text messages from Mary. She wrote that I was a good professor and taught my students well. Then she became more personal. "I've never seen the inside of a professor's house," she wrote. I stopped responding.

I never saw Mary again, but I wasn't deported that day. I didn't feel like I had gamed the system, only survived it. I had no wish to be a hero; I only wished to better understand those who wielded power, who probably saw me as a box on a form that needed to be checked off, a puzzle to complete. All I needed to do was keep my red flags hidden away and my documents in check.

~

The point of gaining game sense in a new system isn't just to survive interrogations or to get across borders, but to change the system somehow, to make it more equitable and just, or otherwise, to burn it all down. Mary's interrogation compelled me to use my game sense from living in China to place myself within a more active and meaningful role. How could I continue to teach students in a context of censorship and banned topics? How could I speak out against the state without getting deported and also without appearing as a Western imperialist merely defending American interests?

My answer was somewhat out of the box: I was going to teach video games. Video games were the perfect combination of youthful nuisance, ambiguous implication, and political provocation. To the Chinese state, games resembled disorder, distraction, queerness, radicalism, even revolution. But they were not the Three Ts.

I had never taught a course on video games before, nor had I met a single professor who taught game studies at my graduate school institution (because there were none). So, I started off light: I created a course, Video Games as Literature, that applied my skills as a literature PhD to video games, and I started hosting events on the topic at the writing centre. My new course focused on non-banned video games that spoke to system change—*Mass Effect*; *Massive Chalice*; *Papers, Please*; and other games about confronting a menacing state power like *This War of Mine*, *September 12th*, and *Prison Architect*. I had students make their own games where they could freely criticize statehood and party politics without ever actually naming China, the Communist Party, or the protests occurring in Taiwan (the Sunflower Student Movement) and Hong Kong (Occupy Hong Kong). Students came to my class to play, unaware that these games might leave them with a revolutionary game sense, with methods to play the system against itself. And what student wouldn't want to take a university course on video games?

~

Teaching video games meant I also had to research them—not just the research of industry statistics and online developer interviews, but the type of research found in textbooks focusing on the labour and material processes that make games possible. Though they often told stories of rebels dismantling evil systems, video games, it turned out, were just as much within the system of global capitalism, American empire, and ongoing forms of colonial violence around the globe.

As digital products, games carry with them the violence of electronics manufacturing, which has always relied upon racialized notions of working bodies, especially for women. Scholar Lisa Nakamura has traced information technology (IT) factories back to Navajo Indian reservations in 1965, when the Fairchild Semiconductor company used ethnic associations of Navajo women with blanket weaving and jewellery making to make them seem naturally fitted to build electronic devices and integrated circuits.⁵⁴ Fairchild was one of the largest private employers in the United States until 1975, when protesters who accused the company of sweatshop labour occupied and shut down its plant. Fairchild then joined the exodus of IT corporations by outsourcing manufacturing to Asian countries like Malaysia and China, where women worked with very low pay and often in prisonlike housing complexes.

Many are familiar now with the way electronics manufacturing can exploit entire populations, often with little regard from the state or the people who use that technology. In 2010, eighteen workers at factories owned by Foxconn, one of the largest electronics manufacturers in the world, attempted suicide by leaping off the rooftops of the prisonlike apartments where they were forced to survive seventy-four-hour workweeks, mostly while standing and inhaling toxic fumes.⁵⁵ Fourteen died. In response, nets were strung up around warehouses to keep workers from leaping over.

Though the company first became infamous for supplying exploited labour to Apple, Foxconn produced game hardware for all three major console companies: Sony, Microsoft, and Nintendo. Even so, Foxconn is just one of many IT companies operating within China's Pearl River Delta, which in the 2010s produced an estimated 90 percent of the world's consumer electronics, providing a seemingly endless supply of labour alongside the protections of the People's Republic of China, with its pervasive internet censorship, unenforced environmental regulations, and the lack of free speech that I and my students strove to evade.

An even more brutal injustice in gaming manufacture has been the ongoing mining of coltan ore, a known conflict mineral present in many electronic devices but especially in gaming consoles. Around 80 percent of coltan ore comes from the Democratic Republic of the Congo, where gaming companies like Sony once purchased the material from any organization willing to sell for the cheapest price.⁵⁶ According to a UN report, this casual indifference resulted in the deaths of thousands, the growth of rebel militias, and child slavery.⁵⁷ As the gaming website *GamesHub* wrote of the conflict, "The correlation in the past two decades between the rise in console gaming and the civil unrest in the DRC is so stark, that the intense conflict in Central Africa has even been referred to as the PlayStation Wars."[58]

Video games are in no way outside our own systems of violence: the exploitation of factory and design work, the natural degradation of e-waste, civil wars in resource-rich countries, and even modern-day enslavement. Many game makers have become outspoken agitators, such as Clint Hocking, game director of *Far Cry 2*, whose speeches at major game expos have focused on the processes of game production, tasking designers to respect that "the processes we use have repercussions into the cultures of our teams and our companies and our society as a whole."[59]

There are dozens of games that literally or metaphorically depict these systems of violence within their manufacture, from Hocking's own *Far Cry 2* to games like *Phone Story*, a smartphone game that takes players through minigames involving managing child slavery at coltan mines, saving Foxconn suicides, and sorting e-waste from smartphones themselves. Such games help us understand the violences of our global systems, not because they are outside it, but because they are the very products of it. Their creators know the scandals, know the labour, know the violence it takes to make video games, and they know it intimately.

~

In their book *Games of Empire*, Nick Dyer-Witheford and Greig de Peuter point out that even though many games were developed through war technology and US Department of Defense funding, game developers themselves have often come from countercultures "of psychedelic drugs and of political dissent" that have been "at odds with the military institutions."[60] In the 1970s, video game arcades were villainized as tantalizing dens of ill repute thought to be gateways to lifestyles that would eventually lead to gambling, asociality, drug dependency, and gang-related violence. To sanitize their image, video game companies sought to erase the countercultures that gaming represented, choosing to downplay and even omit the names of their designers. As one Atari spokesperson admitted, "Management doesn't want us to make rock stars out of them [the designers]."[61] It worked: Americans in 1981 spent 5.7 billion USD on arcade games, twice the gross earnings of all of Nevada's casinos and three times the total revenues for professional baseball, football, and basketball combined.[62]

A broader story of games includes their many radical origins, from the designers who sought to challenge the systems making games, to games that teach players how to create their own revolutionary change. Both the *Red Faction* series and the *Metal Gear* series have remained torchbearers for anti-imperial, anti-war messaging in games, while other game series like *The Elder Scrolls*, *Resident Evil*, *Deus Ex*, *BioShock*, and *Final Fantasy* continually place the player in the role of an insurgent, a hacker, or an eco-terrorist battling an oppressive system that feels eerily similar to our own.

Then there are near-forgotten game makers like Muriel Tramis, known today as the first Black female game designer. After emigrating from her birthplace of Martinique to France to help develop military aircraft, Tramis switched paths in 1986 to create games that spoke to histories of capitalism, militarism, and enslavement.[63] Tramis's first game was *Méwilo*, created in collaboration with the Martinican writer Patrick Chamoiseau, which placed players in a mansion haunted by the ghosts of the 1931 Martinique slave uprising. Five years later, Tramis released an innovative full-motion game, *Lost in Time*, which centres a woman exploring a shipwreck who mysteriously transports back to the era of colonial slavery.

Tramis's most politically ambitious game, *Freedom: Rebels in the Darkness*, released in 1988, doesn't only depict a slave rebellion but also asks the reader to develop and hone strategies for this rebellion—teaching them the tools for radical change based on true-to-life methods of persuasion, mobilization, and direct action. The game opens with the choice of three different roles: "rebellious," "fanatical," or "defiant." Each branch comes with different revolutionary skills—charisma, dexterity, lock picking, climbing, fire setting—as well as different positions on the plantations—craftsman, field hand, "medicine man." The point of these various roles isn't to elevate the importance of one over the others for revolution, but to give us the game sense for seeing how the diverse ecosystem of revolutionary roles is crucial to any social justice–based movement. In risking all with the hopes of gaining freedom for all, even the most minute efforts of pathfinding, gaining knowledge, and sharing your game sense with others can make all the difference.

~

> The more one is able to leave one's cultural home, the more easily is one able to judge it, and the whole world as well, with the spiritual detachment and generosity necessary for true vision. The more easily, too, does one assess oneself.
> —Edward Said, *Orientalism*

After I was interrogated by the Communist Party, I lived for another year and a half in Nanjing, attempting to make a life for myself outside the systems I grew up in. To this day, over a decade later, I still have not returned to live in the US.

Edward Said wrote that exilic otherness purports "restlessness, movement, constantly being unsettled, and unsettling others."[64] For most of my youth I took chances, determined to escape the only life I believed I could live. It took time, friendship, and life-giving artwork to help me understand the systems I grew up in. Writing expressed feeling stuck within an oppressive system; travel awakened me to the histories that created that system; and video games—they taught me how the system worked and how I could strive to resist it by understanding and sharing the transformative possibilities of games themselves.

Though games often feel like pleasure-inducing opiates or exploitative consumerist products, their ability to speak truths about the systems we live in is no flub, no mere glitch. Their very origins come from the deepest violences of our global system. As works of art they will always reflect these violences, whether intentionally or not. As I've learned from my decade-plus of teaching games, radical forms of game sense are everywhere: in the Indigenous community-made games led by Elizabeth LaPensée; in games centring protest like *1979 Revolution: Black Friday*, *All Our Asias*, and *Liberate Hong Kong*; in anti-capitalist games like *Disco Elysium*, *Night in the Woods*, and Chris Kealoha Miller's *Neofeud*; or in queer games like *Butterfly Soup*, a visual novel about four queer and trans Asian Americans growing up in Oakland. These games, which fill my syllabus every year, come from marginalized game makers whose othered positions in games oppose the very systems that make games possible. For their players, they reveal the possibilities and potential consequences of imagining their own otherness otherwise.

CHAPTER 8
Hair, Hips, and Other Blueprints

Gamers often use the phrase *pronoun play* to describe how virtual bodies in games switch pronouns of he, she, and they when we move back and forth among avatars, or in battle parties from healer to paladin to mage. But while inhabiting a familiar game, I feel this sense of pronoun play extending far beyond different in-game characters. Often, my sense of an individual self slips from my body to characters inside the game, then to others who play and know the game, and then even further, to those outside my gaming worlds. These feelings manifest most when I am writing about games and find my descriptions leaving myself behind, the very agent of memory. My narration shifts from "my" play experiences to "our" shared experiences to "yours." "You" hold your breath as "we" fall into a watery abyss. "I" feel the impact of broken bones when "you" fall to "your" death, and "we" have to start over.

In games, *he*, *she*, and *they* become fleeting, while *we*, *you*, and *I* turn toward each other. Every switch feels both out-of-body and comfortably embodied, every moment both ephemeral and stored in personal save points. Our roles in games feel communal, shared with players, audiences, and, eerily, with the characters themselves. Bound to them, we become our "mains"—*she*, *he*, and *they* become the scattered selves of *we*, *you*, and *us*.

~

For most of my youth, my virtual selves of pronoun play were a sacred and untouchable playground for ambiguity. But in 2014, two events in the corporeal world brought pronouns—and the ways we play with them—into sharp and uncomfortable focus. Suddenly, the digital selves we had spent years envisioning were under a media spotlight, and our virtual embodiments were recast in ways that rippled through both culture and code.

The first event in 2014 was the brutal harassment campaign against women journalists and designers later referred to as Gamergate, a watershed moment in gaming cultures that led to new and clearer divisions between the so-called woke gamers demanding more diversity and accountability in games and those who wanted to preserve games from "political correctness." In Gamergate's aftermath, the popular rise of right-wing game commentators like Mike Cernovich, Milo Yiannopoulos, and Adam Baldwin set the stage for the aftershock eruptions of the alt-right movement online. In 2016, the many talking points used against women in games during Gamergate were recycled by the Trump campaign to defeat his rival, Hillary Clinton. As David Neiwert writes in *Alt-America: The Rise of the Radical Right in the Age of Trump*, Gamergate "heralded the rise of the alt-right and provided an early sketch of its primary features: an Internet presence beset by digital trolls, unbridled conspiracism, angry-white-male-identity victimization culture, and, ultimately, open racism, anti-Semitism, ethnic hatred, misogyny, and sexual and gender paranoia."[65] As an outgrowth of gaming culture, Gamergate politicized many young men in opposition to the perceived culture war being waged by the progressive left. For these young men, Gamergate operated as a form of reinstating the boundaries of games to keep out the sordid, contaminated others who lived within the spectrum of femininity: women, trans and non-binary people, queer people, and feminine men.

Gamergate made palpable the stories people told of games in popular media, where gaming had always been depicted as male dominated. While some of this reputation was well deserved—with women making up only 11 percent of the game industry workforce in 2008—the player base for video games was global, diverse, and, in many contexts, had helped reimagine gender in ways that most mainstream audiences could not grapple with while also being inundated by a media landscape that continually reappraised games as toxic masculine products.[66]

But 2014 also witnessed a second form of pronoun play: what *Time* magazine later called the "Transgender Tipping Point." Transgender representation was hitting a threshold in television with the show *Transparent* and the documentary *The T Word*, and in music with Against Me!'s album *Transgender Dysphoria Blues*. At the same time that Gamergate harassment campaigns were rolling through game communities, *Rolling Stone* was announcing an unprecedented moment of gender activism in every other entertainment medium, calling 2014 the "biggest year in transgender history."[67] Western media was finally discovering and giving space to the spectrum of gendered livelihoods, but video games were the odd media out. Gamergate had shaped games as the most *regressive* media, a protective bunker for cisgender white men, one they would defend at all costs.

In 2014 I was twenty-eight, living within China's Great Firewall of blocked information and slow internet. I was terribly—and blissfully—ignorant of how North American media saw video games. I didn't know what Gamergate was, or that video games were being declared the new stronghold for neocons. For many who felt part of a feminized gender spectrum—we neurodivergent, racialized, and feminized queers—video games were still the only media that made us feel like ourselves, the only media that helped us imagine our own bodies and how to inhabit them. Our pronouns had always mixed with the pronoun play of games—the many selves we co-created with games. Gaming communities too became accomplices in our self-multiplying, seeing us in the many ways we could envision *us*.

~

> Home is not where you were born. Home is where all your attempts to escape cease.
> —Naguib Mahfouz

While game communities in North America were rupturing from the new gender wars, I spent 2014 researching and teaching video games to students and then travelling to conferences around Asia to give talks on how video games had always disrupted deeply held notions of gender and race. These talks were based on my own feelings as a gamer emerging from the depths of self-loathing and loss. I began to imagine a new self akin to the selves I had invented in the floating isles of games, my own version of my mains: my own chirpy Princess Peach, my own Filipina Eskrima fighter Talim, my own ponytailed Reno, my own FemShep from *Mass Effect*, my own queer nekocat from role-playing chats.

In June, I attended a conference in Hong Kong on fashion design in fiction, where I was prepared to discuss the economics of buying clothing "skins" in massive multiplayer online role-playing games like *Guild Wars 2* and *Second Life*. In the conference lobby, I saw a woman sitting on a table full of books. Next to her stood a tall older man in a blue-checkered shirt. I approached them and was struck with the sensational feeling of being checked out by them both. In the elevator to the next panel, the three of us made plans to skip the conference for some late-afternoon bar-hopping.

The woman, Y-Dang Troeung, would in two years become my wife, and a year later, mother to our son. The man was her graduate school supervisor, Don Goellnicht, who would become my mentor and close friend. That weekend, Y-Dang, Don, and I tested each other's unabashed lust for living: lingering in queer clubs, skipping lectures to eat fish ball soup in Mong Kok, singing karaoke in Mandarin, dancing in alleyways until the sunrise refracted from Hong Kong's glass skyscrapers. That week, I had an unshakeable feeling that these two people would hold a treasured and lasting place in my heart. Through them, I began to envision countless versions of myself.

There is a moment in many role-playing games that game communities call *getting the mare* or *getting the ship*. This occurs when, after spending much of the game meandering through the game world, slogging up hills and over bridges on foot, the player accesses a new form of travel: a mare in some games, a flying ship in others, or a new tool or power like a jet pack or a grappling hook. By shifting the means of travel, getting the mare changes the game entirely—how one battles or avoids battle; how quickly one can access final episodes in the game; how the game world suddenly opens to new side quests, ecosystems, dungeons, and hidden realms. The impact is so significant that players often talk of two games: the game before the mare, and the game after the mare.

For me, Y-Dang and Don were that mare, summing up my life into two eras: before and after that fated trip to Hong Kong. Meeting Y-Dang and Don allowed me to traverse the world in ways I never believed were possible. We bounced around Asia and North America, to conferences in Xiamen, Kobe, Shanghai, Taipei, Vancouver, and Chicago. At a conference in Seoul, we caught up with my twin brother and his friends, who helped spirit our colleagues to dance clubs and queer bars. We were a queer nomadic family, roping in new-found siblings at every destination, welcoming them into our unconventional commune. All the challenges I had experienced, all the rough terrain, suddenly were replaced by a free and unobscured air.

~

Video games have always been queer.
—Bo Ruberg

There is something about games that allows pleasures and desires to become transformative, to take on what designer and scholar micha cárdenas calls *transreal* forms: the ways that technology can blueprint and prototype our many selves, revealing who we want to be within a space that is relatively safe and familiar.[68] I've spent much of my life in these forms, as have many in my generation who became the targets of harassers and politicians.

Despite their reputation as regressive, right-wing ideas factories, games and their communities have always been transformative to how gamers understand their sexuality, their gender, and themselves. The first trans character in games was Birdetta, a miniboss in 1987's *Super Mario Bros. 2* who shot eggs from her mouth. Once a queer childhood memory, gamers have revived Birdetta into a trans icon, while the mushroom people of Mario's world—the Toads—have been reclaimed as an asexual species who choose their own gender identities.

Prior to 2014, the "biggest year in transgender history," video games had their own year of transgender rupture in 2012, when independent trans designers made efforts to express parts of their own experiences in games. Mattie Brice's *Mainichi* follows a day in the life of a Black trans woman. Anna Anthropy's *Dys4ia* recounts her own hormone replacement therapy through snapshots of WarioWare intensity. And merritt k's LIM follows a dazzling coloured block through a maze of mono-coloured assailants. In that same year, Anthropy also published her classic book, *Rise of the Videogame Zinesters*, a guide for game developers to follow punk rock's culture of zine making to reimagine games from the standpoint of queer and diverse do-it-yourself media.

Importantly, all of the queer and trans designers mentioned above—Mattie Brice, Anna Anthropy, and merritt k—have at one point or another disavowed their games, taken them offline, or written cautions against playing them with the desire to commodify them—to see them as mere objects of empathy.[69] No media, whether memoir or biopic, can capture a life experience that is different for each of the millions of people it represents. So too for marginalized game makers, the obscurity and ambiguity of games cannot be commodified through marketing gimmicks that hash out identities similar to the way other media have. It's not that games are any less apt at telling a life story than other media, but that many marginalized game makers, having been so long excluded from telling their stories in direct and encompassing ways, refuse to be included in those same exploitative and stereotyping marketing schemes. We can use games to show dimensions, reveal familiarities, create new perspectives, but playing a game—like reading a book, watching a movie, or listening to a song—is not the same as having someone else's experience. Our otherness cannot be packaged into something readable, watchable, or downloadable.

While many game developers refused the implications of what became known as "empathy games," the 2012 turn in gaming did seem to green-flag the use of virtual worlds to imagine new selves, to experiment, or, as cárdenas calls it, to *blueprint*: "a kind of rapid prototyping" within virtual worlds.[70] To blueprint is to create test versions of ourselves, built from our limited knowledge of our own desires and shaped by an unknowable future. In 2008, cárdenas staged a form of blueprinting in her art performance piece, *Becoming Dragon*, during which she spent 365 hours in the game *Second Life* living as her main: a giant green-skinned, black-horned dragon. Her immersion as the dragon included spending the entire performance within a head-mounted display, a motion-capture system, and a Pure Data patch that created a grainy, low-toned voice.

For cárdenas, *Becoming Dragon* was both an expression of blueprinting and an attempt to poetically parallel her own experience fulfilling the one-year requirement of "real-life experience" within her gender identity that many transgender people must fulfill in order to receive gender confirmation surgery. The desires of blueprinting speak to the violences we experience when we attempt to inhabit different selves, while the experiments of prototyping give us clues for how we might become other selves. Through this process, we glimpse a life we might lead were our other selves to break free from our mere imaginations.

Blueprinting helps name that feeling I get when I spend over an hour in a character creator, remixing randomly generated bodies, imprinting new versions of myself. Some of these blueprints come from the process of jamming body types together: a self with purple hair streaks, with scaled skin, with breasts, with pronounced hips, with a higher-toned voice, with wings, with long furry ears that seem to defy gravity.

Even in games that have no character creator, I am blueprinting just by choosing my avatar: Do I want to be a Princess Peach and giggle at my enemy's blue turtle-shell explosions, or do I want to be a Rosalina and stare eerily at their misfortune? These choices awaken desires. They propel a promise of becoming, of revealing new ways I might act while away from keyboard—the potentials of biotechnology, body hacks, and new routines. Never solely a blueprint, we become mixtures of our mains.

~

> Beyond the image, *Second Life* offers a social dimension to these constructed identities, in which one feels the moment of being "seen" by another. This is an essential part of becoming, the moment of social interaction and feedback when one's conception of one's self is affirmed and reified by others—the moment of passing.
> —micha cárdenas, "Becoming Dragon"

Being with Y-Dang and Don stripped down all the personas I had invented for the world. Every role I had trained myself to play melted away before them. I was no longer the self made for the world, but the self made within my own world. All my brown, queer, gender-bending selves were realized in their presence.

Y-Dang presented new ways of inhabiting brown femininity, while Don presented new ways of being queer. The three of us went in drag, ambiguously dressed, and frequented queer clubs across Asia. We created our own floating isle of imagination, love, and companionship. Y-Dang and Don were also the first academics who celebrated my work on video games and saw my daily routine of playing games as integral to shaping my own playfulness, openness, humour, and ability to read the systems around me.

Like many within queer family, Y-Dang, Don, and I were connected through our shared desires as well as our shared sense of tragedy and loss. A descendent of Cambodian refugees, Y-Dang had lost most of her family to the genocide of the Khmer Rouge and the decade of US bombings that preceded it. These were horrifyingly unjust events on a massive scale, with afterlives that would last generations. Y-Dang had devoted her life as a scholar and writer to finding meaning in these events and to tracing their effects across histories and nations.

Don, a gay white man raised in Trinidad, had spent most of his life in the straight closet. He coped with his own loss of youth and time by devoting his life to training marginalized students. His legacy as a scholar would always rest with students like Y-Dang, one of many brilliant refugees and diasporic authors he had nurtured. When I explained to Don and Y-Dang my own feelings of loss—losing loved ones, family, and any feelings of belonging in North America—and my ways of coping, I never found judgment, only a willingness to walk through my pain, to ache with the self sunk in grief.

Together, Y-Dang, Don, and I carried the burden of loss, finding in its shared weight a deeper permission to embrace the fragile joys of living. We lived full and free to honour those who could no longer join us, while cherishing those who could. And within months, Y-Dang and I fell into an all-embracing, joyful love. Our love felt cosmic, bound by loss and survival in ways that would reveal themselves with each passing day. After living in Hong Kong together for over a year, we discovered that our first relationships had both ended in tragedy. My first girlfriend, Teal, had died in a car crash, and Y-Dang's first boyfriend had died in a motorcycle accident. Even still, Y-Dang and I laughed about our tragedies, cried in embrace, and celebrated our lives. Somehow, we had survived into our thirties, living and loving in the endlessly vibrant city of Hong Kong.

With Y-Dang and Don, I found new ways of being a scholar, reconciling the abstract theories of academia with my restless pursuit to encounter and grapple with the lived reality around me. With them, I visited the Occupy Hong Kong encampments and participated in talks, marches, and writing workshops condemning the exploitative global elite. We joined the first protests in Asia in solidarity with Black Lives Matter, demonstrating against the deaths of numerous African Americans by police actions: Eric Garner, Michael Brown, Ezell Ford, Tamir Rice, and too many others. Everything was protest, everything was arousal, everything affirmed our co-created selves. Let loose, we envisioned a new world capable of transformation.

~

While the impact of Gamergate in politics may have been disastrous, in games it was followed by the post-Gamergate era: a shift in mainstream gaming away from alt-right, toxic fan bases toward more progressive games with diverse representation (what some would derisively call "woke" games). The gamer's average age was increasing into the mid-thirties, and women were playing games at nearly the same rate as men. Diversity and queerness in games could no longer be a task only for indie designers and story-based role-playing games like *Mass Effect* or *Dragon Age*. Soon, queer and diverse characters were appearing in every game genre, even one that for years had felt like the pleasure dens of white male militarists: the first-person shooter.

In 2016, the transformation of the shooter materialized in the game *Overwatch*, a "hero-based" shooter that featured a motley cast of twenty-one characters, each with unique abilities, who spanned multiple ethnicities, nationalities, sexualities, and genders. Almost instantly, *Overwatch* was as commonly played in Korean PC bangs as in American homes, attracting over twenty million players within months, which grew to forty million by 2018 after the game had earned the coveted IGN Game of the Year award. As the game's distributor, Blizzard Entertainment, was known worldwide as an esports company, the game garnered comparisons to sporting events like the Olympics with its international cast, worldwide audience, and sporting arenas. And like global sporting events, *Overwatch* attempted to give everyone someone to identify with, someone to call their main.

Since the arcade days of *Street Fighter* and *Tekken*, problems with race, like all problems of representation in competitive sports, have been considered mere scruples compared to the problems of balancing the game itself so that it's fair for everyone to play. Both of these issues—representation and fairness—are issues of social justice. Both tend to impact and often exacerbate class, gender, and racial inequities. But since fairness must be established for a game to attract players, games have always taken fairness far more seriously, while seeing representation as a secondary concern, one that can be a bit more funky, a bit more risky, a bit more risqué.

Like many non-white, non-male characters in fighting games, *Overwatch*'s characters are dizzyingly diverse, cartoonish types. These are not empowered rebels fighting against bigotry, but lighthearted and campy depictions that, in other media, would likely be called offensive. Unlike beatific Instagram influencers using photo filters to look like they're sculpted out of clay, *Overwatch* characters look like bouncy parade balloons enticing you to dance in their procession. They are not aspirations but toys, playfully and uniquely asinine.

Players of competitive games like *Street Fighter* and *Overwatch* do not rely on character complexity for nourishment but receive it from other means, like blasting opponents into the sky. These gamers rarely feel hunger for more than surface-level personas. In turn, the heroes of *Overwatch* are not approached with the heaviness of literary memoir or biographical films, but with the exaggerated personas of characters in WWE matches, in Blaxploitation and kung fu films, and in pornography. Like many game characters, *Overwatch* heroes mirror what Susan Sontag once called a "camp sensibility" that perceives a "double sense" of silly and hyperanimated figures whose frivolity signals not a serious representation of racialized people but a quirky style of play.[71] On the surface,

Overwatch's heroes are pure artifice, figures that convert the serious into the absurd, which strikes the player as both offensive and alluring. But this artificial surface also allows the player to recognize the hero as a form of play, inviting theatricality, what Sontag calls "Being-as-Playing-a-Role."[72] The campy heroes of *Overwatch* feel so ridiculous that we embody them less as identities and more as experimental roles we can blueprint, prototype, and slowly reveal to the world.

~

In 2016, about one week after Y-Dang and I got married in two ceremonies, one in Toronto and another in Oahu, we returned to Hong Kong, and I installed *Overwatch*. Immediately after committing myself to one timeless, unceasing relationship, I found another. *Overwatch* seduced me, enticed me, prodded me to test its boundaries and my own. It brightened the city around me in the way a blazing sunset can make an inhospitable world look polished in oil-slicked pinks and purples. I saw the game's dizzyingly diverse universe everywhere.

When I first began playing *Overwatch*, I became hopelessly infatuated with two of its heroes: the cheeky "British" idealist, Tracer, and the visibly queer "Russian" bodybuilder, Zarya. I put both their nationalities in quotation marks here because their national representations echo Sontag's view of camp as seeing "everything in quotation marks."[73] Their "British" and "Russian" origins are tethered to exaggerated accents, such as in Tracer's cartoonish line, "The world could always use more heroes!" and Zarya's nonsensical one-liner, "I want to hug you like big fuzzy Siberian bear!" Players would repeat these lines before each match, jumping in anticipation, and then again after each match, while squatting over the players they just fragged.

Both Tracer and Zarya provided queer blueprints for a nameless, blurry type of queerness. Their teasing sexuality felt both innocent and erotic. For many, Tracer read as a high-energy tomboy fascinated by machines. A pilot with a pixie haircut, she carried visible signs of queerness in ways that many of us did—as stylistic codes that other queer people could recognize but straight people wouldn't think twice about. As gamers, we understood why Tracer couldn't be visibly "out," as she was also the game's mascot, and it felt obvious enough to us that she was in some way queer. Even so, in December 2016, Blizzard confirmed her queerness through a Christmas comic, solidifying *Overwatch*'s place as the first mainstream first-person shooter with a queer mascot.

Despite calls to boycott *Overwatch* over the years for being "too woke," Tracer's coming out has been followed by more heroes: Soldier: 76 was revealed as gay in 2019, Baptiste as bisexual in 2023, Lifeweaver as pansexual in 2023, Pharah as lesbian in 2023, and Venture as non-binary in 2024. Though these moments of coming out routinely make headlines in game magazines and websites, they are less *revelations* of a character's sexuality and more *confirmations* that the obvious signs of queerness observed for years by queer fans are now true for everyone. These confirmations feel nice, but bittersweet and a tad pandering, playing into certain forms of transparent, "official" queerness in order to bolster a company's progressive branding (and indeed, Blizzard has had its fair share of #MeToo-related scandals). Like many gamers, I am often disappointed when a character is "confirmed" as queer. Yes, the celebrated coming out of a fictional character can feel like a cash grab by a multinational corporation. But also, something about the character feels lost. Their being is no longer a mysterious, nameless queer space I can occupy, but a single strictly identifiable type.

Unlike Tracer, the pink and pompy-haired heavyweight hero Zarya has never been confirmed as queer identifying. Yet her image in the game as "the strongest woman in the world" has made her a gay icon, an image once used in LGBTQ2S+ marches.[74] The refusal to confirm Zarya's gender and sexual ambiguity as either cis, straight, or queer allows her to approach different audiences globally. To queer gamers she is a gay icon; to Russians and other gamers who live in nations where queerness is explicitly oppressed and criminalized, Zarya is an incredibly strong woman who fights for the human race and perhaps has behind-the-scenes fun doing it too.

~

Tracer and Zarya opened a realm of queer ambiguity, the possibility of being an eternal question. After months of blueprinting, prototyping, and experimenting with anonymous teammates, my first attempt to embody my mains was at a hair salon, where I presented their cartoonish images as models for my hairdresser—a common practice in Hong Kong that my hairdresser didn't bat an eye at. Showing off my new pompy-pixie undercut, I found my self-presentation overlapping with tomboys, butch dykes, femboys, emo bois, twinks, andros, pixie punks, queerdos, and horny degens. To queer people around me, my newly presented self resembled an untraceable queerness, a tease, a hand appearing through a cracked-open door beckoning for possible fun. To others, especially expatriate white men, my new style was insignificant, a simple sexless fashionable cut that conveyed nothing.

Being both neurodivergent and a "brown boy" Asian, I was always presumed to be queer. So whenever someone named me as a particular type of queer—"confirmed" me—I felt reduced. All my thinking, caring, wandering, and often oscillating sexual preferences felt pancaked into a digestible snack, a two-dimensional puzzle piece that needed to fit into someone else's world view. But the queer ambiguity of Tracer and Zarya prototyped a different form of queerness, one that many gamers have come to call *playersexual*: the way, in many games, non-playable characters of any gender, race, or sexuality can inevitably be attracted to you so long as you can effectively seduce them. In some gaming communities, playersexuality can ring hollow and unrealistic. But to many neurodiverse, queer, and ambiguous players like myself, being playersexual was an aspiration. My own attractions were based far more on enticement, interest, and awe than on someone's confirmed identity type. While many gamers were aghast at how all players and characters could be bisexual, I was comforted by a queerness that always felt open, changeable, and under negotiation.

Queer ambiguity in games also validated a core part of being queer for me, what many call the *bi-cycle*, when someone's long-term attraction toward one particular gender type suddenly bounces to another. On the bi-cycle, one could be attracted to only masculine-presenting people for a while, then fems, then other genders or mixtures to varying degrees. For some, this shifting sexuality can be an exciting process of discovery, while for others, it can be overwhelming and confusing enough to create imposter syndrome, a feeling of never being queer enough or straight enough to be bi. For myself, the queer ambiguity of being playersexual opened ways of staying on the bi-cycle from one terrain to another without a particular destination in sight—a queerness that could only be found through echolocation, a gravitational slingshot from one erotic planet to another.

My queer ambiguity hovered within the eternal question of my tight shirts and my pixie haircut, and it never failed to give me comfort. It was okay to refuse suspicion, to remain *unconfirmed*. Like my mains, I too could tease, entice, and never reveal.

~

Since 2016, I have played *Overwatch* consistently for eight years. I have logged over one thousand hours of in-game play, bi-cycling from one queer crush to another. I have played the game persistently through every game crash, every controversial update, every wave of leavers and newbies, every balancing trial that comes with a new hero (there are over forty now). Throughout these eight years, my mains have shifted several times. Sometimes, a different hero will speak to a new challenge I face or a different part of myself I hope to nurture.

Mei, a Chinese hero inspired by China's ice artist festivals, became my main when I began to miss living in China and started making more frequent trips back. Unlike the normative body types of Chinese film icons, Mei sports a large silhouette. As the chief engineer and climatologist for the *Overwatch* heroes, Mei undermines the vastly male-dominated tech industries in China and carries the striking optimism of combatting climate change even in a country saturated with air pollution: "Everyone is counting on me," Mei says. "Our world is worth fighting for."

Mei's revolutionary optimism was intensely rewarding when I played her. Her chirpy tone could easily turn into a campy stylization of psychological warfare. I repeated her bubbly voice lines while freezing enemies, leaving them struggling in a blind panic, and then executing them point-blank with a blade of ice.

In 2019, Mei's optimistic fierceness was reinvented for a more benign purpose. After Blizzard had banned one of its esports players, Blitzchung, for making statements calling for the liberation of Hong Kong, pro-democracy protesters claimed Mei's image as a mascot and created posters that featured her voice lines advocating for change.[75] Mei became not only an icon, but a character with her own voice—someone who could and would condemn the arrest of protesters and the banning of free speech. In their last demonstrations against the government before a city-wide ban on protests began, protesters in Hong Kong held up signs of Mei stating, "Mei is fighting for her rights."

~

In 2017, while living in Hong Kong, I was in my second year of marriage, was fast becoming a recognized teacher and scholar, and had just become a father. Marriage, professionalization, and fatherhood were all life events that many people hold as life goals since childhood. For me, they were happenstance, a result of choosing to stay in graduate school rather than risk the Great Recession, of building a new self that Y-Dang and I imagined together. Marriage, professionalization, and fatherhood were all systems I had fundamentally disagreed with, structures I had sought to escape. Sure, I presented as genderqueer and had my erotic kink life, but to my former self, I was a stranger. Not an outsider to the system but a shiny, unbreakable cog within it.

Around that time I also became infatuated with a different *Overwatch* character, an anti-hero who would become my most reliable main for the next seven years. Because *Overwatch* audits my play time, tallying every minute I spend in each character's skin, I know that I have spent over 165 hours of in-game play as this character in over a thousand matches.

This hero is a cunning Mexican hacker who faked her own death only to resurface under a new name: Sombra. My *main* main, Sombra is the epitome of inaccessible coolness: aloof, eyes elsewhere, she will never reveal her plans or her true self. Hidden in invisible camouflage, Sombra can infiltrate enemy back lines, assassinate a target, then taunt them with a trolling voice line: "Amateur hour," "You were boring me," or "Kudos for trying, güey."

Like Sombra, I had left my life in America behind and resurfaced under a new name, Kawika Guillermo: the name I had used for years as a short story author. Kawika was my matrilineal name, my mother's maiden name, and the name she had intended for me. It was also the name I saw manifested in the floating isles shared with friends, family, gamers, and readers alike. This name amplified my own racial and gender ambiguity with its curious combination of Kawika—the native Hawaiian word for the colonizer name David—and Guillermo, the first name of the Spanish friar whom my family had once worked for in the Philippines. It was a complex name full of history and baggage, but its complexity and refusal to turn away from these histories also spoke to my multiple lineages and to my many selves. As Kawika, I could remake these histories into aspiring futures. As Kawika, I could turn depression not to joy, but to expression—to create, create, and create. As Kawika, I could hack into the networks of the elite, the academic, the literary. I could truly speak my mind, reveal the hypocrisies of the systems we inhabited, dwell in the dark sides of ourselves—that darkness I shared with Teal, with my uncle Danny, with my brother, with Y-Dang and Don, with the living and the dead.

Sombra too is a pen name pointing to ambiguity. In Spanish it means "shadow, shade, enwrapped darkness." Through her play style, her personality, her background, and her mysterious, unconfirmed identity, Sombra became more than a blueprint or a prototype. Sombra was the familiar at my side who always found playful ways to manoeuvre through conversations with colleagues and expats; she was the spirit I summoned when academic committees asked me to "put out fires" when I would much rather dance around them. Like Sombra, I sought to hide my plans to sabotage the systems that held me through a carefree and friendly demeanour. Like Sombra, I had entered the system not to rise within it, but as a hacker intent on sabotage, a virus carrying radical change, a glitch meant to rupture its solid architecture.

~

Ten years into the post-Gamergate era, video games have begun to shift their reputation from a hideaway for white male militarism to a place of queer immaturity. Games are now becoming a sign of racial otherness (especially Asianness), of queerness, of gender deviation, of "woke feminism." Whereas games were once proof of unrestrained toxic masculinity, today they are used as evidence of a simplistic, overbearing belief that trans and gender-nonconforming people are just confused adults addicted to virtual worlds.

In *Glitch Feminism*, Legacy Russell pinpoints the foundational anxiety that permeates right-wing pundits' arguments about games: that our queer gender identities are as fake and imagined as our online, virtual ones. For them, games perpetuate an asocial, pathological disease they name "gender ideology." Yet for Russell, many marginalized gamers—in her discussion, Black queer women—find fulfillment from these identities and have found ways to flourish through virtual bodies marked as "cosmic" and "inconceivably vast."[76] In virtual worlds we do not just embody a polygonal self, we become *bodied* as a verb. Our blueprinting, prototyping, and enacting are acts of creation, of bodying, of "giv[ing] material form to something abstract."[77]

For many, Gamergate was proof of the misogyny that video games always represented. But for me and many queer and marginalized gamers, Gamergate was not an indicator of how regressive games were but a reaction to how progressive, transformative, and revolutionary games had become: the DIY tools that queer and of colour indie designers used to express themselves; the slippages in gender, race, and pronouns we inevitably felt for our mains; the focus on story, poetry, and meditative pacing that gave players time to think and dwell with their characters. For us, games were no protective bunker for white male rage but a space where new selves could incubate, emerge, and *become*.

~

> The glitch is for those selves joyfully immersed in the in-between, those who have traveled away from their assigned site of gendered origin.
> —Legacy Russell, *Glitch Feminism*

In 2018, Y-Dang and I decided to leave Hong Kong and move to Vancouver, Canada. We had secured teaching positions in a city with less hustle, less political turmoil, and with a much more viable and affordable daycare system for our son.

While Y-Dang was exhilarated by this new prospect, I was terrified. I thought about this new, ambiguous self I had cultivated in Asia and how, in every single instance I could recall of being queer bashed, ridiculed, or attacked for being effeminate or Asian or for dressing in bright florals, the attacker had always been a white man. Whenever I visited a majority-white city, whether Sydney, Las Vegas, Seattle, Portland, or Vancouver, I was always afraid of being assaulted, or worse. My return to North America symbolized the end of pride and self-love. It was back to being invisible, unwanted, left-swiped.

Vancouver had the reputation of being both the most Asian city in North America and the most *anti*-Asian city in North America, a place where anti-Asian racism was so ubiquitous that it didn't even seem to count as racism. The city was a techno-orientalist dreamscape with a brutal history of anti-Asian riots, a place where an all-white band could name themselves Japandroids, and where its most popular company, Lululemon, had *on record* named itself Lululemon because the founder, Chip Wilson, thought it would be funny to watch Japanese people try to pronounce a name with three *L*'s in it.[78] While learning all of this, I also learned that I could say nothing about the city's racism in front of white residents without being marked as a typical arrogant American, or a threatening angry brown man. In Vancouver's always-conditional welcome, I learned what many people of colour called "the non-white man's burden": the imperative to smile and be nice to your white hosts, *or else*.

The day we moved into our new apartment near our university, I could not wait to unpack my computer. I loaded up *Overwatch* and spent time with my mains. I also spent time with my main loves—Y-Dang, our son, Kai, and Don when he came to visit us from Toronto. With them, it didn't matter that so many people on our campus stared at me as I walked by, not with the curious tease I was used to, but with looks of concern, of upset at some form of trespass. While walking my son in his stroller, uninvited questions about our identity were relentless: "Welcome to Canada, where are you from?" "What kind of accent is that?" "Is your family from Mexico? The Philippines?" "His mother must be Chinese, right? I can see it in his eyes." Though it was dressed under a different name, the need to be identified, the ongoing demand to *confirm* my being, the hunger for life story—only from the marginalized—was as strong in Vancouver as anywhere else I had lived.

I felt the familiar walls of North American bigotry closing in. And yet, this time was different: I had play styles, strategies, game sense, blueprints and prototypes, and pride in being the gender-bendy, nameless, and unconfirmed self that changed as constantly as the video game I was playing. And I had my new family: Y-Dang and Don, who would be joined by many more in Vancouver, until we had a full-fledged queer community greater than any dizzyingly diverse video game roster. I began to feel like a role model for my students—not a difficult thing, as there weren't many other flashy, brown, queer femboy professors around. The weight of my presence in white and Western academia no longer felt like that of an imposter or mere anomaly, but a glitch in an otherwise stifling institution. By simply being myself in a harsh and unyielding system, perhaps I too could blueprint the radical hope for something more.

CHAPTER 9

Of Dark Dungeons

When we received a call at ten in the morning on a Sunday, I knew something had to be wrong. Sunday mornings are a time for calm and reflection—for going to church, for nursing a hangover. On this Sunday morning, I was with my wife, Y-Dang, and our two-year-old son in a large indoor mall, a retreat from Vancouver's October rain. While Y-Dang talked on her phone, I walked ahead, pushing our son in his stroller, anxious of the news. Who calls on a Sunday morning, if not to report a tragic end?

Two stores away, I heard her choked cry.

The friend was Don Goellnicht, Y-Dang's graduate school supervisor, our mentor and friend who was with us the night we met, who fed us wisdom while chewing on scallops in Kobe, who made us laugh until our stomachs hurt on the back of a bus in Xiamen, who came out of the closet in his fifties and lived so freely and fully that we, for the first time, had begun to imagine a future where we might age with the same youthful spirit.

I didn't need Y-Dang to communicate the details. Having witnessed death already, I had come to expect it. I knew when I felt that familiar numbness, that whiplash of reality: *Don is dead*, I thought, heaving a sigh that felt like blowing out a candle. Another quenched flame.

~

Video games have been present throughout my life for every joy, every change, and every sorrow. But rarely do we consider games in the worst times, in times of ineffable turmoil and loss. So why, when disease, trauma, and death immersed me, nearly drowned me, did I still play games? Years after my loved ones passed, I enter the ocean of memory through the games I played at the time. Their presence was with me in hospital waiting rooms, was shared with loved ones debilitated in their beds.

Trauma, as my therapist reminds me, is the rupture of our ability to forget. To accept and incorporate traumatic memory, I was told to turn to poetry. I often did. But I also played games. In moments of grief, I found a different poetics of memory: I remember my uncle Danny's death through the underground world of *Super Mario 64*, while trying to use the lava floor to propel myself to new heights; I remember my first girlfriend Teal's death through the game *Vagrant Story*, where players descend a dungeon and perform impeccably timed strikes against enemies, creating rhythm within the catacombs; I remember my grandmother Prisca's death through the platform worlds of Mario and Sonic, where falling into an abyss was just as routine as rebirth. Games help me receive these memories, to dwell upon those isles where the memories of lost loved ones can be pulled out of a long dormancy, allowing parts of the past to dissolve and others to grow.

~

Ten months before Don's death, I spent a night in an ambulance watching paramedics try to breathe life back into my unconscious one-year-old son, who was in the midst of his second major seizure. He survived, but for the next year, Y-Dang and I were in and out of hospitals, following the instructions of a dozen doctors who asked us to repeatedly take his blood, insert needles, and feed him medication, all while singing his favourite nursery rhymes. In time, I grew accustomed to teaching college courses through my laptop from ammonia-scented hospital bathrooms.

I recall the surreal irony of once sitting next to my son's hospital bed while teaching a virtual class on video games and health. The rhythm of his beeping vital-signs monitors underscored my lecture describing how, in the game *Depression Quest*, you can see multiple dialogue options but can only choose the ones you have the energy and capacity to follow; how in the game *Curtain*, an abusive relationship manifests through the confinement of text boxes, blurriness, and feeling trapped in the same unresolvable arguments. Immersed in the relentless tides of caregiving and illness, I found plenty of games exploring these emotional states: *That Dragon, Cancer*, chronicling a child's cancer diagnosis; *Life Is Strange* and *Mixed Messages*, grappling with suicidal ideation; and *Gris*, *Dear Esther*, and *What Remains of Edith Finch*, which turn grief into haunting, tangible landscapes.

Researchers in the medical sciences have demonstrated how games can affect mental health by shifting one's brain state.[79] Rather than name games a pathology, this recent research has attempted to lift games into a new form of self-medication used to cope with PTSD and other stressful situations. This research argues that short-burst interactions with games can transform one's brain state and help players think more positively. Just ten minutes in a game can squash cravings and calm down anger or a panic attack; twenty can result in a Zen-like state. For these researchers, there is little interest in the content of a game. What's important is how a game makes you feel: you can put together *Tetris* blocks, collect cats, or blow things up, so long as the game results in a sought-after mood shift.

Despite teaching these points about games, when I was going through my own experiences with depression and grief, I found them only momentarily helpful. While mourning Don's death, I avoided games *about* mourning. They felt too close to home, and most seemed to be about empathizing with an experience that I was too deep within. As well, I avoided using games merely to shift my mood. Video games have that unique ability to keep you going during depression, but also to elongate it, turning your one shitty day into a dreadfully depressive month. Instead, I absorbed myself in games that were not about loss explicitly but that gave metaphor for the loss I was experiencing, reimagining my wearisome world through play.

~

Before 2020, I had never stepped foot inside a therapist's office. My therapy, for better or worse, was in counselling with anonymous players in a video game. In my early twenties, one of these random healing seshes resulted in a friendship with a boy from Southern Texas: Jesús Franco, the best friend I ever made through video games. When we first met, Jesús and I shared game experiences as well as poetry, short stories, and traumas. Queer and Latino, Jesús taught me how to understand my own queerness as a subject of fun, random encounter, and inspiration, rather than shame.

Many games show how healing and understanding occur in games through anonymous players who share health experiences. *Cibele* recounts the developer Nina Freeman's real-life relationship with a stranger in an online game, where she found unexpected emotional depth and connection. In *Depression Quest*, while unable to get out of bed in a dark room, you can find energy and understanding in an online friend who dwells with you in that depressive space. Jesús was that online friend who ached with me. We were both insomniacs, and we often talked each other through 4 a.m. panic spells.

I use the past tense to write about Jesús not because we lost touch, but because he died suddenly and tragically in late 2022. I found out through a Facebook post, where I discovered I wasn't the only random online encounter whom Jesús had helped through their worst possible moment. I joined the ranks of other nameless players, penning a brief memorial to my friend: "I remember Jesús as a vivid and dependable soul in the internet realm. He was also the best and funniest flirt. Rest in peace, Jesús, and deep condolences to the family."

Jesús was an avatar for myself: queer, brown, fat, gamer, writer. Like me, he suffered deep self-hate. Unlike me, he always came out of it, stubbornly proud of being fat, queer, and brown. Only after he died did I realize he was all of these things. His beauty came from them, because he wasn't ashamed. Surely, if I had died first, he would have heard the news and written on some webpage that he thought I too was beautiful.

~

> You are deeply depressed. Even activities you used to
> enjoy hold little or no interest for you, and you exist
> in a near-constant state of lethargy.
> —*Depression Quest*

Often when I encounter illness or death, I can only describe that numb, automated feeling of shock and absorption through the games I've played. For weeks, I feel split in two, like I am playing *The Sims*: I am both the Sim being led about from one task to another, pleading to the heavens in a nonsensical language, and I am the player instructing the Sim, barking orders, giving them pathways to work, to eat, to breathe, even to piss and shit, because they can no longer do it themselves.

When I first encountered the numbness of loss, it felt like waking up and realizing that I, and most everyone I knew, had always been a Sim. With almost perfunctory automation, most people choose routes of progress, achievement, money, consumerism, and build their lives on the goals of winning a game, a game we were born into. To encounter death felt like getting unplugged from this game. It caused me to question my own mortality, my moral being, my meaning.

But when I experienced loss later in life, I needed simulation. My body was in so much pain and shock and stress that it needed to disassociate, to run on autopilot. The result was two mes: the me feeling all the pain, and the me outside the game, telling myself to go to work, to pick up my son from school, to make lunch. The me on the ground could only do what a robotic body could do. And I needed that automaton, that unthinking simulation, to hold steady, unburdened by the anguish of simply staying alive.

~

Like many games, *The Sims* features permanent death. Once a Sim dies, that's it.

Is there something perverse about video games that allows you to create characters based on people you know—to shape their dress, their face, their name, to replicate your friends and family—only to see them scrubbed from the virtual world, just as they will one day be pulled away from our real world?

~

In some sense, our society already acknowledges that virtual worlds contain ways of ceaselessly facing death. We call digital success "going viral." Games are routinely checked for "bugs" and "toxicity." Magazines encourage us to protect our health by going through a "digital detox." These metaphors of illness and disease help us understand the digital and how virtual worlds play vital roles in times of debilitation and loss. When we cannot get out of bed, we pick up a device to communicate with others. We dress our avatars when we cannot dress ourselves.

In 2021, my step-grandmother, Vee Guillermo, passed away from Alzheimer's. Less than a year later, my uncle Cameron Dickens tragically passed in a hospital. Two months after that, his son, my younger cousin Kamalona, took his own life. Each of these deaths came with visits to Hawaiʻi where my mother, sister, and brother would mourn and cry and fight on streets filled with wealthy tourists.

The division between my grieving family and the wealthy landowners and tourists in Hawaiʻi seemed to echo Susan Sontag's description of mourning as being cast in "the night-side of life" or "the kingdom of the sick."[80] But the separations actually ran much deeper. My grandmother was a descendent of Filipino plantation workers. My uncle was a proud Indigenous Kānaka Maoli man, and his son, my cousin, inherited a mixture of these histories as well as their presences in the constant buying and stealing of land, in pollution and toxicity, in a dismantled health care system, in the presence of military bases, and in the sunburned tourists around him. All my loved ones in Hawai'i met their tragic ends in someone else's island paradise.

In grief, I relied on games to avoid the real world, with its clichés, its mandatory positivity, its insistence on straightness and masculinity even in times of mourning. The real world was not just unequal in wealth and health, but unequal in death. Death was not democratic, not universal. It came in degrees. And those on the other side of the fence, they who could exalt death and use it to enter the "kingdom of the sick," did not know us, did not see us. We were the peasants of their kingdom, dwelling in its shadowed slums.

~

> Madness ... our old friend.
> —*Darkest Dungeon*

I have what many call a low baseline: I am often depressed but not debilitatingly so, I am an insomniac who gets just enough sleep to take my son to school in the morning, I am a self-loathing loner even when surrounded by friends. For moody and morose pessimists like myself, games are a substitute for the uppers of self-medication; they are the jolts of a caffeine high, the kick of a sugar rush. While going through the motions of life, games help me feel *something*, even if that something is descending into a dark and terrifying place.

Descending into caves, castles, or underground lairs is a routine activity in games. Since the popularity of Dungeons & Dragons, these dark liminal spaces have all been referred to as dungeons: hellish zones separate from the main game where the player fights hordes of enemies, challenges a boss, and gains loot. Since the early 2010s, games like *Spelunky*, *Dead Cells*, and *Hades* have popularized the dungeon crawler game (also called the Rogue-like), where dungeons *are* the main game.

In these, players descend into dungeons with short runs that last around five to twenty minutes and often result in some small foundational change: upgrades are gained, and one might change or lose certain characters or abilities.

In 2016, the game *Darkest Dungeon* took dungeons far beyond their role as dens of monsters and thieves. Here dungeons meant imprisonment, torture, distress, suicidal ideation, and PTSD. Players hire mercenaries, send them into dungeons, and—assuming these poor "heroes" survive—find ways to tend their wounds, physical and psychological. Each adventurer has a visible stress meter so players can bring them to the brink of psychological breakdown before pulling them out of the dungeon. If too late, the mercenaries develop a psychological condition: paranoia results in refusal to fight; masochism results in purposefully setting off traps; abusive results in hitting and even killing teammates; anorexia results in an inability to heal; a heart attack results in instant death.

In *Darkest Dungeon*, trauma, anxiety, and depression do not turn mercenaries into heroes. Trauma bends reality, resulting in cycles of violence. Trauma damages the nervous system, putting its victims in a constant loop of hypervigilance. Trauma hijacks minds, turning friends into enemies. Trauma jerry-rigs digestive tracks, turning nourishment into poison. But trauma is nothing new, nothing others haven't faced before.

In *Darkest Dungeon*'s medieval setting, adventurers have access to forgotten forms of healing. They can visit the tavern to drink, gamble, or patronize the brothel, or go to the abbey to meditate, pray, or flagellate themselves. The hero's form of care depends on their own personality, quirks, and fetishes, but there is always a way to heal. And, once recovered, there is always a compelling reason—whether gold, glory, or god—to go back into that dungeon.

~

In the classical myths of Homer and Virgil, journeys into the underworld are referred to as katabasis, meaning "a going down." Perhaps the most famous tale of katabasis is of the poet and musician Orpheus, who travels to the underworld to rescue his wife, Eurydice, a forest nymph who died while fleeing Apollo's son Aristaeus, who was attempting to rape her. Eurydice's death also occurs from a descent; while fleeing her assailant, she falls into a den of poisonous vipers.

The mourning of Eurydice, whose name means "a far-reaching justice," is the grief of injustice, of a wound that can never heal so long as injustice remains. The poet Rainer Maria Rilke called her a woman who was loved so much "that a whole world was made from mourning."[81]

Orpheus's descent into hell to rescue Eurydice illustrates the dread of illness, of pursuing love within loss, of a strained, dwindling hope kept alive only through poetry, music, and sheer will. Orpheus slips past the creature Cerberus by playing music to lull him to sleep. With poetry, he softens the heart of Hades, who allows him to pass. But after that, Orpheus's katabasis is left to interpretation. For Plato, Orpheus finds only an apparition of Eurydice and gives up. For Virgil, Orpheus pulls Eurydice from the underworld only to lose her again just as he exits. In most myths, Orpheus meets his own death soon after entering the underworld—a punishment for his descent, a death for seeking to overcome death.

The story of Orpheus and Eurydice has been revised across centuries in poetry, films, and video games. In the game *Hades*, Orpheus appears as a shadow of his former self. He can no longer sing or write poetry, having lost the will to chase his passions. Though even in this video game, katabasis is beset by tragedy, the player offers some hope, as he can descend deeper into the underworld to communicate with Eurydice. Perhaps, with time and commitment, Orpheus and Eurydice might one day meet again in the underworld they've made home.

~

> As a fruit is filled with its sweetness and darkness
> she was filled with her big death, still so new
> that it hadn't been fathomed.
> —Rainer Maria Rilke, "Orpheus, Eurydice, Hermes"

In November 2021, two years after Don passed, I was in Hawai'i, on the island of Oahu, on my first trip after the COVID-19 lockdowns, to bury my step-grandmother. I had just been poked with a COVID test at Walgreens and was eating pulled pork from a takeout box on the back of a rental truck when Y-Dang called me, panicking over the results of an ultrasound. She sent me a picture. Little white specks dotted her intestine, her liver, her lungs, her insides.

I returned to Vancouver. Her stomach pain had become unbearable. We left our apartment in a torrent of rain. Somehow all the windows in our car had been left fully open, even the sunroof. Our bodies sank into soggy puddles of rainwater as I drove to the ER. We dried ourselves off during an emergency CT scan. During our weeklong hospital stay, we watched rain whip the windows of our downtown hospital room, while rainbow colours snuck in from the queer district below us, leaving fluorescent streaks on the walls. On the day of her biopsy, the storm finally let up to reveal a real rainbow arching over the city skyline. We took it as a symbol of hope.

Her biopsy results took that hope away.

For weeks, I couldn't speak the illness's name. "My wife has C," I would say. "The worst kind of C you can have."

During the first month after my wife's diagnosis, I kept myself from playing games, dry heaving at every loading screen. I should be helping her. I should be grading, attending to class. Games were frivolous, childish, and offered nothing to the land of the dispirited, the mourning, the dying. Games belonged to those carefree others, the winged ones posing in sunshine. We had become creatures with broken wings, still and fragile, our bodies withering, weathered.

Video games were for the young. She would never get old. And I would never be young again.

~

Without games, I became unmoored. I lingered restlessly until I heard a single note of music and became a sobbing mess. If I saw a screen or went to answer a message, I started gasping for air. Everything sparked a short-circuit in my blood-brain barrier, pulling me back into a nauseous, spinning void.

When I returned to games, I could finally exhale. And once I gave some brief moments in my day to games, all other habits of self-care began to reignite. With games, I was often distracted, tense, and unsettled. Without games, I was an utterly helpless wreck, in a constant state of upheaval and breakdown. Nothing else could soothe my twitching impulse spasms, my insomnia. During my wife's illness, games were outlets to let out anger (*Overwatch*), to escape (*Paradise Killer*), to feel nostalgia (*Halo*), to be with friends and family (*Gunfire Reborn*). But more importantly, games gave me new ways to understand trauma (*Subnautica*), illness (*Celeste*), and death itself (*Spiritfarer*).

~

> Hear, o gods, my desperate plea
> To see my love beside me
> Sunk below the mortal sea
> Her anchor weighs upon me
> —Orpheus, from *Hades*

In *Subnautica*, you descend into the unexplored ocean of an alien planet. The fears of the underwater dungeon come not from darkness, but from vastness. At any moment you could lose the energy to swim and suffocate in the salted sea. Stay on an island for too long, and you'll run out of resources and die of starvation. Go too far into the ocean depths, and you'll be torn apart from underwater pressure, run out of oxygen, or become food for a monstrous leviathan. The water is both gorgeous and terrifying, contemplative and nerve-racking, aswarm with wondrous life and a thousand things deadly to your own.

I was in the bathroom, hearing Y-Dang talk to someone on the phone. How many times had I imagined, when overhearing her conversations, that she might start jumping and screaming in joy, and in that uproar I would rush out to see what was the matter, and she would start shouting, *It's a misdiagnosis! They confused my chart with someone else's! It turns out I only have scars, or gallstones, or whatever!*

The chances of it all going away: three, maybe four lightning strikes. But I left room for these magnetisms.

We were in a storm, our guts drooping down, weighing us. In those times, playing games felt like being buoyed out to sea, moving with the waves, waiting for some lifeline to tug me back to shore. It was a struggle. But if I stopped playing, I fell out of the game's current, and a cold undertow would pull me into the depths.

My wife and I were stone remnants, sinking, watching the rest of humankind swarm around us, dipping past in wavering currents. The buzz of work and study, once enthralling, became background noise, echoes of rain on a surface miles above us, distant as sunlight. With every passing day we sank further, down into the dungeon, into the mud, into that soul-stirring sea. Every time we thought we'd found a branch to grasp, it turned out to be lifeless seaweed.

One day, while waiting for Y-Dang in a hospital room, I finally started to feel bad for myself. I began to see the way others saw me: a thirty-six-year-old man who might lose the love of his life, who might be widowed, who might raise a four-year-old child all on his own, while juggling an incredibly demanding job, mortgage payments, care for his in-laws, and his own wavering mental health. How could anyone survive this?

In *Subnautica*, you learn the terror of the deep blue sea. As a lone survivor, stranded on a remote ocean planet, your every minute comes with a tinge of imminent doom. You learn dizziness, how waves can pummel you, driving you deeper under. The ocean is unreasonable, inescapable, and indifferent to your small drowning body.

How could anyone survive this?

~

The first time I saw my wife enjoy a video game was while she was in recovery from a brutal round of chemotherapy that included three types of refined chemical toxins. I bought a Nintendo Switch for our son thinking it was actually for me, but it turned out to be for her. "A lot of debilitated people can play video games," she said from our bed, where she spent most of the day. "I see why. I finally get the appeal."

She had broken two pairs of earbuds with her toxic sweat. But she could hold a controller.

In a way, video games had equipped me for this. Cancer was a basic rescue-the-princess narrative, a puzzle to complete, a boss to defeat, a dungeon to emerge from, victorious.

In the same way, nothing had ever equipped me for this.

~

> Health is wasted on the healthy, and life is wasted on the living.
> —Julie Yip-Williams, *The Unwinding of the Miracle*

Witnessing my own emotional breakdowns, my wife referred me to her therapist. In our first session, I told him why the two previous therapists I'd seen had not worked for me: "I'm neurodivergent. I like to be challenged rather than validated. I will often laugh and make terrible jokes about my own issues, and I have no intention of stopping that. If you expect tears and seriousness, you are expecting me to mask, and this will not work. And also: video games. If you pathologize them, I'm out."

"Tell me about the games you play," my new therapist asked me. "What are they about?"

His question caught me off guard. Never had a therapist or counsellor taken an interest in the games I played.

I told him about a game I was playing just before our session, *Celeste*. You play as Madeline, a girl who chooses to climb the dauntingly dangerous Celeste Mountain. Submerged in states of depression and anxiety, Madeline must climb to get out of her own head. Otherwise, her only outlets are drinking and "getting mad at people on the internet."

My therapist asked for more. Info dumping, I told him about how the Celeste Mountain shows you things you're not ready for. You see monuments built in honour of the dead who perished along the way, but also shadows of your darker selves.

I admitted to getting incredibly frustrated playing *Celeste*—some of the jumping and platforming felt impossible. My frustration burned whenever I died, my virtual body turning to little sparkles upon the same damn spikes, again and again. Eventually, I realized I could just turn around, find a different direction. I could keep going up the summit, even if I didn't know every secret on the way.

My therapist spoke like an acupuncturist, getting right into needling the pressure points. "And how are you climbing that mountain now?"

~

Living one day at a time is maddening. The welling up of anger, the slow drip of torture, the wearing down of the daily checkpoints, the chipping away of your self-defences, the degree-by-degree drop in temperature until you can no longer feel your hands.

Whiteness is the cold and desolate Celeste Mountain. Whiteness is the ghosts who haunt it, the cancer that harms us, the blood cells that turned against her, the chemotherapy bags meant to kill those blood cells. Cancer transforms white cells from good to evil, from healers to killers. With chemotherapy, the good blood cells have to die as well.

During COVID-19, every time I left the house I put her life at risk. Panic attacks became frequent. Bodily dissociation came with dizziness, paralysis, feelings of suffocation when the air suddenly became thin. Even my joints began to let go, and my feet refused to move another step.

In *Celeste*, a panic attack hits when you are suspended in a broken gondola. Caught in another snowstorm, this time, you see no way out. Your friend Theo gives you advice he learned from his grandfather: imagine a feather and try to keep it suspended in the air with your breath.

A red feather appears on screen, and the player must keep it from falling.

Madeline breathes, eyes closed, her body in a fit of shakes. I am only pressing a button, but I am breathing with her. Together, we keep that feather afloat.

~

> Badeline: "You have no idea what you're getting into. You can't handle this."
> Madeline: "That is exactly why I need to do this."
> —*Celeste*

Madeline feels the need to climb the Celeste Mountain after her grandmother's death. The mountain is not merely her desire to overcome grief, but her need to face her darkest selves that surface in times of grief: paranoia, jealousy, rage. These self-reflections, manifest in Madeline's alter ego, Badeline, tell her she cannot climb this mountain. She cannot ever rid herself of herself. She will never be worthy of this world of the living.

Y-Dang continued with chemotherapy, her body changing, her hair drifting away with the cold of winter, her pain intensifying in the turn to spring, her joy returning with the summer sun. Eight months crested and crumbled. Painful nights came and went. Sleep mercifully seeped into our bed. Coming and going: the nausea, the waves of sadness, the heights when we felt she might survive longer, the falls that came when scans revealed growth. In July, we realized she had survived longer than expected—something we wanted to celebrate, but couldn't face, because it also meant we were living on stolen time. Coming and going: tugs of pain, panic attacks, bits of bad news pushing us closer to a cliff's edge.

I was daunted by the mountain before us. I could not see its summit, and the climb felt infinite. But like Madeline, there were things I could do—focus on where I was, and find some way to get to that next checkpoint. Maybe there would be a rest house there, a place to camp, or a message left by someone who felt just as alone in the world. All I had to do was get us there. Whatever came after, I would worry about later.

For the summer, we lived as well as we could, flung across spheres of illness, determined not to just sit in wait of death. As Y-Dang put it, we no longer waited for that raspberry jam to go on sale before buying it.

In August, we took the last trip out of Vancouver we would ever take together. With our son, who had just turned five, we rode a gondola up Whistler Mountain. In the middle of our ride, our gondola paused, stuck. We sat and practised slow breathing, keeping the feather afloat. Soon, the machine started again, and we resumed our climb.

~

In October 2022, nearly a year after Y-Dang's diagnosis, we left for the ER again. She was confident it would be a quick visit and didn't bother to say goodbye to the house, as we sometimes did when we weren't sure if she was ever coming back. The sky above was clear, and the wind was quiet. But I could not escape a feeling that we were starting another climb.

The game *Spiritfarer* teaches us not to be afraid of the descent into death. You play as Stella, taking over the role of ferry master from the Greek god Charon. But as ferry master, you don't just carry souls across a river. You care for them over time, across a vast sea of islands. Along the way you find new spirits. You bring them aboard, comfort them, feed them, and hug them as they prepare to enter the Everdoor, the gateway to the other side.

Spiritfarer is a game about caregiving for people at death's door. You do not fulfill last wishes so much as dwell with these souls: you cook for them, bring them things that remind them of home, go shopping for them, fish for them, talk to them, and sometimes you do nothing but let time pass. For a video game, there is a lot of waiting.

The longer Y-Dang stayed at the hospital, the more I brought items from our apartment to help make her room into a new home: clothing, blankets, pillows, cuddly toys, toothbrushes, and robes. The nurses told us our hospital room felt like a place of joy and often mistook us for newlyweds. We joked and came up with kooky scenarios about her potential death, my life after her death, and my own death too. We decided that being reincarnated into worms would be fine, so long as all our organs were in the right place and we weren't constantly in pain. Wriggling around in dirt, our slimy bodies entwined, felt like a waking dream.

In that hospital room we laughed, we ached, and we dreamt. We returned to the floating isle we'd created when we first met, when the world seemed to shape itself around us.

~

Emotional capacities are heightened upon *Spiritfarer*'s boat. In the game, preparing others for death does not happen through direct conversation. The work of daily caregiving takes time, and stories come through the work.

One of the souls, Uncle Atul, has a hankering for popcorn. But when you finally grow corn and upgrade your kitchen so you can cook it, Atul reveals that he doesn't actually like the taste. Popcorn reminds him of his family, of his kids falling asleep on him as they watched television late into the night, eating popcorn. In the game, giving him popcorn will sour his mood (resulting in two down arrows for "remembering his family"). A soul's memories can be difficult and inaccessible, even in death. It can take time for the souls to process their meaning, if they ever do. Your role is only to give them time.

The goal of *Spiritfarer* is not to make souls happy or to help them grow, but to be present with them, to provide space and comfort in their final days. In conversing with them, there are no dialogue choices, no talking back, no anxiety over how you should respond. Just being present and listening is enough.

A soul's happiness does not establish a win. It is the same as their sadness: another part of the process toward accepting their fate. Happy or not, they are still another day closer to approaching their end. When they enter the Everdoor, their bodies become cosmic constellations. Ephemeral starlight: what they were before they were born, what they will become when they return.

~

In her hospital room, my wife and I often talked about the places we had been and the different people we used to be. She loved drama class, being "in character" pretending to be other people, living in that world of imagination. When we'd first met, people often thought we were brother and sister. We wouldn't correct them, and then later would start making out in front of them. Together we'd invented our scholar personas. Hers was serious, calm, soft-spoken; mine was jocular, abrasive, and direct.

From our floating isles, we watched the ocean, as well as the night sky above. Every tide below us was pulled and pushed by the cold and barren moon above us. Cosmic indifference tilted the waves.

~

Spiritfarer can get stressful when you have a full boat. Sometimes you don't notice when one of the souls hasn't left their room for days, or when one goes missing, or when one begins to starve. You do your best to help them, but you have to meet your own capacities. If you collapse, they will all pay.

Some souls will never grow. Some will never overcome their fears. Some will continue to be distant, as dismissive of others' feelings as they are of their own. In some sense, most will never really be ready to meet death.

When the spirit Gwen tells me she is ready to go to the Everdoor, I am confused, because she is still haunted by jellyfish. My understanding as a gamer is that the fears and anxieties of these spirits are something to overcome, to cure, to win. But her fear of jellyfish—or whatever they are an allegory for—is never overcome and is not something she seeks to overcome. She goes through the Everdoor, ever afraid.

It can be shocking when a spirit tells you they are ready to go. You've been so caught up in caretaking, and you've gotten so used to having them around, to listening to their complaints and foraging for their food. As they remember that this ship is not their home, you wonder how this ship will ever go on without them.

~

Every day after dropping off our son at school, I would bring breakfast to my wife's hospital room. Often, she would brighten up and smile when I walked in. Other times, she would look weak, drained, still reeling from a night of unfathomable pain. "Thank god you're here," she would say, striking me with some tinge of guilt—a minuscule pain compared to hers. But one that endures.

~

While accompanying a spirit, you can hold their hand. You can hug them. If they ask you not to smother them, you can keep your distance. You can give them space.

All the spirits have different nicknames for you: Sweet Pea, Big Hat, Sprout, Scout. They appear as different non-human creatures: Atul is a flute-playing frog, the brothers Mickey and Bruce are a bull and a hummingbird. Some will teach you how to garden, cook, mine, gather, meditate, and sail. Some never express their regrets, their hopes, and never really trust you. But the ship changes with each of them, and they change you.

Stanley appears as a curious and creative spirit with four arms and a mushroom head. He flaps his hands, says non sequiturs, and fiddles his fingers. Later, he reveals he is an eight-year-old child whose last memories are of lying in a hospital bed, trying to be brave for his parents.

His presence can be unsettling to others. Even amid death there is room for youth.

To care for Stanley, the player helps him put on a play. His desire to express himself results in a child's imagining of death: "A big rumble! Explosion! Wind! Dust! Smoke everywhere. Everything is quiet for a second. Then, we don't get to see our friend again. That's when the real pain starts. The end."

Stanley's play results in a soured mood—some spirits belittle him, while others can't help but show disappointment. Not long after, Stanley decides to go to the Everdoor. He confides in his last speech that he disappointed everyone, including his parents, who had to watch him die. At death's door, he tells you he is still afraid. "I hope it's like falling asleep," he says.

Stanley's absence on the ship is deeply felt. His childish creativity, his need to impress others, his lacklustre artistry—it all lingers in the minds of the other spirits. His play may have been disappointing, but its lesson was wise: one day, we don't get to see our friend again, and the real pain starts.

~

I remember that meeting, when words tumbled out of two young doctors.
    one
        to
                two
    weeks
    left
                    to
              live

It felt like finally hitting the ground. A levelling pain, a fall you never get up from.

Then, there's nothing to do. No rush, no work, no need to stay hopeful.

You just lie there. You don't even breathe.

~

On the ship I learn to dwell with the dying until they are ready to go. In this game, we do not see others as games—as forms of value, of investment, of exchange. Whether they bring us stress or joy, we honour their continued presence with our own.

~

While I sit holding her hand, missing her voice, I realize I will soon miss being here, holding her hand, missing her voice. For now, I still get to touch her and talk to her. Even if she can't communicate. And that's a lot. Soon, I will think about how lucky I am right now.

~

The people I mourn all died young, in their own way. My grandmother, who passed just days after getting to hold her two infant grandchildren. Uncle Danny, ever marked as a queer child. Teal, a defiant seventeen-year-old whose rebellion never had the chance to take shape. Don, who spent his last decade living the queer youth he'd never had. And Y-Dang, who lived with an intensity that fulfilled her every dream but who saw only the faint beginnings of her legacy—her work, her youth, her love—before departing. One day, I too will be unready, but I will still embark. I too will swim in the same sea, climb the same mountain, float toward the Everdoor, and take my place among their constellations.

~

> You've opened your heart to the suffering of others,
> And, in return, their spark warms your heart and
> shapes your fate.
> —*Spiritfarer*

Before that last hospital stay, I believed I had already experienced death. But with Y-Dang's loss, it was the difference between having a wound and missing a limb. I was not the same person; I never would be again. And of course the comparison is still only scratching the surface. I would gladly have given up a leg, an arm, for her to continue living.

The soul wounds remain in how I remember her impact on my life. She had helped bring me out of my suicidal ideation. She was my cure, and I was hers. But if she left, I didn't want to put that on someone else, especially not our son. Life, in itself, would have to be worth living.

For months, I dwelt within our floating isles. Slowly, they became another dungeon. I watched everyone outside with the same indifference as the stars who looked down on me. I knew I could not stay on those arid islands. Eventually, I would need to return. For the sake of our son and myself.

~

Y-Dang's passing was a loss for many people. For the students and scholars who bonded with her, for the Cambodian refugee communities who found their own experiences in her book, *Refugee Lifeworlds*, which was published only two months before her death, and for all her future readers who would read her family memoir, *Landbridge*, published a year after she died. We made a world in her loss, a mourning world capable of nurturing new life.

I am present now for myself, for my son, and for the communities I am part of. And I still spend time in my dark dungeons. I still return to climb the Celeste Mountain and to ferry spirits home. And with a tilt of a joystick, a push of a button, I still float. I float above the waves striking before me, spreading far and wide, and watch them glimmer under the lunar light.

game hips isles
system roles you terror
playing pleasures blueprints path
dungeons would straying

CONCLUSION

A Poetics of Interaction

hair war continue world dark sensing
like floating other fantasies
open teenagers final

I first imagined writing this book in 2020, at the height of the COVID-19 epidemic, when I and many other introverted academics who had always *urked* at the idea of giving public speeches about our own work suddenly found an unexpected joy in doing just that. My first book on video games, *Open World Empire*, had just come into the world, and thanks to the pandemic, my book tour took place in the only space I felt truly comfortable: the virtual space, my home turf. For the first time, I did not shift in discomfort when someone asked, "What is your personal relationship to games?" or "Why did you come to study games, and how have they impacted you?" The more I tried to answer these questions, the more I came to realize that the importance of video games for me went far beyond my interests as a researcher and hobbyist. It was through these live streamed conversations with students, colleagues, and readers that I came to understand how video games had cradled me as a child, had been my quirky, cool uncle, and in my darkest hours, had nursed me back to health.

Death is the only certainty in life, and in games. Just when we allow ourselves to mourn, a new death comes. The more death returns to us, the more determined we become for the next incarnation. Games had been my enemy, my therapist, my death doula, my addiction, and my lover. As I became used to opening myself up, to delivering cringeworthy details about my life on the digital stage, I began to return my audiences' inquiries: Did anyone else feel this way about games? Yes, many of my audience members did, and they wrote to me with their stories. Had anyone ever written about games in this way before? Yes, there were stories in games journalism, on Reddit, and in YouTube video essays. But I could not find a single book that dealt with games as an intimate, personal, and person-shaping experience, spread over a lifetime of play.

Of Floating Isles is my attempt to write such a book. At first, I imagined it as a cross between essays by queer cultural theorists like Roland Barthes, Eve Sedgwick, and José Esteban Muñoz and essays by contemporary authors like Jia Tolentino, Roxane Gay, Tom Bissell, and Carmen Maria Machado. But then, in 2021, with the sudden deaths of family members and friends and the diagnosis of cancer that would later take my wife's life, *Of Floating Isles* transformed into a meditation on mourning, with a more poetic rendering of what games have meant for a life that has remained, in many ways, within the ever-grinning spectre of death.

~

I am finishing the final draft of this book in January 2025, over two years after Y-Dang's death, and nearly five years since I began writing it. I write now from an apartment in Hong Kong, entering the fifth month of an nine-month trip in Asia. I am on another pilgrimage, retracing the steps Y-Dang and I once took across Asia, seeking the fragments of memory within every city we visited while living here. And I am showing these places to our son, who was born here. I am also showing him how to mourn, how to treasure the time you have, how to cherish those around you, and how, when facing unimaginable loss, we can always keep moving. With every move we awaken the past, rediscover once-forgotten moments, and hold fast to our ever-fleeting world.

CONCLUSION

In the early stages of writing this book, I was led by the fear that my memories were being consumed by the autism narrative. But this fear soon became overwhelmed by the fear of forgetting those I've lost, of losing them again in memory, this time forever. I had never kept a journal or a diary, but for the first time, I wanted to conquer my faulty memory and document my life story, because doing so would also mean preserving theirs. But with every attempt to delve into the past, I had to first pass through the gate of games. By remembering the games I played during pivotal moments of my life, I was able to retrieve long-forgotten feelings, experiences, and dreams from the blurred depths. And I was able to see just how deeply video games had shaped every part of my self: my anger, my queerness, my suicidal ideation, my attitudes toward race, class, and the systems that seek to control us, and my understanding of death. Throughout this process, I have clung to the quiet hope that there are readers who won't find these comparisons outlandish or absurd, but will see in my experiences faint glimpses of their own.

Central to my experience is one that I know many gamers share: when we are in times of crisis, we hide our sorely pained spirit and our ill health behind a facade. We create real-world avatars, while the avatars we play in video games become surrogates of our real feelings, our hurt and aching selves. In the outside world we cannot speak; we are strangers. In games we show our face. And when this outside figure, this automated body that we've constructed, begins to break down and we're running on low batteries, the only way to reach us is through games. The only way *we* can reach *ourselves* is through games.

~

Games assure us that we are real, because through them we seek to escape the real, the places of non-control. Video games do not replace life but remind us that life happens phenomenally in time.

The game *That Dragon, Cancer* works in abstraction, in non-meaning. Though it is based on the designers' (Ryan and Amy Green's) experience of seeing their infant son diagnosed with terminal cancer, the game tells this story in scattershot fragments, tousling memories, making the traumatic past playable.

In the beginning, we control a duck in a pond. A blocky, faceless child, Joel, kneels on the shore. We leave the water and play with Joel through different objects: swing sets, bathtubs, playpens. We aren't told about Joel's experiences; we play them: we levitate holding balloons and evading monstrous cancer cells, we drive a wagon through medications and blood tests, we wade through a flood of trauma as a doctor's office turns into a boundless ocean. Our play is not based on pleasure or pain but on dwelling and reflection, on longing. These moments feel less like playing a story and more like pausing in the white space of a poem. As the doctor sits to discuss Joel's tumour growth, his words become echoes, drifting across a poetic page.

~

> There isn't pleasure without trial, without going through consensual pain.
> —Mattie Brice, "Play and Be Real About It"

In 2020, with the release of *Open World Empire*, I also began development on my own video game, *Stamped: an anti-travel game*, an adaptation of my first novel about travelling and living in Asia. The development process was slow and measured, lasting nearly four years. Even so, it helped me grasp games as creative projects on every level, from the narrative and dialogue to the rules and choices to the backgrounds and sprites. As a poet and fiction author, I could not think of a comparable art that had so many levels of creative detail. The possibilities felt endless.

Strange as it might sound, some of the best advice I received on how to make games was through another interactive type of play: kink, or BDSM play. As the designer Anna Anthropy has argued, viewing games through the lens of kink helps explain their transformative experiences—how they get us to understand the rules we follow so we can make our own, how they teach us to negotiate with others and ourselves.[82] In kink, power, consent, and control are not seen as flaws or objectives but as contexts that must be understood if we are to establish ethical and caring habits.

Expanding on Anthropy's desire to find kinky ways of playing games, the designer Mattie Brice has pointed out that video games already provide an opportunity to practice kink's "experience arc."[83] First comes *negotiation*. Players must agree to consensual practices and to ways of provoking play while keeping aware of prior agreements, fetishes, and power dynamics. What do we want, and what do we seek from the games we play? If a game makes us angry, or spiteful, or sad, or bored, then perhaps this is not a defect of the game, but exactly what we are seeking. And if so, how does this feeling relate to something we may be going through outside the game?

Second, players establish a *scene*. They enter the game knowing what they are seeking and attempt to get there while knowing it may not work out. Playing a game is interactive in challenging ways: it is collaborative, unpredictable, and can result in messy outcomes. In games, I often find a troubling reversal of power—my power fantasy in *Far Cry 2* will shut down the second my gun jams up or I feel the vision-blurring effects of malaria. The point is not to see these moments as defects but as disclosures: Why was that power fantasy so important to me that disrupting it left me emotionally sore? Might that soreness have something to do with me—my nationality, my masculinity, my desires, my self-imagining?

The third and most transformative part of kink is not in gaining consent or in the practice of sex itself. It is in the moments, days, and years that follow the experience, the *aftercare*. This is the space we create for debriefing, for shared understanding, where meaning is made. What was pleasurable about playing this game, and why? Did we feel tortured by the scene? Did we feel dabbled in degradation? How might we return to ourselves as different and perhaps better-informed people?

~

The game *Hurt Me Plenty* explores the sequential nature of kink culture and what happens when you break boundaries. The game begins with the negotiation phase, shaking hands to decide the intensity, clothing, and safe word. Then the play: spanking while measuring the screams of "No, no!" and "Ow!" and "Stop!" with the presence or absence of the agreed-upon safe word. (Remember it?)

In the aftercare phase of *Hurt Me Plenty*, you can select "Caress tenderly to help unpack feelings (and listen to your partner ...)." The conversation begins with raw emotions—"I'm exhausted"—followed by memories—"You were rough!"—to new agreements or boundaries—"You're really dangerous and scary ... stay away from me."

As in many games, there are consequences to your decisions. If you abuse your partner, they refuse to meet with you again, and you must wait to replay the game ... for eighteen days. Not pretend days—real days. Even though the character is virtual, the hurt you caused and the trust you betrayed feels real because there is a real consequence. You feel spurned, embarrassed, and hurt yourself. So why did you do it?

Hurt Me Plenty is a stunning and sensational game. But it is not exceptional in how games impact us. As in kink, games give us a safe space to experiment, to learn about ourselves, and to transform. They feel safe, but our time in them can have real consequences. What we do, how we live, who we are, are all partially results of these consequences.

~

Though the impetus for this book emerged in 2020, portions of it are taken from passages written throughout my life during moments of gaming aftercare, when I wanted to reassemble the feelings and ideas that seemed to break apart as soon as I picked up the controller. These scattered musings came from the depths of my digital lives, from my fansites, blogs, and academic papers to unfinished projects like comics, e-zines, and notations, to conversations in chat rooms, direct messages, and emails.

In an aftercare moment in 2016, I wrote a blog post that gave this eccentric practice of writing about games a new name. I used a term akin to *machinima* (machine cinema), a genre of filmmaking that uses video game cameras and engines. I called it *machphrasis*: prose inspired by the machinations of video games, their universes, their puzzles, their social and physical systems of logic, their rules and boundaries, and their emotional resonances.[84] The term was a play on the word *ekphrasis*, meaning the art of representing something visual (like a painting, sculpture, or photograph) using only words. Ekphrasis is a technique most famously used in poems like John Keats's "Ode on a Grecian Urn," a poem about a work of art that is not really meant to interpret that art but to share feelings and ideas inspired from it—to allow that art to transform us in some way.

My musings about video games, and the stories and poems I wrote inspired by games, were also an ekphrastic art. Like ekphrastic poems, the task of machphrasis is not to showcase or analyze an art object but to capture the range of unique experiences it holds, experiences that broach new ways of seeing and appreciating the machinations of the outside world.

Machphrasis occurs in those moments when something in a game makes us lie back in wonder, trying to figure out what just happened. Most games don't actively encourage us to reflect on these moments but to bypass them, to see them as defects, or to move on quickly to the next adrenalin rush. But we actually dwell in these moments all the time. Sometimes we hit the pause button and wait for our breath to return. Sometimes we skip to a YouTuber, a reviewer, or a friend to see how someone else reacted to the same moment. And sometimes we write that moment down and share those thoughts online for readers to one day stumble upon, to feel less alone in our own worlds.

~

Games are constantly staging encounters with otherness, with other ways of imagining and relating to others. As the philosopher Édouard

Glissant wrote in *Poetics of Relation*, we are not merely opposed to others but entangled with them, co-constituting each other's sense of self through poetic, chaotic, and often playful encounters. In many machphrastic writings, games stage a poetics of interaction with others, dissolving what we thought we knew of them and ourselves.

In the game *Journey*, players rove about a desert landscape solving puzzles. While some puzzles can be solved alone, others need the help of a friend: a randomized player who could be from anywhere around the world, someone who can only communicate in gestures and chirps. In *Journey*, completing puzzles means discovering new ways to speak, to mime signals like "Up there!" merely with jumps. We learn that without language, we can convey meanings from the need to actively see, mimic, and listen.

The Tumblr blog *Journey Stories* is a collection of machphrastic writings about *Journey* in which gamers share ephemeral, communal experiences from the game. One author, who played the game while sick with fever, was abandoned by another player who "made me feel more crap" and whose desertion made "the pain in my chest worsen." Later on, the player met a new friend, and as the author began to exhaust herself from fever, the new player

> came running towards me, repeatedly chirping like he was panicking and so worried asking if I was alright. Looking at my character on the screen, I was in tears. I can't help but think my character is on the verge of dying. I even thought that maybe I really can't make it. He kept chirping and chirping at me like he's telling me not to lose hope, that I could do this, and we can finish this together.[85]

Our roles in games always extend to the others we are defined by: those we help, those we adventure with, those we battle, those who sell us their wares. *Journey*'s absence of words allows new experiences to emerge—some so unlikely and unpredictable that they require the reflection of aftercare, of picking up the pen.

~

Machphrasis isn't just a summary of a game's events. It gives space and time to ponder how the emotions we feel while playing translate into the world, sometimes breaking past the screen and into experiences of prejudice and assault.

In 2016, not long after the rise of the Black Lives Matter movement, games journalist Gita Jackson wrote a story about how the game *Dragon Age: Inquisition* laid bare her hatred for a certain kind of racist solidarity. Jackson noted how the Elvish nobleman Solas will compliment the player in the way a racist person might like a person of colour for being "one of the good ones":

> He likes an aspect of you, but he thinks you're disgusting at the core. Somehow, he tells you, he has gotten over his instinctual response of a deep and pointed loathing when he is around you. That version of Solas still thinks you are worthless—you're just a little less worthless than your countrymen, and he admires you for that.[86]

Jackson's interactions with Solas dredged up the type of white racism she experienced in the suburbs of Connecticut, being one of "the only non-white family on the street" who was frequently complimented for being an "Oreo." Solas's racist "compliments" loop back during times of anti-Black violence, particularly the police killings of Black men. When Jackson saw that "Philando Castile was murdered during a traffic stop," she recalled her interactions with Solas, who made her feel like "one of the good ones" despite his repugnance for her entire race.

In *Dragon Age: Inquisition*, Jackson played a Qunari, a monster seen as dumb, violent, and impetuous. In real life, as the police officer

Jeronimo Yanez hadn't yet been charged for killing an unarmed Black man (he was later acquitted), Jackson could see that the views of *Dragon Age: Inquisition* were part of the same social machinations of white supremacy leading to the unjust killing of Black men and women.

Unable to write a traditional review, Jackson admitted that her writing had led to something else: "It's so hard to explain how this [game] makes me feel, because it's so tightly wrapped up into the fabric of my life."[87]

~

> If you have spent your life staring at a thing, you can write about it with knowledge. You can write about it with love. But it is almost impossible to write about it with wonder.
> —Fane, *Divinity: Original Sin II*

Our writings on games connect us to each other, to the world around us, and to ourselves, exploring the emotions and memories we sometimes cannot approach otherwise. But because we are never entirely comfortable writing about games, because relating games to our lives is always cast as eccentric at best or shameful at worst, games still hold an otherworldly quality in our writing—spectral evocations of our real world, leaving us in wonder.

When I began the fantasy role-playing game *Divinity: Original Sin 11*, I chose to play as the mystic musician Lohse, drawn to her description as a magician whose mind has become "a playground for sprites and spirits and worse." Throughout the game, Lohse's journey involves talking to and overcoming an evil spirit lurking inside her psyche, threatening to warp her into something sinister. Near the end of the game, I as Lohse finally learn the identity of the spirit possessing me: an ancient archdemon named Adramahlihk.

I arrive in Arx to confront Adramahlihk, but my friend Malady—a half-demon you can trust—tells me that this demon is far more powerful than any I've faced before. He is too strong to challenge directly. But

I can weaken him from the inside; I can travel to his home plane—the inner psyche where his stolen souls are held captive—and "destroy it."

Malady takes me inside the demon's plane. Surrounded by Greco-style walls, pillars, and howling dog statues, Malady describes the realm as the demon's "private playground where no prying eyes can interfere with their ... fun." I find a candle made of black wax encasing a soul in its flickering warmth. As Lohse, I am spirit-sensitive and can sense the soul inside the flame. It belongs to a woman named Prudence, an innkeeper who made a sorry deal with the demon. Now, she is trapped inside him in perpetuity, her essence ceaselessly siphoned for his dark power.

I am given the choice of snuffing the candle out or leaving it be and fighting the demon at full strength. But eviscerating the candle won't just kill Prudence. Unlike other souls, Prudence will be denied an afterlife. She will never reach another plane of existence. She will simply cease to be.

The candle burns in a raw wince of light. I pinch the wick, and the flame vanishes in a gasp of smoke.

But I'm not done. Malady takes me farther into the plane. I come to another stone island, this one with two candles, both yearning for my ear. One is a humble father who is willing to sacrifice himself to weaken the demon. The other is a murderer filled with fury who begs me not to send him into the darkness, the nothingness of death.

I snuff them both out, two souls lost to the ether.

But we're still not finished. Malady takes me farther, not to a room or an island, but to a cliff. Before my eyes, a sea of candles twinkles like a star-filled sky—an endless expanse of spirits whose only purpose is to suffer. Lohse's knees weaken. "All these people ... all these people ... all these precious people ... they're all like me. Every last one of them."

I feel a kinship with these souls. The darkness possessing me is the same that possessed them. The only difference is that I have the power to overcome it. But that doesn't make me feel their pain any less. In that moment of moral choice, I realize how easy it would be to join them, "to step off the edge and float away. There's nothing to me anymore. Nothing at all."

The candles glimmer. I tell Malady to summon a storm. Rain douses every last flame. The game points me to the next objective, but I cannot move. I have to sit and dwell with the silence. After a moment, I feel a peace in the nothingness. The poetic ending we all must face.

Years later, I still think of this moment in *Divinity* whenever I am faced with a sea of statistics. A thousand people are a thousand candles, a thousand souls, lost to wars, massacres, guns, disease, famine, the toxicities of modern life. I think of all the people killed by men with unrestrained power, whose deaths only add up and up: the darker-skinned teenager picking a candy bar from his pocket, the family who must cross a border or a sea to seek a better life, the people bombed and bombed and bombed only because they were born within an occupied nation. Like Lohse, I feel the weight of their loss, of "All these people ... all these people." I have no words, no reasoning, except that some of us have power, and they did not.

So too do I think of the souls within my own realm. I've felt like I died with them and am merely floating here, with their candles, the flames of all whom I mourn. I start to think of myself not as an individual, but as *they*. I cannot trap them, because their memory will always pour over, their flames will always spread. I envision their strength, their voices, their hearts, their tenderness, as always part of me. Together, we make a wordless wish for time.

~

> Life is no "brief candle" for me. It is a sort of splendid torch which I have got hold of for the moment, and I want to make it burn as brightly as possible before handing it on to future generations.
> —George Bernard Shaw

I end this book offering strange and off-putting ideas about games, kink, aftercare, and machphrasis, because writing about how games have impacted me deeply and personally feels so strange and off-putting. I have often felt embarrassed to write about the loss of my grandmother, my uncle, my cousin, my first girlfriend, my mentor, and my wife through the video games I played while witnessing and processing their deaths. Sometimes I've felt the possible reactions of friends and family who might curse me for dishonouring their memories. In those times, I watched gamers on Twitch and YouTube speak about their struggles while streaming games to an audience of single digits. When I could find no one, I wrote with only a single guiding light: that I had these feelings, experienced these emotions, and that throughout every challenge, games have changed me in ways I could not, would not share with anyone, until now.

This is machphrasis: an art of writing that reveals our memories not in dull-toned sepias but in the blue blurs of a passing sky, the fog of a forsaken land, the glittery bursts of a well-placed headshot, all expressed through the pleasures, pains, and longings of play. Machphrasis is an art that manifests not from retreats or sanctuaries but from the frenetic intimacy of chat room role play, gaming forums, and public streams, and from the seemingly endless time where we perform as—and become—our mains. It is an art that strays from the smoothed-out paths before us, that belies the systems we are born into, that expresses the adventures of our floating isles and dwells within the dark dungeons where our fantasies meet their end.

I hope this book changes the ways we think about games and the ways we write about them. But more so, I hope it gives you, the reader, permission to be as weird, personal, off-putting, and fantastical as you can be in seeing your own life through games. I hope someday we can talk about games alongside bigotry, religion, suicide, kink, and death without having to overcome the wrinkled brows of others and our own inner demons whispering our shames. I have spent my life writing about games, not as a hobby but as a necessity. It took many years before I felt comfortable sharing these writings with friends, colleagues, and strangers. To do so, I had to publish an academic book about games and teach a decade's worth of college classes about games—basically, I had to become a PhD-certified *games expert*. I hope that the reader of this book understands they need no such credentials—heck, they don't need to identify as a gamer or even play games themselves. To deny our relationship to games is to deny ourselves a certain poetry, a way of understanding the restless yet vibrant parts of ourselves that only emerge in moonlight: ready to go, and eager to play.

Acknowledgments

The ideas in this book do not stand on the shoulders of giants. *Of Floating Isles* builds on the work of thousands of lesser-known, rarely acknowledged, and often-ignored scholars, writers, journalists, game makers, and players. These mere mortals make a community of distinct voices, a chorus whose melodies rarely harmonize but can create sensational sonic force. Their works are listed in the bibliography that follows. I thank several friends and mentors who have helped guide my way: Tara Fickle, Lisa Nakamura, Amanda Phillips, Edmond Chang, Melos Han-Tani and Marina Kittaka, Chris Kealoha Miller, Robert Yang, Minh Le, Naomi Clark, and the *Game Studies Study Buddies* podcast.

Portions of this book were revised from previously published writings. Many of the sections on the *Far Cry* series, *Final Fantasy VII*, and *Counter-Strike* were revised from my book *Open World Empire: Race, Erotics, and the Global Rise of Video Games*. Many of my thoughts on race and Asian America came from my edited collection with Tara Fickle, *Made in Asia/America: Why Video Games Were Never (Really) About Us*. Some sections on my childhood and adolescence were revised from my prose-poetry book *Nimrods: a fake-punk self-hurt anti-memoir*. Some of the sections on chat room role-playing and the art of machphrasis came from writings for *decomp* journal, ANMLY, and my blog *Critical Plunge*.

I wrote *Of Floating Isles* intensely from 2021 to 2024 on the suggestion of my agent, Laura Cameron, who cherry-picked the project out of a short list of book ideas I had been tinkering with for years. Thank you to Laura and to my editors, to Brian Lam and everyone at Arsenal Pulp Press, and to my supporters during this time: Y-Dang Troeung and the Troeung family, Kai Basilio Troeung, Cameron Patterson, Chanel Guillermo, Dion Guillermo Glenn, Justin Alger, Madeleine Thien, Mary Tsoi, and my friends and colleagues in Vancouver: Elif Sarı, Danielle Wong, David Chariandy, Kimberly Bain, Christine Kim, Jasbir Puar, Crystal Webster, JP Catungal, and many others. Thank you to everyone who showed me new sides of games throughout my life: Matt, Justin, and Nolan in Portland; Josh, Mikee, and Kristy in Las Vegas; Chris in Seattle; Jesús; Sunshine and Winter in Nanjing; and the many students in my games courses in Hong Kong and Vancouver. Thanks to those who gave companionship and support while I revised this work in Asia: Ah-mee Kim, Andy Wang, Collier Nogues, Jia Tan, Alvy Wong, and Doretta Lau. Thank you to Academia Sinica in Taipei and the Chinese University of Hong Kong for helping host my stays.

Though I pursued this book over a five-year period, *Of Floating Isles* was written over a lifetime of ecstatic love, remorseful love, and the love of grief and loss. I thank everyone whose name appears in this book. I hope my depictions showcase the love I felt in writing about us, and that—when time demands it—they can reawaken the roles, communities, and adventures we once imagined together.

Notes

1. Jacques Rancière, *The Ignorant Schoolmaster: Five Lessons in Intellectual Emancipation*, trans. Kristin Ross (Fayard, 1987), 84.
2. Tristan Donovan, *Replay: The History of Video Games* (Yellow Ant, 2010), 8–9.
3. Michiel Buijsman, "The Global Games Market Will Generate $187.7 Billion in 2024," Newzoo, August 13, 2024. https://newzoo.com/resources/blog/global-games-market-revenue-estimates-and-forecasts-in-2024.
4. "2023 Essential Facts About the U.S. Video Game Industry," Entertainment Software Association, accessed February 10, 2025, https://www.theesa.com/resources/essential-facts-about-the-us-video-game-industry/2023-2/.
5. Anita Sarkeesian and Katherine Cross, "Your Humanity Is in Another Castle: Terror Dreams and the Harassment of Women," *The State of Play: Creators and Critics on Video Game Culture*, eds. Daniel Goldberg and Linus Larsson (Seven Stories Press, 2015), 103–26.
6. Colin Milburn, *Mondo Nano: Fun and Games in the World of Digital Matter* (Duke University Press, 2015), xviii.
7. Milburn, *Mondo Nano*, xviii.
8. "2024 Essential Facts About the U.S. Video Game Industry," Entertainment Software Association, accessed May 2, 2025, https://www.theesa.com/resources/essential-facts-about-the-us-video-game-industry/2024-data/.
9. Mary Ann Buckles, "Interactive Fiction: The Computer Story Game *Adventure*," (PhD thesis, University of California San Diego, 1985), 178.
10. Tom Bissell, *Extra Lives: Why Video Games Matter* (Vintage, 2011), 27.
11. Melanie Remi Yergeau, *Authoring Autism: On Rhetoric and Neurological Queerness* (Duke University Press, 2018), 1.
12. Yergeau, *Authoring Autism*, 193.
13. Yergeau, *Authoring Autism*, 182.

14 Rudyard Kipling, "The White Man's Burden: The United States & The Philippine Islands" (1899), *Rudyard Kipling's Verse: Definitive Edition* (Doubleday, 1929).

15 Michael T. Saler, *As If: Modern Enchantment and the Literary Prehistory of Virtual Reality* (Oxford University Press, 2012), 189.

16 Julian Dibbell, *My Tiny Life: Crime and Passion in a Virtual World* (Holt Paperbacks, 1998); Lisa Nakamura, "Race in/for Cyberspace: Identity Tourism and Racial Passing on the Internet," *Works and Days* 13, no. 1–2 (1995): 181–193.

17 Colin Milburn, *Respawn: Gamers, Hackers, and Technogenic Life* (Duke University Press, 2018), 200.

18 Milburn, *Respawn*, 207.

19 Judith Butler, *Gender Trouble: Feminism and the Subversion of Identity* (Routledge, 2002), 187.

20 Albert Chan, "Headshot! An In-Depth Analysis of the Success of *Counter-Strike* as a Team-Oriented First Person Shooter and Its Effects on Video Game Culture Around the World," Stanford University, accessed March 30, 2017, http://web.stanford.edu/group/htgg/cgi-bin/drupal/sites/default/files2/achan_2002_1.pdf.

21 Henry Jenkins, *Fans, Bloggers, and Gamers: Exploring Participatory Culture* (New York University Press, 2006), 208; Christopher B. Patterson, *Open World Empire: Race, Erotics, and the Global Rise of Video Games* (New York University Press, 2020), 104, 200.

22 Natasha Dow Schüll, *Addiction by Design: Machine Gambling in Las Vegas* (Princeton University Press, 2012), 206.

23 Schüll, *Addiction by Design*, 203.

24 Kawika Guillermo, "Race, Terror and *Counter-Strike*: Interview with Minh Le (Gooseman), Co-Creator of *Counter-Strike*," Medium, April 14, 2017, https://medium.com/anomalyblog/race-terror-and-counter-strike-interview-with-minh-le-gooseman-co-creator-of-counter-strike-bfee27b28fab.

25 Guillermo, "Race, Terror and *Counter-Strike*"; Minh Le, "I Am Minh Le, aka. Gooseman, Co-Creator of the Original *Counter-Strike* and Now *Tactical Intervention*, AMA!" Reddit, May 2, 2013, https://www.reddit.com/r/IAmA/comments/1dkeht/iam_minh_le_aka_gooseman_cocreator_of_the/.

26 Chan, "Headshot!"

27 Luke Winkie, "We Caught Up with FPS Doug, Gaming Culture's Original Meme," *The Daily Dot*, May 27, 2021, https://www.dailydot.com/unclick/catching-up-with-fps-doug/.

28 Geoff Lapaire and Jarett Cale, "*Pure Pwnage*—FPS Doug cs:s," KylePP, July 6, 2006, video, 3:42, www.youtube.com/watch?v=a9qXbgrx9rg.

29 Patterson, *Open World Empire*, 104.

30 Zack Zwiezen, "Here Are the Best-Selling Games Every Year for the Past Two Decades," *Kotaku*, October 25, 2024, https://kotaku.com/best-selling-games-ever-20-years-madden-call-of-duty-1851680848.

31 Jeremy Parish, *A History of Video Games*, read by the author (The Great Courses, 2020), Audible, 4 hr., 4 min.

32 Timothy Blake Donohoo and Zack Millsap, "Nintendo's Forgotten History with the Japanese Mafia," CBR, April 4, 2024, https://www.cbr.com/nintendo-japanese-yakuza-history.

33 Sam Pettus, *Service Games: The Rise and Fall of SEGA*, Enhanced Edition (Pub. by the author, 2013), 9.

34 Andrew Park, "*GameSpot*'s All-Time Greatest Game Hero Draws to a Close. And the Winner Is...," *GameSpot*, October 15, 2009, https://www.gamespot.com/articles/gamespots-all-time-greatest-game-hero-draws-to-a-close-and-the-winner-is/1100-6233560/.

35 Alexander Smith, "One, Two, Three, Four I Declare a Space War," *They Create Worlds*, February 2, 2017, https://videogamehistorian.wordpress.com/2014/08/07/one-two-three-four-i-declare-a-space-war/.

36 Steve Bloom, *Video Invaders* (Arco Publishing, 1982), 114.

37 Bloom, *Video Invaders*, 118.

38 Rhacel Salazar Parreñas, "'White Trash' Meets the 'Little Brown Monkeys': The Taxi Dance Hall as a Site of Interracial and Gender Alliances Between White Working Class Women and Filipino Immigrant Men in the 1920s and 30s," *Amerasia Journal* 24, no. 2 (1998): 115–134.

39 "Sakaguchi Discusses the Development of *Final Fantasy*," MCV/*Develop*, December 13, 2007, https://mcvuk.com/development-news/sakaguchi-discusses-the-development-of-final-fantasy/.

40 Maureen Corrigan, "Chang-Rae Lee Stretches for Dystopic Drama, but Doesn't Quite Reach," National Public Radio, January 14, 2014, https://www.npr.org/2014/01/14/262386113/chang-rae-lee-stretches-for-dystopic-drama-but-doesnt-quite-reach.

41 VoodooExtreme, "Development Team Chat," Planet Elder Scrolls, July 19, 2000, archived on October 19, 2007, at https://web.archive.org/web/20071019071012/http://planetelderscrolls.gamespy.com/View.php?view=Articles.Detail&id=27.

42   Jun-Sok Huhh, "The 'Bang' Where Korean Online Gaming Began: The Culture and Business of the PC Bang in Korea," in *Gaming Cultures and Place in Asia-Pacific*, eds. Larissa Hjorth and Dean Chan (Routledge, 2009), 103.

43   Roland Barthes, *The Pleasure of the Text* (Hill and Wang, 1975), 15.

44   Roland Barthes, *Empire of Signs* (Hill and Wang, 1982), 3.

45   Dulcey Simpkins, "Rethinking the Sex Industry: Thailand's Sex Workers, the State, and Changing Cultures of Consumption," *Michigan Feminist Studies* 12 (1997–98), http://hdl.handle.net/2027/spo.ark5583.0012.005.

46   Barthes, *Pleasure of the Text*, 14.

47   Bissell, *Extra Lives*, 69.

48   Bissell, *Extra Lives*, 69.

49   Natalia Duong, "Rhizophora: Queering Chemical Kinship in the Agent Orange Diaspora," in *Crip Genealogies*, ed. Mel Y. Chen et al. (Duke University Press, 2023), 148.

50   John Walker, "*Far Cry 3*'s Jeffrey Yohalem on Racism, Torture and Satire," *Rock Paper Shotgun*, December 19, 2012, https://www.rockpapershotgun.com/far-cry-3s-jeffrey-yohalem-on-racism-torture-and-satire.

51   Jessica Clement, "Leading Gaming Markets Worldwide 2023, by Gaming Revenue," Statista, July 11, 2024, https://www.statista.com/forecasts/308454/gaming-revenue-countries.

52   Mary Pilon, "The Secret History of Monopoly: The Capitalist Board Game's Leftwing Origins," *The Guardian*, April 11, 2015, https://www.theguardian.com/lifeandstyle/2015/apr/11/secret-history-monopoly-capitalist-game-leftwing-origins.

53   Edward W. Said, *Orientalism* (Vintage, 1979), 48.

54   Lisa Nakamura, "Indigenous Circuits: Navajo Women and the Racialization of Early Electronic Manufacture," *American Quarterly* 66, no. 4 (2014): 919–41.

55   Fiona Tam, "Foxconn Factories Are Labour Camps: Report," *South China Morning Post*, October 11, 2010, https://www.scmp.com/article/727143/foxconn-factories-are-labour-camps-report; Jenny Chan, Ngai Pun, and Mark Selden, "The Politics of Global Production: Apple, Foxconn and China's New Working Class," *New Technology, Work and Employment* 28, no. 2 (2013): 100–15.

56   Jini Maxwell, "Videogames Have a Conflict Mineral Problem," *GamesHub*, November 24, 2020, https://www.gameshub.com/news/features/videogames-have-a-conflict-mineral-problem-261507-2297/.

57 "Final Report of the Panel of Experts on the Illegal Exploitation of Natural Resources and Other Forms of Wealth of DR Congo (S/2003/1027)," ReliefWeb, October 23, 2003, https://reliefweb.int/report/democratic-republic-congo/final-report-panel-experts-illegal-exploitation-natural-resources.

58 Maxwell, "Videogames Have a Conflict Mineral Problem."

59 Kawika Guillermo, "Clint Hocking's Call to Make Games Well," *Critical Plunge*, February 3, 2016, https://critplunge.wordpress.com/2016/02/03/clint-hockings-call-to-make-games-well/.

60 Nick Dyer-Witheford and Greig de Peuter, *Games of Empire: Global Capitalism and Video Games* (University of Minnesota Press, 2009), 8.

61 Bloom, *Video Invaders*, 114.

62 Bloom, *Video Invaders*, xix.

63 Elijah Lee, "Muriel Tramis | A First Lady of Gaming | The First Black Female Game Designer," *The Icon*, September 25, 2020, https://www.theicon.com/a-first-lady-of-gaming/.

64 Edward W. Said, *Representations of the Intellectual* (Vintage, 1996), 53.

65 David Neiwert, *Alt-America: The Rise of the Radical Right in the Age of Trump* (Verso Books, 2017), 215.

66 Patterson, *Open World Empire*, 186.

67 Samantha Allen and Nico Lang, "11 Ways 2014 Was the Biggest Year in Transgender History," *Rolling Stone*, December 23, 2014, https://www.rollingstone.com/politics/politics-news/11-ways-2014-was-the-biggest-year-in-transgender-history-188238/.

68 micha cárdenas, "Becoming Dragon: A Transversal Technology Study," *CTheory* (2010): 4–29, https://journals.uvic.ca/index.php/ctheory/article/view/14680/5550.

69 Anna Anthropy, "On *Dys4ia*'s Return," *Dys4ia*, October 13, 2023, https://w.itch.io/dys4ia/devlog/620323/on-dys4ias-return; Bo Ruberg and Mattie Brice, "Radical Play Through Vulnerability," in *The Queer Games Avant-Garde: How LGBTQ Game Makers Are Reimagining the Medium of Video Games*, ed. Bo Ruberg (Duke University Press, 2020), 135; merritt k, "Interview—Merritt Kopas, Part 1: Feminist Porn, Games, & Capital," *First Person Scholar*, June 25, 2014, https://www.firstpersonscholar.com/interview-merritt-kopas/.

70 cárdenas, "Becoming Dragon."

71 Susan Sontag, *Against Interpretation and Other Essays* (Noonday Press, 1966), 277.

72 Sontag, *Against Interpretation*, 280.

73 Sontag, *Against Interpretation*, 280.

74 Cecilia D'Anastasio, "Zarya from *Overwatch* Has Become a Gay Icon, Ironically," *Kotaku*, June 29, 2016, https://kotaku.com/zarya-from-overwatch-has-become-a-gay-icon-ironically-1782833947.

75 Nicole Carpenter, "Protestors Are Trying to Get *Overwatch* Banned in China, Using Memes of Popular Hero Mei," *Polygon*, October 9, 2019, https://www.polygon.com/2019/10/9/20906320/overwatch-mei-blizzard-hong-kong-protest-banned-memes.

76 Legacy Russell, *Glitch Feminism: A Manifesto* (Verso, 2020), 41.

77 Russell, *Glitch Feminism*, 41.

78 Scott Deveau, "Yoga Mogul Has Critics in a Knot," *The Tyee*, February 17, 2005, https://thetyee.ca/News/2005/02/17/LuluCritics/.

79 See Jane McGonigal, *Reality Is Broken: Why Games Make Us Better and How They Can Change the World* (Penguin, 2011); Jamie Madigan, *Getting Gamers: The Psychology of Video Games and Their Impact on the People Who Play Them* (Rowman & Littlefield, 2015); Jane McGonigal, *SuperBetter: The Power of Living Gamefully* (Penguin, 2016); and Anthony M. Bean, *Working with Video Gamers and Games in Therapy: A Clinician's Guide* (Routledge, 2018).

80 Susan Sontag, *Illness as Metaphor* (Farrar, Straus and Giroux, 1978), 3.

81 Rainier Maria Rilke, *The Unknown Rilke: Expanded Edition*, trans. Franz Wright (Oberlin College Press, 1983), 43.

82 Anna Anthropy, "How to Make Games About Being a Dominatrix," Auntie Pixelantie, May 7, 2013, http://www.auntiepixelante.com/?p=2182 (site discontinued).

83 Mattie Brice, "Play and Be Real About It: What Games Could Learn from Kink," in *Queer Game Studies*, eds. Bo Ruberg and Adrienne Shaw (University of Minnesota Press, 2014), 80.

84 Kawika Guillermo, "The Art of Machphrasis: Stories Inspired by Video Games," Medium, October 14, 2016, https://medium.com/anomalyblog/the-art-of-machphrasis-stories-inspired-by-video-games-11261e9087d9.

85 *Journey Stories*, May 2012, https://www.tumblr.com/journeystories.

86 Gita Jackson, "Guest Column: On Monsters, Role Playing, and Blackness," *Giant Bomb*, August 15, 2016, https://www.giantbomb.com/articles/guest-column-on-monsters-role-playing-and-blacknes/1100-5479/.

87 Jackson, "Guest Column."

Bibliography

Activision. *Call of Duty 4: Modern Warfare*. Released November 5, 2007. Windows.

Allen, Samantha, and Nico Lang. "11 Ways 2014 Was the Biggest Year in Transgender History." *Rolling Stone*, December 23, 2014. https://www.rollingstone.com/politics/politics-news/11-ways-2014-was-the-biggest-year-in-transgender-history-188238/.

Anthropy, Anna. "How to Make Games About Being a Dominatrix." Auntie Pixelantie, May 7, 2013. http://www.auntiepixelante.com/?p=2182 (site discontinued).

Anthropy, Anna. "On *Dys4ia*'s Return." *Dys4ia*, October 13, 2023. https://w.itch.io/dys4ia/devlog/620323/on-dys4ias-return.

Anthropy, Anna. *Rise of the Videogame Zinesters: How Freaks, Normals, Amateurs, Artists, Dreamers, Drop-Outs, Queers, Housewives, and People Like You Are Taking Back an Art Form*. Seven Stories Press, 2012.

Barthes, Roland. *Empire of Signs*. Hill and Wang, 1982.

Barthes, Roland. *The Pleasure of the Text*. Hill and Wang, 1975.

Bataille, Georges. *Erotism: Death and Sensuality*. City Lights Publishers, 1986.

Bean, Anthony M. *Working with Video Gamers and Games in Therapy: A Clinician's Guide*. Routledge, 2018.

Bethesda Softworks. *The Elder Scrolls III: Morrowind*. Released May 2, 2002. Windows.

Bissell, Tom. *Extra Lives: Why Video Games Matter*. Vintage, 2011.

Blizzard Entertainment. *Overwatch*. Released May 24, 2016. Windows.

Bloom, Steve. *Video Invaders*. Arco Publishing, 1982.

Bogost, Ian. *Persuasive Games: The Expressive Power of Videogames*. MIT Press, 2007.

Brice, Mattie. "Play and Be Real About It: What Games Could Learn from Kink." In *Queer Game Studies*, edited by Bo Ruberg and Adrienne Shaw. University of Minnesota Press, 2014.

Buckles, Mary Ann. "Interactive Fiction: The Computer Story Game *Adventure.*" PhD thesis, University of California San Diego, 1985.

Buijsman, Michiel. "The Global Games Market Will Generate $187.7 Billion in 2024." Newzoo, August 13, 2024. https://newzoo.com/resources/blog/global-games-market-revenue-estimates-and-forecasts-in-2024.

Butler, Judith. *Gender Trouble: Feminism and the Subversion of Identity.* Routledge, 2002.

Butterworth-Parr, Francis. "Machphrasis: Towards a Poetics of Video Games in Contemporary Literary Culture." *Games and Culture* 19, no. 3 (2024): 373–390.

Cameron, Barbara. "'Gee, You Don't Seem Like an Indian from the Reservation.'" In *This Bridge Called My Back: Writings by Radical Women of Color,* edited by Cherríe L. Moraga and Gloria E. Anzaldúa. Kitchen Table: Women of Color Press, 1983.

Capcom. *Street Fighter II: The World Warrior.* Released March 7, 1991. Arcade.

cárdenas, micha. "Becoming Dragon: A Transversal Technology Study." *CTheory* (2010): 4–29. https://journals.uvic.ca/index.php/ctheory/article/view/14680/5550.

Carpenter, Nicole. "Protestors Are Trying to Get *Overwatch* Banned in China, Using Memes of Popular Hero Mei." *Polygon,* October 9, 2019. https://www.polygon.com/2019/10/9/20906320/overwatch-mei-blizzard-hong-kong-protest-banned-memes.

Chan, Albert. "Headshot! An In-Depth Analysis of the Success of *Counter-Strike* as a Team-Oriented First Person Shooter and Its Effects on Video Game Culture Around the World." Stanford University, accessed March 30, 2017. http://web.stanford.edu/group/htgg/cgi-bin/drupal/sites/default/files2/achan_2002_1.pdf.

Chan, Jenny, Ngai Pun, and Mark Selden. "The Politics of Global Production: Apple, Foxconn and China's New Working Class." *New Technology, Work and Employment* 28, no. 2 (2013): 100–15.

Clare, Eli. *Exile and Pride: Disability, Queerness, and Liberation.* South End Press, 1999.

Clement, Jessica. "Leading Gaming Markets Worldwide 2023, by Gaming Revenue." Statista, July 11, 2024. https://www.statista.com/forecasts/308454/gaming-revenue-countries.

Corrigan, Maureen. "Chang-Rae Lee Stretches for Dystopic Drama, but Doesn't Quite Reach." National Public Radio, January 14, 2014. https://www.npr.org/2014/01/14/262386113/chang-rae-lee-stretches-for-dystopic-drama-but-doesnt-quite-reach.

Crenshaw, Kimberlé, Saidiya Hartman, and N.K. Jemisin. "Under the Blacklight—Storytelling While Black & Female: Conjuring Beautiful Experiments in Past & Future Worlds." African American Policy Forum, August 5, 2020. YouTube, 1:33:00. https://www.youtube.com/live/xGS5aP5Vi7g?si=H31LKOsWPGYe7MKX.

D'Anastasio, Cecilia. "Zarya from Overwatch Has Become a Gay Icon, Ironically." *Kotaku*, June 29, 2016. https://kotaku.com/zarya-from-overwatch-has-become-a-gay-icon-ironically-1782833947.

Danico, Mary Yu, and Linda Trinh Vo. "'No Lattes Here': Asian American Youth and the Cyber Café Obsession." In *Asian American Youth: Culture, Identity, and Ethnicity*, edited by Jennifer Lee and Min Zhou. Routledge, 2004.

Deep Silver. *Dead Island*. Released September 6, 2011. Windows.

Deveau, Scott. "Yoga Mogul Has Critics in a Knot." *The Tyee*, February 17, 2005. https://thetyee.ca/News/2005/02/17/LuluCritics/.

Dibbell, Julian. *My Tiny Life: Crime and Passion in a Virtual World*. Holt Paperbacks, 1998.

Donohoo, Timothy Blake, and Zack Millsap. "Nintendo's Forgotten History with the Japanese Mafia." CBR, April 4, 2024, https://www.cbr.com/nintendo-japanese-yakuza-history.

Donovan, Tristan. *Replay: The History of Video Games*. Yellow Ant, 2010.

Double Fine Productions. *Massive Chalice*. Released June 1, 2015. Windows.

Duong, Natalia. "Rhizophora: Queering Chemical Kinship in the Agent Orange Diaspora." In *Crip Genealogies*, edited by Mel Y. Chen, Alison Kafer, Eunjung Kim, and Julie Avril Minich. Duke University Press, 2023.

Dyer-Witheford, Nick, and Greig de Peuter. *Games of Empire: Global Capitalism and Video Games*. Minneapolis: University of Minnesota Press, 2009.

Edney, Andrew. "Talking About *Far Cry Four* with Creative Director Alex Hutchinson." *Huffington Post* UK, October 16, 2014, https://www.huffingtonpost.co.uk/andrew-edney/talking-about-far-cry-4-w_b_5987562.html.

Electronic Arts. *Crysis*. Released November 13, 2007. Windows.

Electronic Arts. *Dragon Age: Inquisition*. Released November 18, 2014. Windows.

Electronic Arts. *Mass Effect 2*. Released January 26, 2010. Windows.

Electronic Arts. *Mass Effect 3*. Released March 6, 2012. Windows.

Fickle, Tara. *The Race Card: From Gaming Technologies to Model Minorities*. New York University Press, 2019.

"Final Report of the Panel of Experts on the Illegal Exploitation of Natural Resources and Other Forms of Wealth of DR Congo (s/2003/1027)." ReliefWeb, October 23, 2003. https://reliefweb.int/report/democratic-republic-congo/final-report-panel-experts-illegal-exploitation-natural-resources.

Gallagher, Marina Janette. "Pastoral and Anti-Pastoral Music and Landscapes in *Final Fantasy X, XII, XIII,* and *XV.*" PhD dissertation, University of British Columbia, 2023.

Gallagher, Rob. "From Camp to Kitsch: A Queer Eye on Console Fandom." G|A|M|E *Games as Art, Media, Entertainment* 1, no. 3 (2014): 39–50.

Glissant, Édouard. *Poetics of Relation.* Translated by Betsy Wing. University of Michigan Press, 1997.

Glück, Louise. *Ararat.* The Ecco Press, 1990.

Gramsci, Antonio. *Letters from Prison, Volume 1.* Columbia University Press, 1994.

Guillermo, Kawika. "The Art of Machphrasis: Stories Inspired by Video Games." Medium, October 14, 2016. https://medium.com/anomalyblog/the-art-of-machphrasis-stories-inspired-by-video-games-11261e9087d9.

Guillermo, Kawika. "Clint Hocking's Call to Make Games Well." *Critical Plunge,* February 3, 2016. https://critplunge.wordpress.com/2016/02/03/clint-hockings-call-to-make-games-well/.

Guillermo, Kawika. *Nimrods: a fake-punk self-hurt anti-memoir.* Duke University Press, 2023.

Guillermo, Kawika. "Race, Terror and *Counter-Strike*: Interview with Minh Le (Gooseman), Co-Creator of *Counter-Strike.*" Medium, April 14, 2017. https://medium.com/anomalyblog/race-terror-and-counter-strike-interview-with-minh-le-gooseman-co-creator-of-counter-strike-bfee27b28fab.

Guillermo, Kawika. *Stamped: an anti-travel novel.* Westphalia Press, 2018.

Harvey, Auriea, and Michaël Samyn. "Realtime Art Manifesto." Mediaterra Festival of Art and Technology. Athens, Greece, 2006. https://tale-of-tales.com/tales/RAM.html.

Hayot, Eric. "Video Games & the Novel." *Daedalus* 150, no. 1 (2021): 178–187.

hooks, bell. *The Will to Change: Men, Masculinity, and Love.* Washington Square Press, 2004.

Huhh, Jun-Sok. "The 'Bang' Where Korean Online Gaming Began: The Culture and Business of the PC Bang in Korea." In *Gaming Cultures and Place in Asia-Pacific,* edited by Larissa Hjorth and Dean Chan. Routledge, 2009.

Jackson, Gita. "Guest Column: On Monsters, Role Playing, and Blackness." *Giant Bomb*, August 15, 2016. https://www.giantbomb.com/articles/guest-column-on-monsters-role-playing-and-blacknes/1100-5479/.

Jenkins, Henry. *Fans, Bloggers, and Gamers: Exploring Participatory Culture*. New York University Press, 2006.

Johnston, David. "The Making of Dust: Architecture and the Art of Level Design." In *The State of Play: Creators and Critics on Video Game Culture*, edited by Daniel Goldberg and Linus Larsson. Seven Stories Press, 2015.

Jordan, June. *On Call: Political Essays*. South End Press, 1985.

Joudah, Fady. "[…]." Poets.org, April 2, 2024. https://poets.org/node/719306.

Journey Stories, May 2012. https://www.tumblr.com/journeystories.

k, merritt. "Interview—Merritt Kopas, Part 1: Feminist Porn, Games, & Capital." *First Person Scholar*, June 25, 2014. https://www.firstpersonscholar.com/interview-merritt-kopas/.

Kang, Han. *Human Acts*. Translated by Deborah Smith. Hogarth, 2017.

Kent, Steven L. *The Ultimate History of Video Games, Volume 1: From Pong to Pokémon and Beyond … The Story Behind the Craze That Touched Our Lives and Changed the World*. Crown, 2010.

Kipling, Rudyard. *Rudyard Kipling's Verse: Definitive Edition*. Doubleday, 1929.

Lapaire, Geoff, and Jarett Cale. "*Pure Pwnage*—FPS Doug CS:S." KylePP, July 6, 2006. YouTube, 3:42. https://www.youtube.com/watch?v=a9qXbgrx9rg.

Larian Studios. *Divinity: Original Sin II*. Released September 14, 2017. Windows.

Le, Minh. "I Am Minh Le, aka. Gooseman, Co-Creator of the Original *Counter-Strike* and Now *Tactical Intervention*, AMA!" Reddit, May 2, 2013. https://www.reddit.com/r/IAmA/comments/1dkeht/iam_minh_le_aka_gooseman_cocreator_of_the/.

Lee, Elijah. "Muriel Tramis | A First Lady of Gaming | The First Black Female Game Designer." *The Icon*, September 25, 2020. https://www.theicon.com/a-first-lady-of-gaming/.

Maddy Makes Games. *Celeste*. Released January 25, 2018. Windows.

Madigan, Jamie. *Getting Gamers: The Psychology of Video Games and Their Impact on the People Who Play Them*. Rowman & Littlefield, 2015.

Malkowski, Jennifer, and TreaAndrea M. Russworm. *Gaming Representation: Race, Gender, and Sexuality in Video Games*. Indiana University Press, 2017.

Martin, Randy. *Critical Moves: Dance Studies in Theory and Politics.* Duke University Press, 1998.

Maxis. *The Sims.* Released February 4, 2000. Windows.

Maxwell, Jini. "Videogames Have a Conflict Mineral Problem." *GamesHub,* November 24, 2020. https://www.gameshub.com/news/features/videogames-have-a-conflict-mineral-problem-261507-2297/.

McGonigal, Jane. *Reality Is Broken: Why Games Make Us Better and How They Can Change the World.* Penguin, 2011.

McGonigal, Jane. *SuperBetter: The Power of Living Gamefully.* Penguin, 2016.

Microsoft Game Studios. *Mass Effect.* Released November 20, 2007. Windows.

Midway Games. *Mortal Kombat.* Released October 1992. Arcade.

Milburn, Colin. *Mondo Nano: Fun and Games in the World of Digital Matter.* Duke University Press, 2015.

Milburn, Colin. *Respawn: Gamers, Hackers, and Technogenic Life.* Duke University Press, 2018.

Molleindustria. *Phone Story.* Released September 9, 2011. iOS (iPhone).

Nakamura, Lisa. "Indigenous Circuits: Navajo Women and the Racialization of Early Electronic Manufacture." *American Quarterly* 66, no. 4 (2014): 919–41.

Nakamura, Lisa. "Race in/for Cyberspace: Identity Tourism and Racial Passing on the Internet." *Works and Days* 13, no. 1–2 (1995): 181–193.

Neiwert, David. *Alt-America: The Rise of the Radical Right in the Age of Trump.* Verso Books, 2017.

"Newzoo's Global Games Market Report 2023 | May 2024 Update." Newzoo, February 8, 2024, https://newzoo.com/resources/trend-reports/newzoo-global-games-market-report-2023-free-version.

Nintendo. *GoldenEye 007.* Released August 25, 1997. Nintendo 64.

Nintendo. *Super Mario Bros.* Released October 1985. Nintendo Entertainment System.

Numinous Games. *That Dragon, Cancer.* Released July 12, 2016. Windows.

Parish, Jeremy. *A History of Video Games.* The Great Courses, 2020. Audible, 4 hours, 4 minutes.

Parreñas, Rhacel Salazar. "'White Trash' Meets the 'Little Brown Monkeys': The Taxi Dance Hall as a Site of Interracial and Gender Alliances Between White Working Class Women and Filipino Immigrant Men in the 1920s and 30s." *Amerasia Journal* 24, no. 2 (1998): 115–134.

Patterson, Christopher B. *Open World Empire: Race, Erotics, and the Global Rise of Video Games*. NYU Press, 2020.

Patterson, Christopher B., and Tara Fickle, eds. *Made in Asia/America: Why Video Games Were Never (Really) About Us*. Duke University Press, 2024.

Payne, Matthew Thomas. *Playing War: Military Video Games After 9/11*. NYU Press, 2016.

Pettus, Sam. *Service Games: The Rise and Fall of SEGA, Enhanced Edition*. Pub. by the author, 2013.

Pilon, Mary. "The Secret History of Monopoly: The Capitalist Board Game's Leftwing Origins." *The Guardian*, April 11, 2015. https://www.theguardian.com/lifeandstyle/2015/apr/11/secret-history-monopoly-capitalist-game-leftwing-origins.

Rancière, Jacques. *The Ignorant Schoolmaster: Five Lessons in Intellectual Emancipation*. Translated by Kristin Ross. Fayard, 1987.

Red Hook Studios. *Darkest Dungeon*. Released January 19, 2016. Windows.

Rilke, Rainier Maria. *The Unknown Rilke: Expanded Edition*. Translated by Franz Wright. Oberlin College Press, 1983.

Rockstar Games. *Grand Theft Auto IV*. Released December 2, 2008. Windows.

Ruberg, Bo. *Video Games Have Always Been Queer*. New York University Press, 2019.

Ruberg, Bo, and Adrienne Shaw, eds. *Queer Game Studies*. University of Minnesota Press, 2017.

Ruberg, Bo, and Mattie Brice. "Radical Play Through Vulnerability." In *The Queer Games Avant-Garde: How LGBTQ Game Makers Are Reimagining the Medium of Video Games*, edited by Bo Ruberg. Duke University Press, 2020.

Russell, Legacy. *Glitch Feminism: A Manifesto*. Verso Books, 2020.

Said, Edward W. *Orientalism*. Vintage, 1994 (1979).

Said, Edward W. *Representations of the Intellectual*. Vintage, 1996.

"Sakaguchi Discusses the Development of *Final Fantasy*." MCV/Develop, December 13, 2007. https://mcvuk.com/development-news/sakaguchi-discusses-the-development-of-final-fantasy/.

Saler, Michael T. *As If: Modern Enchantment and the Literary Prehistory of Virtual Reality*. Oxford University Press, 2012.

Sarkeesian, Anita, and Katherine Cross. "Your Humanity Is in Another Castle: Terror Dreams and the Harassment of Women." In *The State of Play: Creators and Critics on Video Game Culture*, edited by Daniel Goldberg and Linus Larsson. Seven Stories Press, 2015.

Schüll, Natasha Dow. *Addiction by Design: Machine Gambling in Las Vegas.* Princeton University Press, 2012.

Sega. *Sonic the Hedgehog.* Released June 23, 1991. Sega Genesis.

Simpkins, Dulcey. "Rethinking the Sex Industry: Thailand's Sex Workers, the State, and Changing Cultures of Consumption." *Michigan Feminist Studies* 12 (1997–98). http://hdl.handle.net/2027/spo.ark5583.0012.005.

Smith, Alexander. "One, Two, Three, Four I Declare a Space War." *They Create Worlds*, February 2, 2017. https://videogamehistorian.wordpress.com/2014/08/07/one-two-three-four-i-declare-a-space-war/.

Sontag, Susan. *"Against Interpretation" and Other Essays.* Noonday Press, 1966.

Sontag, Susan. *Illness as Metaphor.* Farrar, Straus and Giroux, 1978.

Sony Computer Entertainment. *Journey.* Released March 13, 2012. PlayStation 3.

Spivak, Gayatri Chakravorty. "Can the Subaltern Speak?" In *Can the Subaltern Speak? Reflections on the History of an Idea*, edited by Rosalind Morris. Columbia University Press, 2010.

SquareSoft. *Final Fantasy VII.* Released January 31, 1997. PlayStation.

Stefanescu, Alina. "Solmaz Sharif by Alina Stefanescu." BOMB, Winter 2022. https://bombmagazine.org/articles/solmaz-sharif-alina-stefanescu/.

Stockton, Kathryn Bond. *Gender(s).* MIT Press, 2021.

Supergiant Games. *Hades.* Released September 17, 2020. Windows.

Swink, Steve. *Game Feel: A Game Designer's Guide to Virtual Sensation.* CRC Press, 2008.

Tale of Tales. *The Path.* Released March 18, 2009. Windows.

Tam, Fiona. "Foxconn Factories Are Labour Camps: Report." *South China Morning Post*, October 11, 2010. https://www.scmp.com/article/727143/foxconn-factories-are-labour-camps-report.

3909 LLC. *Papers, Please.* Released August 8, 2013. Windows.

Thunder Lotus Games. *Spiritfarer.* Released August 18, 2020. Windows.

TRIAL and Pro Juventute. "Playing by the Rules: Applying International Humanitarian Law to Video and Computer Games." TRIAL, October 2009. https://trialinternational.org/wp-content/uploads/2016/05/Playing_by_the_Rule.pdf.

"2023 Essential Facts About the U.S. Video Game Industry." Entertainment Software Association, February 10, 2024. https://www.theesa.com/resources/essential-facts-about-the-us-video-game-industry/2023-2/.

"2024 Essential Facts About the U.S. Video Game Industry." Entertainment Software Association, accessed May 2, 2025. https://www.theesa.com/resources/essential-facts-about-the-us-video-game-industry/2024-data/.

Ubisoft. *Far Cry*. Released March 23, 2004. Windows.

Ubisoft. *Far Cry 2*. Released October 21, 2008. Windows.

Ubisoft. *Far Cry 3*. Released November 29, 2012. Windows.

Ubisoft. *Far Cry 4*. Released November 18, 2014. Windows.

United States Army. *America's Army*. Released July 4, 2002. Windows.

Unknown Worlds Entertainment. *Subnautica*. Released January 23, 2018. Windows.

Valve. *Counter-Strike*. Released November 9, 2009. Windows.

VoodooExtreme. "Development Team Chat." Planet Elder Scrolls, July 19, 2000. Archived on October 19, 2007, at https://web.archive.org/web/20071019071012/http://planetelderscrolls.gamespy.com/View.php?view=Articles.Detail&id=27.

Voorhees, Gerald. "Neoliberal Multiculturalism in Mass Effect: The Government of Difference in Digital RPGs." In *Dungeons, Dragons, and Digital Denizens: The Digital Role-Playing Game*, edited by Gerald A. Voorhees, Joshua Call, and Katie Whitlock. Bloomsbury Publishing, 2012.

Walker, John. "Far Cry 3's Jeffrey Yohalem on Racism, Torture and Satire." *Rock Paper Shotgun*, December 19, 2012. https://www.rockpapershotgun.com/far-cry-3s-jeffrey-yohalem-on-racism-torture-and-satire.

Wark, McKenzie. *Gamer Theory*. Harvard University Press, 2007.

Wilde, Oscar. *The Decay of Lying*. Penguin UK, 2022.

Wilde, Poppy. "I, Posthuman: A Deliberately Provocative Title." *International Review of Qualitative Research* 13, no. 3 (2020): 365–380.

Williams, Raymond. *Resources of Hope: Culture, Democracy, Socialism*. Verso Books, 2016.

Winkie, Luke. "We Caught Up with FPS Doug, Gaming Culture's Original Meme." *The Daily Dot*, May 27, 2021. https://www.dailydot.com/unclick/catching-up-with-fps-doug/.

Yang, Robert. *Hurt Me Plenty*. Released December 2, 2014. Windows.

Yergeau, Melanie Remi. *Authoring Autism: On Rhetoric and Neurological Queerness*. Duke University Press, 2018.

Yip-Williams, Julie. *The Unwinding of the Miracle: A Memoir of Life, Death, and Everything That Comes After*. Random House Trade Paperbacks, 2020.

Zwieien, Zack. "Here Are the Best-Selling Games Every Year for the Past Two Decades." *Kotaku*, October 25, 2024. https://kotaku.com/best-selling-games-ever-20-years-madden-call-of-duty-1851680848.

Photo credit: Nathalie Green

Kawika Guillermo is the award-winning author of five books, including two novels, the prose-poetry collection *Nimrods: a fake-punk self-hurt anti-memoir* (Duke University Press), and two academic books, including *Open World Empire: Race, Erotics, and the Global Rise of Video Games* (NYU Press). They co-edited the anthologies *Made in Asia/America: Why Video Games Were Never (Really) About Us* (Duke University Press) and *Transpacific, Undisciplined* (University of Washington Press) and designed the video game *Stamped: an anti-travel game* (Analgesic Productions), based on their first novel. They currently teach game studies at the University of British Columbia.
kawikaguillermo.com